Kathy Gude
Michael Duckworth
Louis Rogers

Cambridge English Proficiency MASTERCLASS

Student's Book with Online Skills & Language Practice

Contents

Contents (continued)

Introduction & exam overview

Introduction

About *Proficiency Masterclass*

This fully-updated and revised edition of *Proficiency Masterclass* provides material which gives prospective candidates appropriate preparation and practice for the 2013 *Cambridge English: Proficiency* (CPE) exam. The material in this course also provides opportunities for candidates to develop their English on a broader level for success in the real world beyond the exam.

The units in this **Student's Book** contain practice of exam-type tasks for all the parts of each paper in the exam. High-level vocabulary and grammar are developed throughout the course. The grammar syllabus is supported by a *Grammar notes* section (page 149) written by linguist George Yule. The *Review* section (page 166) contains exercises that review and consolidate the language covered in the main units.

The **Online Skills and Language Practice** (your unique access code is on the card at the back of this book) contains over 150 exercises which build on and extend the language and skills covered in the Student's Book. It includes:

- exam practice tasks for each part of the four papers in the exam, including speak-and-record tasks
- skills-training exercises
- text-analysis tasks
- vocabulary exercises
- grammar exercises
- **Oxford Advanced Learner's Dictionary 8th Edition* search box
- *feedback on your answers.

(*Available if your teacher sets assignments from your Online Skills and Language Practice 'with help' or with self-study use.)

The access code for your Online Skills and Language Practice also gives access to a full **online practice test**.

We hope you enjoy using *Proficiency Masterclass* to help you to prepare for the *Cambridge English: Proficiency* exam.

About the exam

Revisions to the *Cambridge English: Proficiency* (CPE) exam for 2013 ensure that it is up to date with the latest methodological approaches to communicative language testing. It is a C2-level exam, at the highest end of the CEFR framework. It is proof that successful candidates have achieved an exceptional level of English. As such, it attracts candidates who require English for higher levels of academic study and/or those who wish to enhance their career options and professional development. *Cambridge English: Proficiency* is recognised by a wide range of organisations, including universities, government agencies and international companies. For more information about recognition see www.cambridgeesol.org/recognition.

The revised *Cambridge English: Proficiency* (CPE) exam for 2013 consists of four papers:

- **Reading and Use of English** (1 hour 30 minutes)
- **Writing** (1 hour 30 minutes)
- **Listening** (approx. 40 minutes)
- **Speaking** (approx. 16 minutes).

The exam is approximately 3 hours and 56 minutes long.

More information

For more details and the most up-to-date information about the 2013 *Cambridge English: Proficiency* exam, go to www.cambridgeesol.org.

Reading & Use of English (1 hour 30 minutes)

This paper consists of seven tasks which test a variety of reading skills. In the first four parts the focus is largely on testing language knowledge – vocabulary and grammar, while the last three parts (Parts 5–7) focus on more extensive reading skills with tasks based on longer texts than in Parts 1–4.

The texts are taken from a wide range of authentic sources including newspapers, magazine articles, fiction, guides, letters and reports. There are 53 questions in total in this paper and it carries 40% of the total marks.

	Task type	Number of items/ marks	What you do	What it tests	Exam strategies
Part 1	Multiple-choice cloze	8 items; 8 marks	Choose the correct word(s) from a set of four options to fill each gap in one short text.	Accuracy with vocabulary and some grammar (meaning of single words, phrases, phrasal verbs, etc.).	*page 133*
Part 2	Open cloze	8 questions; 8 marks	Think of a single word to complete each gap in a short text.	Accuracy with grammar and some vocabulary in context.	*page 133*
Part 3	Word formation	8 questions; 8 marks	Use the given root word to form the correct word to fill each gap in one short text.	Accuracy with vocabulary, particularly with word-building, including compound words and the use of prefixes and suffixes.	*page 133*
Part 4	Key word transformations	6 questions; 12 marks (1 mark for each part of the answer, max. 2 marks per question)	There are 6 unrelated sentences, each followed by a single word and a gapped sentence. Use the word given to complete the gapped sentence (in 3–8 words) so that it means the same as the first sentence.	Accuracy with a wide range of grammar and vocabulary, including collocation, phrasal verbs and lexical phrases.	*page 134*
Part 5	Multiple choice	6 questions; 12 marks	There is one longer text for this part. Answer each question about the text by choosing the correct option from a set of four.	Understanding of detail, opinion, attitude, tone, purpose, main idea, implication, exemplification, reference, etc.	*page 134*
Part 6	Gapped text	7 questions; 14 marks	There is one text from which 7 paragraphs are missing. Choose from a choice of 8 paragraphs to fill the gaps.	Understanding of text structure, links between parts of text.	*page 134*
Part 7	Multiple matching	10 questions; 10 marks	There is one text divided into sections OR there are several short texts. Match ten statements / pieces of information to the relevant section(s) of the text(s).	Understanding of detail, opinion, attitude, specific information, etc.	*page 134*

Writing (1 hour 30 minutes)

This paper consists of two parts and carries 20% of the total marks. Each part carries equal marks. Part 1 is a compulsory essay question. In Part 2 you must choose one of four questions. These may include: articles, reviews, letters, reports, essays (for the set text questions only).

	Task type	Word limit	What you do	What it tests	Exam strategies/ Writing guide
Part 1	Essay (compulsory)	240–280 words	Identify, summarize and evaluate the key points in two short texts in an essay that incorporates your own opinions. Candidates must do this task.	Ability to identify and evaluate key information and incorporate this into a coherent essay using own words, expressing and supporting your opinions.	*page 135* *pages 138–139*
Part 2	Choose one question from Questions 2–4. These can include an article, report, review, letter. OR Choose one question about the set books from Questions 5a and 5b. These can include an article, report, review, letter or essay.	280–320 words	Choose one task from Questions 2–4 OR one of the set text questions (there are two set books for the exam which change periodically).	Ability to put together relevant ideas and express them clearly for the reader within the format of the task.	*page 135* *pages 140–148*

Listening (approx. 40 minutes)

This paper consists of four parts and takes about 40 minutes. It carries 20% of the total marks.

The recorded text may include the following:
- for monologues: radio programmes, lectures, talks, anecdotes, speeches
- for interacting speakers: interviews, conversations, discussions.

The speakers will have a variety of accents.

Each recording is heard twice. At the end of the exam, candidates are given 5 minutes to transfer their answers to the answer sheet.

	Task type	Number of items/ marks	What you do	What it tests	Exam strategies
Part 1	Multiple choice (3-option)	6 questions; 6 marks	Listen to 3 short unrelated pieces (monologues or conversations). For each one, answer a question by choosing one option from a set of three. There are two questions per piece.	Understanding of detail, gist, opinion, feeling, attitude, purpose, agreement between speakers, course of action.	*page 136*
Part 2	Sentence completion	9 questions; 9 marks	Listen to one monologue and complete each of 9 sentences with a word or short phrase from the recording.	Understanding of specific information given in the piece.	*page 136*
Part 3	Multiple choice (4-option)	5 questions; 5 marks	Listen to an interview or discussion (two or more speakers). For each question, choose one option from a set of four.	Understanding of opinion, attitude, detail, gist, inference.	*page 136*
Part 4	Multiple matching (2 tasks)	10 questions; 10 marks	Listen to 5 short themed monologues. Match what each speaker says to one of 8 options in Task 1 and one of 8 options in Task 2.	Understanding of detail, gist, opinion, feeling, attitude, purpose, agreement between speakers, course of action.	*page 136*

Speaking (approx. 16 minutes)

This paper consists of three parts and takes approximately 16 minutes. Paper 4 carries 20% of the total marks.

There are normally two candidates and two examiners. One examiner assesses, while the other gives instructions and interacts with candidates. In some circumstances, three candidates may sit the test together, this will increase the time.

You will be assessed throughout the test on:
- accurate use of grammar
- range and use of vocabulary
- pronunciation
- communication
- discourse management
- successful completion of tasks
- ability to take part in different kinds of interaction.

	Task type	Timing (examiner + two candidates)	What you do	What it tests	Exam strategies
Part 1	Conversation between candidates and examiner	2 minutes	Answer the examiner's questions.	Ability to use general and social language to talk about personal topics relating to the candidate.	*page 137*
Part 2	2-way conversation with decision-making task	4 minutes	Answer a question about one or more of the pictures you are shown and do a decision-making task.	Ability to exchange ideas, give and justify opinions, make suggestions, agree/disagree, reach a decision through negotiation.	*page 137*
Part 3	Individual long turn and topic related discussion	10 minutes	Each candidate speaks alone for 2 minutes, based on a prompt card; each candidate is also asked a question about what the other candidate said. This is followed by a discussion between candidates and examiner on the same topics.	Ability to speak continuously on a given topic, and to comment on what someone has said. Also ability to exchange ideas, give and justify opinions, agree/disagree.	*page 137*

Unit 1 People & places

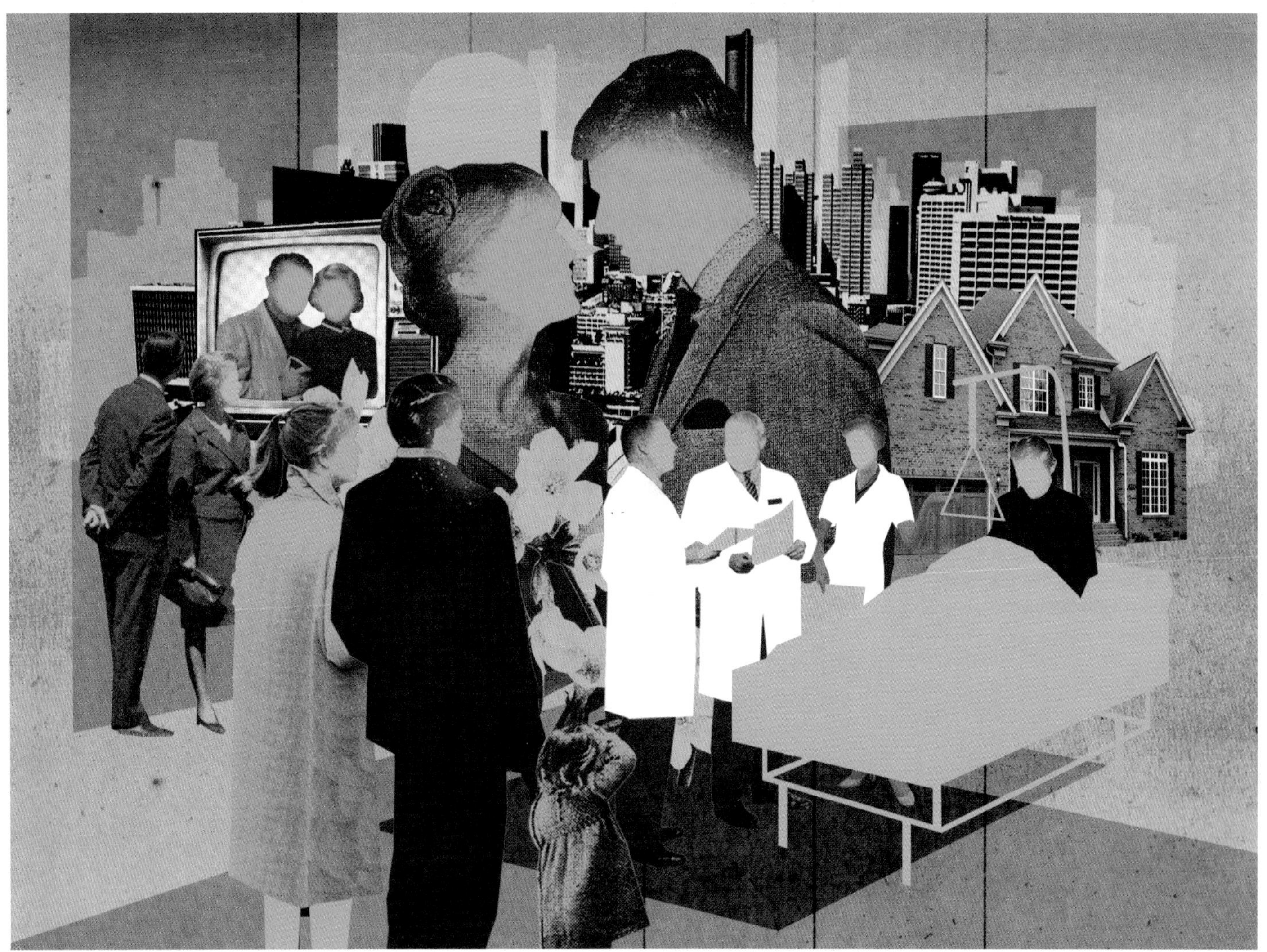

Introduction

1 A study identified four groups of soap opera viewers. With a partner, discuss what you think the attitudes of these people are likely to be.

Fanatics Ironics Non-committed Dismissives

2 🔊 1·01 Now listen to three people describing their attitudes towards watching soap operas. As you listen, decide which category of viewer in 1 they fit into.

3 Match the words in list A with those in list B to form collocations. Sometimes more than one collocation is possible.

A: *hackneyed mundane eccentric compulsive corny cliffhanger unconvincing atrocious negative glamorous topical far-fetched contrived*

B: *stereotypes storylines viewing situations endings characters issues acting settings plot*

4 Which category of viewer in 1 would you put yourself in? Use words from 3 to explain reasons for your choice.

5 Discuss these statements.

a *Soap operas offer an accurate depiction of real-life people who live and work in the places that the soap is set in, e.g. school, country/area/community, hospital, university, etc.*

b *Soap operas can be an effective tool to convey important social messages. They can raise awareness of and help address problems in society.*

c *By publishing the heroism of ordinary life, soaps announce the communality of human crisis; tragedy is the same whether in ghetto or palace.* (Stewart Dakers)

Reading & Use of English

Part 5

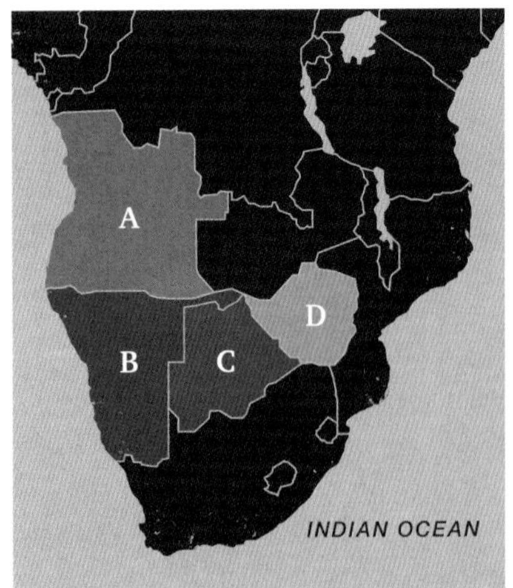

Tip

In this type of text the multiple-choice questions often focus on the writer's implied meaning. Read the question carefully to find words that ask for this kind of interpretation.

1 You are going to read an extract from a novel set in Botswana called *The No.1 Ladies' Detective Agency* by Alexander McCall Smith. The main character, Mma Ramotswe, has set up a detective agency in Botswana with the money she inherited from her father. Before you read the extract, answer these questions.

a Identify these countries on the map: Botswana, Zimbabwe, Angola and Namibia.

b What image does Botswana conjure up in your mind?

2 Now read the text. How similar was your image of Botswana to that in the text?

Exam practice

3 For questions 1–6, choose the answer (A, B, C or D) which you think fits best according to the text.

1 What is the writer implying in the first paragraph?
- A Memories need to be recalled to make sure they do not disappear.
- B We have no control over our memories but they are a part of us.
- C Few people are interested in the lives of ordinary people.
- D Obed Ramotswe was a most unfortunate man.

2 What is suggested about the local boys?
- A They often tried to rob the people.
- B The railway employees had little control over how they behaved.
- C They were reluctant to get too close to the railway track.
- D The passengers were rather irritated by their presence.

3 When talking about Mahalapye, Obed paints a picture of
- A a group of houses reflecting a social divide.
- B a village which was arranged neatly around the railway line.
- C children receiving an education which was inadequate.
- D local children who were encouraged to pursue their own culture.

4 What point is Obed making in paragraph F?
- A The doctor was reluctant to tell him any bad news.
- B He refuses to despair when hearing bad news.
- C People react to bad news in very similar ways.
- D Bad news is never as bad as it seems.

5 What does Obed imply in the last paragraph?
- A He would like to see more of his only child.
- B His life has been a hard struggle to make ends meet.
- C He has found living in Africa a solitary experience.
- D Despite problems, his achievements have been praiseworthy.

6 The overall impression Obed gives of life in Africa in his day is that it was a land where
- A the problems of everyday life could easily be forgotten.
- B there were opportunities for people to take advantage of.
- C the geography had a profound effect on people's character.
- D strong family ties and loyalties were paramount.

Text analysis

4 Work through a–f, referring to paragraphs A–G in the text.

a How effective is the simile that the writer uses? (A)

b What device does the writer use to engage the reader in the narrative? (A)

c What surprises the reader at the beginning of the second paragraph? (B)

d Why do you think Obed compares the passengers on the train to ghosts? (C)

e How does the writer create an impression of what Africa was like in the past? (E)

f How does Obed effectively convey the atmosphere of Africa? (G)

All those years ago

A We don't forget, thought Mma Ramotswe. Our heads may be small, but they are as full of memories as the sky may sometimes be full of swarming bees, thousands and thousands of memories, of smells, of places, of little things that happened to us and which come back, unexpectedly, to remind us of who we are. And who am I? I am Precious Ramotswe, citizen of Botswana, daughter of Obed Ramotswe who died because he had been a miner and could no longer breathe. His life was unrecorded; who is there to write down the lives of ordinary people?

B I am Obed Ramotswe, and I was born near Mahalapye in 1930. Mahalapye is halfway between Gaborone and Francistown, on that road that seems to go on forever. It was a dirt road in those days, of course, and the railway line was much more important. The track came down from Bulawayo, crossed into Botswana at Plumtree, and then headed south down the side of the country all the way to Mafikeng, on the other side.

C As a boy, I used to watch the trains as they drew up at the siding. They let out great clouds of steam, and we would dare one another to run as close as we could to it. The stoker would shout at us, and the station master would blow his whistle, but they never managed to get rid of us. We hid behind plants and boxes and dashed out to ask for coins from the closed windows of the trains. We saw the white people look out of their windows, like ghosts, and sometimes they would toss us one of their Rhodesian pennies – large copper coins with a hole in the middle – or, if we were lucky, a tiny silver coin we called a tickey, which could buy us a small tin of syrup.

D Mahalapye was a straggling village of huts made of brown, sun-baked mud bricks and a few tin-roofed buildings. These belonged to the Government or the Railways, and they seemed to us to represent distant, unattainable luxury. There was a school run by an old Anglican priest and a white woman whose face had been half-destroyed by the sun. They both spoke Setswana, which was unusual, but they taught us in English, insisting on the pain of a thrashing that we left our own language outside in the playground.

E On the other side of the road was the beginning of the plain that stretched out into the Kalahari. It was a featureless land, cluttered with low thorn trees, on the branches of which there perched the hornbills and the fluttering molopes, with their long trailing tail-feathers. It was a world that seemed to have no end, and that, I think, is what made Africa in those days so different. There was no end to it. A man could walk, or ride, forever, and he would never get anywhere.

F I am sixty now, and I do not think God wants me to live much longer. Perhaps there will be a few years more, but I doubt it; I saw Dr Moffat at the Dutch Reformed Hospital in Mochudi who listened to my chest. He could tell that I had been a miner, just by listening, and he shook his head and said that the mines have many different ways of hurting a man. As he spoke, I remembered a song the Sotho miners used to sing. They sang: 'The mines eat men. Even when you have left them, the mines may still be eating you.' We all knew this was true. You could be killed by falling rock or you could be killed years later, when underground was just a memory, or even a bad dream that visited you at night. The mines would come back for their payment, just as they were coming back for me now. So I was not surprised by what Dr Moffat said. Some people cannot bear news like that. They think they must live forever, and they cry and wail when they realize that their time is coming. I do not feel like that, and I do not weep at the news the doctor gave me. The only thing that makes me sad is that I shall be leaving Africa when I die. I love Africa, which is my mother and my father. When I am dead I shall miss the smell of Africa, because they say that where you go, wherever that may be, there is no smell or taste.

G But I can look back over my sixty years and think of everything that I have seen and of how I started with nothing and ended up with almost two hundred cattle. And I have a good daughter, a loyal daughter, who looks after me well and makes me tea while I sit here in the sun and look out to the hills in the distance. When you see the hills from a distance, they are blue; as all the distances in the country are. We are far from the sea here, with Angola and Namibia between us and the coast, and yet we have this great empty ocean of blue above and around us. No sailor could be lonelier than a man standing in the middle of our land, with miles and miles of blue about him.

From *The No.1 Ladies' Detective Agency* by Alexander McCall Smith

Vocabulary

Word knowledge: *get*

5 **The *Oxford Advanced Learner's Dictionary* lists 26 meanings for the verb *get*. Look at this extract from the text on page 13. What does *get* mean here?**

A man could walk, or ride, forever, and he would never get anywhere.

6 **What is the meaning of *get* in a–j? How could each use be paraphrased?**

a Just to get to meet him was a thrill, but I got to work with him, too!
b I get the impression that he doesn't like me very much.
c He couldn't get the car to start this morning and was late again.
d I shall quite enjoy getting used to this lifestyle.
e We had a bite to eat and got talking.
f You get all sorts in here, from accountants to film stars.
g I can't go out. I've only just got in.
h What gets me is how we have to pay through the nose for petrol.
i It's far from ideal but we're getting there.
j I just don't get it – why on earth would you want to go there?

7 **Write sentences with *get* that are true for you. For each sentence, try to use the word *get* in a different way.**

Collocations: *memory*

8 **Divide these adjectives which collocate with *memory* into the four categories a–d below. Some words might fit more than one category.**

vivid distant short-term long-term dreadful faded cherished nostalgic fuzzy precious treasured bitter-sweet haunting vague disturbing bitter traumatic lingering fleeting

a duration
b clarity
c positive
d negative

9 **Which of these verbs which collocate with *memory* do you think have a negative meaning?**

bury erase bring back evoke rekindle push aside push away spark stir (up) trigger conjure up block (out) blot out hold come flooding back fade

10 **Talk to a partner about memories. Try to use some of the vocabulary in 8 and 9.**

Your views

11 **Look back at the text on page 13. Would you be interested in reading the rest of the book? Why/Why not?**

Grammar *See notes page 149*

Past tenses

12 **Complete a–j with a suitable past tense of the verbs in brackets. Where more than one tense is possible, does it create a difference in meaning?**

a When I lived abroad, my mother (always/phone) me at dinner time.
b After the railway (disappear), life in the town changed dramatically.
c I (hope) to take a really long holiday last year but it didn't work out.
d When I (do) all the housework, I sat down and had a nice cup of tea.
e I (visit) the island at least three times a year.
f We all stood up and left the room when John (sing) his latest song.
g I (study) French in Paris when I first met Marc.
h I got the job because I (have) a good knowledge of the surrounding area.
i I (have) dinner with my boss last night and he (say) that things are looking up for the company.
j As soon as he (open) the present, his face lit up.

Past verb forms with present or future meaning

13 **What effect do the past tenses have in each of the sentences in a–g?**

a Supposing we didn't go on holiday next year, what would we do instead?

b I'd rather you didn't come tomorrow as I'm quite busy today.

c I know you love me, but would you follow me wherever I went?

d I think it's time we left for the airport.

e I thought you might like to know that I passed all my exams.

f Did you want to come round and see us tonight?

g I was hoping we could get this sorted out this week.

Word knowledge: *would*

14 **Read this extract from the text on page 13. What meaning is the writer trying to convey with the use of *would*? Is there any difference between the use of *would* and *used to*?**

... I used to watch the trains as they drew up at the siding. They let out great clouds of steam, and we would dare one another to run as close as we could to it. The stoker would shout at us, and the station master would blow his whistle, but they never managed to get rid of us.

15 **What is the function and meaning of *would* in a–f?**

a When Susie first saw the house, she knew that one day she would live there.

b She would happily get up at the crack of dawn to make the kids their breakfast.

c I wanted Tim to start looking for another job but he wouldn't hear of it.

d I would say that this would be a difficult place to settle down in.

e Would you pop this in the post on your way to work?

f Typical! You would tell him about the party!

16 1·02 **When would you normally contract *would* in a–f above if they were spoken? Listen and check.**

Personalization

17 **Prepare a short paragraph about people and/or places from your past like the one in 14. Use the pictures below for some ideas. Then read it out to a partner.**

Speaking

Part 1

1 ◀)) 1·03 **Part 1 of the speaking test lasts for two minutes. In the first part of the test, the examiners will introduce themselves and ask some brief questions. Listen to the introduction to this part of the speaking test. Make a note of the six questions the examiner asks.**

2 **Tick the kinds of questions in the list below that you think the examiner will ask after the introductory ones. How many questions do you think the examiner will ask the candidates?**

...... requiring candidates to justify their opinions
...... developing topics
...... focusing on decision making
...... focusing on exchanging ideas
...... about candidates' lifestyle and surroundings
...... requiring more speculative answers
...... related to an exam task
...... focusing on general interactional language

3 ◀)) 1·04 **Look at these three Part 1 questions. Listen to some candidates answering them. Make a note of the strengths and weaknesses of each candidate's response. How might they improve their answers?**

a You said you are from … What do you like about living there?
b How do you like to spend your leisure time?
c If you could do any job, what would you choose?

Vocabulary

Link words

4 **The following link words a–i will help you to structure your responses. Match them to their uses 1–7.**

a because	1 to introduce another point of view
b so that	2 to confess that something is true
c on the other hand	3 to speculate
d if	4 to give yourself time to think
e actually	5 to preface what you really think
f I must admit	6 to give an explanation or reason
g I have to say	7 to express a result
h so	
i well	

Exam practice

Tip

Before you answer a question, quickly take a deep breath and, as you breathe out, try projecting your voice a little. Both examiners need to be able to hear you.

5 ◀)) 1·05 **Listen to four Part 1 questions. After each one, discuss with a partner what might be a suitable reply to the questions as in the example below. Quickly thinking of two or three different angles for each question will help you to start talking immediately, and expand on and structure your response.**

Example: *How important is it for you to travel?*

(**Ideas:** *trips or travelling you have already done; trips you would like to go on; why you are or are not interested in travel,* etc.)

6 **Now take it in turns to practise asking and answering the questions.**

Reading & Use of English

Part 1

1 Look at these pictures. What do you think it would be like to live in these places?

2 Read the text below, ignoring the gaps, and find out what kind of place Nuuk is to live in. How would you feel about living there?

Exam practice

3 Read the text again. For questions 1–8, decide which answer (A, B, C or D) best fits each gap. There is an example at the beginning (0).

Northern light

All roads do not lead to Nuuk. In fact, no roads lead to Nuuk. Songwriter and Nuuk native, Nive Neilson, tells us why it's worth the trip.

Nuuk is different. For a start, it's not (0) ___B___ to other places in Greenland. If you want to quit town, you need a boat, a helicopter or a propeller plane. Nuuk really is off the (1) ________ track. On the other hand, we've got mountains, the coastline, a vast expanse of water and icebergs – a landscape that's as fascinating as it is inspiring, above all for artists. And there are plenty of those here. I love the albums of Ole Christianson. His surreal lyrics are wonderful. He sings in Greenlandic but his lyrics alone were reason enough to encourage people to (2) ________ with our language.

I like to start my day at the only place in Nuuk where you can get (3) ________ coffee. The espresso is strong and tastes excellent. But although it's difficult to find good coffee, it's easy to (4) ________ hook, line and sinker for Greenlandic cuisine. In my favourite restaurant (5) ________ on the harbour, you get smoked reindeer, fish and musk ox. Places such as Qoornoq are just as (6) ________ as the local cuisine. It's a (7) ________ village on an island just off Nuuk. There's nothing there apart from a few holiday homes. But (8) ________ heed if you go there: the clouds of mosquitos can be really bothersome in summer. That's why people use mosquito nets on boat trips. It looks pretty funny but, as I said, Nuuk is just different.

Tip

Even if you think you have found the correct word to fill the gap, try the other options in the gap to make sure they do not collocate with the other words in the phrase or sentence before you make your final choice.

	A	B	C	D
0	*A combined*	*(B) connected*	*C related*	*D united*
1	A forged	B beaten	C formed	D worked
2	A activate	B encounter	C involve	D engage
3	A appropriate	B suitable	C presentable	D respectable
4	A fall	B drop	C jump	D dive
5	A fixed	B placed	C established	D located
6	A evocative	B reminiscent	C suggestive	D inducing
7	A stranded	B deserted	C vacant	D derelict
8	A keep	B make	C take	D give

Listening | Part 1

1 **Do you agree with this statement? Why/Why not?**

The only way to give effective help to people in need is to go and give it yourself.

Exam practice

2 **1·06 You will hear three different extracts. For questions 1–6, choose the answer (A, B or C) which fits best according to what you hear. There are two questions for each extract.**

Extract 1: You hear two friends talking about a trip to help someone in need.

1 The woman seems surprised that the man and his colleagues
  A found time to organize the trip.
  B managed to fit all the toys and clothing into two lorries.
  C were able to find the money to finance the trip.

2 When the lorries arrived, the man felt
  A proud of his achievements.
  B sympathetic for the children's predicament.
  C determined that he would return.

Extract 2: You hear a presenter making a charity appeal on TV.

3 The man emphasizes the fact that
  A making a donation is not the only way to help people in need.
  B whatever help we can give is welcome.
  C it's up to us all to ensure funds reach their target.

4 In the man's opinion, anyone making a donation will
  A be motivated to do more in future.
  B feel guilty for not having done so earlier.
  C have a clear conscience tonight.

Extract 3: You hear two people on a radio programme talking about sponsoring a child.

5 Why did the man find Opportunity International inspiring?
  A It's prepared to advertise in newspapers.
  B It interviews sponsors personally.
  C It cooperates with the local population.

6 The man regards the donation he makes as
  A a means of obtaining information.
  B a small contribution towards a good cause.
  C an insignificant gesture given the circumstances.

Tip

Always read all the questions and the options through carefully before the recording starts. You will be given time to do this in the exam. As you listen for the first time, put a dot beside the option you think is correct.

Your views

3 **Which of the methods of helping people mentioned in the extracts do you consider to be the most effective? Why?**

Vocabulary

Word knowledge: *help* and *give*

4 **Replace the words in *italics* in a–g using an expression with *help* or *give*.**

a Lynn's tried not to lose her temper so often, but she *can't stop herself*.

b The best way to handle children is not to *let them do just what they want to*.

c *Have some of* these olives everybody – they're delicious.

d I'm going to be late, but *it's not my fault* that the traffic is so bad.

e Things seem bad right now but if you *wait a little while* they might get better.

f When I was struggling to set up my business, he *lent me some money*.

g You are a hard worker – I'll *admit that's true*.

Writing

Part 2, Set text

1 Discuss these questions.

a Do you like reading? Why/Why not?

b What type of things do you like and dislike reading?

c How often do you read?

d Thinking about the things you read, why do you read them?

e Where do you like to read?

f Have your reading habits changed over the years? If so, how?

Preparing for the tasks

2 Here is a list of things you should do when preparing for the set text task. Some of the guidance is wrong. Cross out the guidance that is incorrect.

a Make a list of the main events and note which characters are involved in each event.

b Make notes on how the relationships between the key characters develop.

c Learn your notes by heart and plan to reproduce them exactly in the exam.

d Prepare short character profiles for the main characters.

e Make notes where relevant on attitudes that differ to those of the modern day.

f Link attitudes in the novel to other aspects such as character motivation.

g Write a short summary of each chapter.

h Just watch the film version.

i Spend as much time studying the minor characters as the main characters.

3 Can you think of any other ideas to add to the list above?

Vocabulary

4 Read these extracts from some literature essays and reviews. Complete a–g with a suitable word from the list below in the correct form. There may be more than one possible answer.

heart foot laden culminate mount mirror paint nod doom tend breath compel backdrop play emerge resonate plot lie grip mar

a The theme at the ________ of the book ________ in the narrator's relationship with his sister – a relatively square girl who joins the army after her marriage ends in tatters.

b O'Grady ________ fresh life into the genre with a ________ and evocative novella, having one ________ in the esoterically fogeyish world of eccentric men of letters.

c Narrative suspense ________ around the seemingly trite question of who will lead her through this transformation from child to woman. Against this ________, questions of freedom and alienation ________ as all the more complex.

d The power relations at ________ in the encounters described are ________ in Paulo's small rural community, helping to ________ a lucid picture of turn of the century small town America.

e The novel is ________ with images of concealment, carefully placed within the first section and ________ throughout, ________ in a spine-chilling finale.

f With more than a passing ________ to history, this sentimental novel describes the ________ relationship between a young, impressionable farmhand and a sophisticated, but shallow countess.

g Gilbert popularizes an intricate story well, ________ it intermittently by a ________ to overdramatize an already interesting ________.

Exam practice *See Writing guide page 148*

5 Read each of the exam questions and answer the questions that follow.

a Your local newspaper has invited readers to send in articles entitled 'People thought differently then'. Write an article about your chosen book, focusing on how the attitudes of society affect the relationship between two of the main characters.

1 What kind of balance should there be between characters, events and details about society in your answer?
2 Who are the target readers? What will they expect to learn from such an article?
3 Should the style of the article be formal or informal?

Tip

Only choose a set text question in Part 2 if you have read the text in full or seen the film version.

b 'Their relationship was doomed from the beginning.' Write an essay for your tutor discussing this statement, describing how the relationship between two of the characters in your chosen book begins and develops. Write about the pressures they meet through their own differences in personality and circumstances, and the opposition of society and other people in their lives.

1 What is the main focus in this question?
2 What four paragraphs would you definitely have to include?
3 What style should the essay be in?

c A magazine has decided to start a book review page that focuses on novels in which the protagonist successfully resolves a problem. It is asking its readers for suggestions. Write a letter to the magazine recommending your chosen book. You should briefly describe the character and circumstances of the protagonist, and state why you think readers will be able to relate to him/her.

1 Who are your target readers? What are you trying to achieve through your letter?
2 What should you include in your letter?
3 What kind of style and tone should you adopt?

d A newspaper has asked you to write a review of a book saying whether you think young people are still likely to relate to its themes. Write your review focusing on the main characters and their situations and relationships, and stating how relevant their circumstances are today.

1 Who are your target readers?
2 What is the main purpose of your review?
3 What kind of style should you use?

e The head of English at your college has asked you to comment on the appropriacy of your chosen book for students studying on your course in the future. Write a report commenting on how the book may help students learn about the culture and history of the country in which it is set, and recommending ways of keeping the students interested in the book on future courses.

1 Who is the target audience?
2 What points of style and organization are important when writing a report?
3 What must you include in the report?

6 Choose one of the tasks a–e and write your answer in 280–320 words.

Unit 2 Our environment

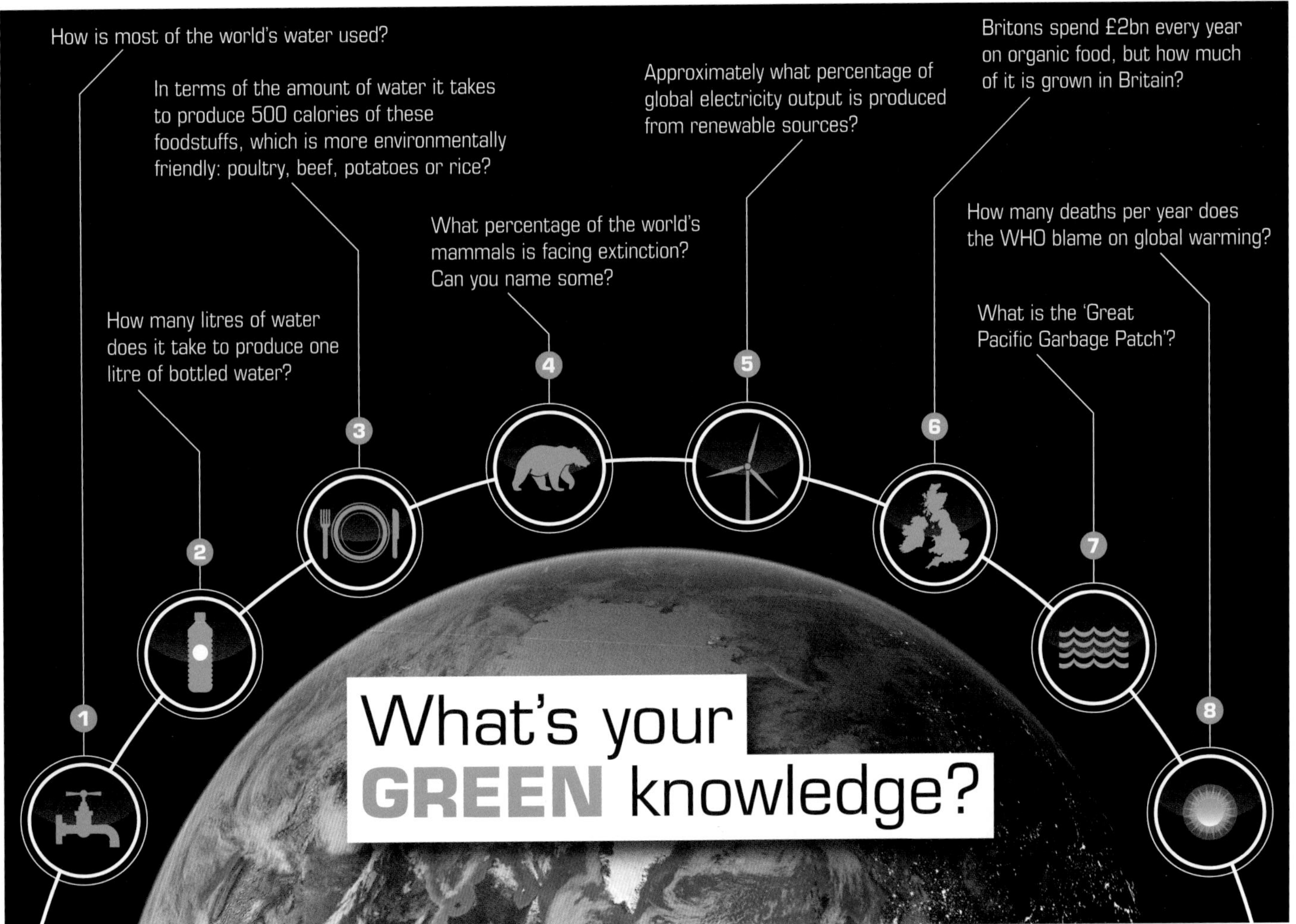

How is most of the world's water used?
How many litres of water does it take to produce one litre of bottled water?
In terms of the amount of water it takes to produce 500 calories of these foodstuffs, which is more environmentally friendly: poultry, beef, potatoes or rice?
What percentage of the world's mammals is facing extinction? Can you name some?
Approximately what percentage of global electricity output is produced from renewable sources?
Britons spend £2bn every year on organic food, but how much of it is grown in Britain?
What is the 'Great Pacific Garbage Patch'?
How many deaths per year does the WHO blame on global warming?
1
2
3
4
5
6
7
8
What's your GREEN knowledge?

Introduction

1 **Discuss the questions in this quiz and find out how much you know about the world we live in. Check your answers on page 163.**

2 1·07 **Listen to two students taking part in a discussion about the environment. Tick the problems they mention.**

- .... greenhouse gases
- .... the exploitation of food sources
- .... the depletion of natural resources
- .... throwaway society
- .... the impact of global warming
- .... the threat of species becoming extinct
- .... climate change
- .... the excessive consumption of energy

3 **Make statements about the issues in 2 using words from list A and list B and any prepositions you may need. There are a number of possible answers.**

Example: *The massive increase in the emission of greenhouse gases is bound to increase global warming.*

A: *reprehensible massive real gross increasing irreversible detrimental burgeoning indiscriminate excessive*

B: *exploitation reduction impact threat depletion prevention effect consumption increase emission*

4 1·07 **Now listen again. Make notes about what the students say.**

5 **Discuss these questions.**

a How do the students differ in their points of view?

b Who do you think put forward the most convincing arguments? Why?

Reading & Use of English

Part 2

1 Discuss these questions.

a What do you think is the purpose of the building shown below?

b What kinds of buildings do you think we might live in in the future?

2 Read the text below, ignoring the missing words. Find out whether your prediction in 1 above was correct.

Can the Earth keep up with human consumption?

The long-term consequences of rising consumption have already been demonstrated empirically. In an experiment in sustainability, four intrepid 'bioneers' were sealed in Biosphere 2, a massive airtight structure covering 1.25 hectares of the Arizona desert. After two years, the occupants quit (0) ___*due*___ to the inability of the ecosystems to sustain human life, and returned to Biosphere 1: Earth.

The experiment clearly shows that 1.25 hectares provide (1) ______ from enough resources for four people. The average Briton requires about five hectares to support their lifestyle, a North American twice that, whereas the average Mexican gets (2) ______ on less than half the UK level.

The problem is that we only have so (3) ______ land to share out. The planet's 10 billion hectares sound a lot (4) ______ one considers the size of the population and the fact that it is going to rise. By 2050, space per global citizen will have reduced to one hectare.

More nations will be approaching US consumption levels in years to (5) ______ and previous data suggests that at least four additional Earths will be needed to sustain (6) ______ a level. (7) ______ the inhabitants of Biosphere 2, when Biosphere 1 fails, we will have (8) ______ else to go.

Exam practice

Tip

The words before and after each space give valuable clues about the type of word missing. Try saying each gapped sentence in your head to help you decide what type of word is missing.

3 Look at these suggestions for words to complete gaps 1–8 in the text. Which ones are correct? Correct the ones that are wrong.

1 more ______
2 away ______
3 little ______
4 if ______
5 come ______
6 many ______
7 like ______
8 nowhere ______

Grammar *See notes page 150*

Future forms

4 Find five examples of future forms in the text on page 22. Match them to a–d.

a predictions or statements of fact about the future based on past experience or knowledge

b a process that we think will have begun at a particular time in the future

c a process that we think will be completed by a particular time in the future

d a prediction based on current evidence

5 Choose the correct structure in *italics* to complete a–f.

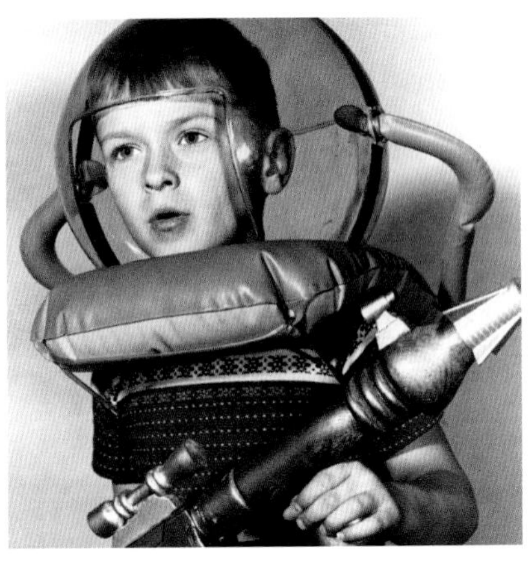

a Excuse me. Could you tell me what time the wildlife centre *opens / shall open*?

b Nuclear waste *will continue / is continuing* to damage the environment for many years.

c We'd better cancel our end-of-term picnic. They say it *rains / 's going to rain* tomorrow.

d I'm afraid I'm busy this afternoon – I *will go / 'm going* to an exhibition of wildlife photography with my colleagues.

e I've sold my car because I *'m going to start / 'll start* cycling to work from now on.

f There are so many empty bottles that I think I *'ll take / 'm taking* them to be recycled.

6 Complete sentences a–f with a suitable future form, using the words in brackets.

a A hundred years from now, we ________ to fix the damage to our environment that we're causing today. (try)

b I ________ of flying to Spain, but I decided to go by train instead. (think)

c The government has announced that the nuclear power plant ________. (close)

d By 2050, space per global citizen ________ to one hectare. (fall)

e By the time we realize the damage we're causing, we ________ the world for too long. (already/pollute)

f I'm ________ solar panels on the roof next year. (install)

Tenses in future time clauses

7 Which present tense is used in a–c? Explain the effect of each form.

a Once Biosphere 1 *fails*, we won't have anywhere to go.

b When you*'ve read* the report, please tell me what you think.

c We will only recognize the problems when resources *are running* out.

Future phrases

8 What is the difference in usage between the phrases in *italics* in the TV news item below?

The Prime Minister's plane *is about to* land in Zurich. He *is due to* address the conference on Environmental Protection tomorrow where he *is to* deliver a warning that much more needs to be done to protect the environment.

9 Complete the missing words in the future phrases in a–g.

a Ted is *s*________ *to* succeed in his aims if he works hard enough.

b Aren't you ready yet? Everyone is all *s*________ *to* depart.

c The Green Party is *b*________ *to* win some seats in the next election. It has quite a following in this country.

d I think we're *u*________ *to* achieve our aim of cutting emissions by 50%.

e Wind farms are *c*________ *to* be a controversial issue over the next few years.

f There's *l*________ *to* be a storm tonight. Look at those dark clouds!

g We'd better hurry *i*________ *we're to* get to the lecture in time.

10 Now use the future phrases from 9 in sentences of your own.

11 Write a short TV news item like the one in 8 about something you expect to happen in your country.

Reading & Use of English | Part 6

1 **Look at a–d, which are periods of geological time. Which refers to:**

590 million years ago? 144 million years ago?
248 million years ago? 0.01 million years ago?

a Cretaceous (first flowering plants; the extinction of dinosaurs; deposits of chalk)
b Cambrian (the explosion of many forms of invertebrate life)
c Jurassic (evidence of many large dinosaurs and the first birds)
d Holoscene (evidence of human development; extinction of large mammals)

2 **Read the text below, ignoring gaps 1–7 for the missing paragraphs and the words in *italics*. What is the text about?**

Geologists press for recognition of Earth-changing 'human epoch'

I These are epoch-making times, literally. There is now "compelling evidence", according to an influential group of geologists, that humans have had such an impact on the planet that *we are entering a dramatic new phase of geological time.*

1 ______

II Now, the scientists are pushing for the new epoch to be officially recognised as *what they call the Anthropocene.* 'We don't know what is going to happen in the Anthropocene,' says geographer Professor Erle Ellis of the University of Maryland. 'But we need to think differently and globally, to take ownership of the planet.'

2 ______

III Geologists predict that our geological footprint will be visible, for example, in radioactive material from the atomic bomb tests, plastic pollution, increased carbon dioxide levels and human-induced mass extinction. 'Geologists and ecologists are already using the term "Anthropocene", so *it makes sense to have an accepted definition,*' says geologist Dr Jan Zalasiewicz of the University of Leicester.

3 ______

IV In the past, geological changes on a scale big enough to merit a new epoch have been *the result of events such as the eruption of a supervolcano or a catastrophic meteor strike* – things a lawyer might describe as acts of God.

4 ______

V The Anthropocene Working Group of the International Commission on Stratigraphy, which is the body charged with formally designating geological time periods, met in London last month *to discuss evidence* for the planet having crossed into a new geological epoch.

5 ______

VI Putting humans at the centre of our planet's activity represents a paradigm shift in the way geologists usually think of our species – as a mere blip on the long timescale of Earth. *But there have been seven epochs since the dinosaurs died out around 65 million years ago.*

6 ______

VII *Now, however, the effect on the climate and our fellow species is having a global impact.* 'The fossil record will reveal a massive loss of plant and animal species, and also the scale of invasive species – how we've distributed animals and plants across the globe,' says Zalasiewicz. The working group still has some more evidence to gather before it presents its findings to the stratigraphy committee, 'and then the real battle will commence,' he says. 'These are slow, nit-picky debates, fraught with acrimony and issues of nationalism.'

7 ______

VIII *But others feel that the new epoch is upon us* and we should come to terms with its implications for the planet. 'We broke it, we bought it, we own it,' Ellis says. 'Now we've got to take responsibility for it.'

From *The Guardian*

Tip

The paragraph may link with words or information that come before or after the paragraph in the text.

Exam practice

3 Now read the missing paragraphs and, using the words in *italics* to help you, try to decide where the paragraphs belong in the text. Choose from the paragraphs A–H the one which fits each gap (1–7). There is one extra paragraph which you do not need to use.

Missing paragraphs

A *And the last time we passed a geological boundary*, entering the Holocene around 12,000 years ago at the end of the last ice age, *we were an insignificant species*, just one of a couple of hominids struggling to survive in a world where so many of our cousins, like *Homo erectus*, had failed to make it.

B *And there is plenty of geological proof to consider*, for example, industrial-scale mining, damming, deforestation and agriculture, as well as the concentration of carbon in the atmosphere and nitrates in the oceans. Even the presence of the first human-produced chemicals like PCBs, radioactive fallout and the humble plastic bag could be measured millions of years hence.

C *There is some friction because some members are very cautious* and think it's premature to define the Anthropocene, because the Holocene has only been around for a short period in geological terms. Other epochs have lasted millions of years.

D *Millions of years from now, these experts say, alien geologists would be able to make out a human-influenced stripe in the accumulated layers of rock*, in the same way that we can see the imprint of dinosaurs in the Jurassic, or the explosion of life that marks the Cambrian.

E *But this is not just a question of everyone agreeing unanimously on an epithet*. Formal recognition of the epoch could have wider significance beyond the geology community. By officially stating that human actions are having an effect on the make-up of the Earth, it may have an impact on, say, the law of the sea or on people's behaviour.

F However, the end of *the Jurassic period* did not witness any major extinction event. The start and end of the period are defined by carefully selected locations, rather than specific dates.

G *The term for the new epoch was conceived in 2002 by Nobel laureate Paul Crutzen*. It means 'the Age of Man', recognizing the ascent of our species to a geophysical force on a par with Earth-shattering asteroids and planet-cloaking volcanoes.

H *But nowadays, it is humans, not ecological disasters, that have become the determining factor*. We are the guiding, controlling species – and many of our changes will leave a permanent mark in the rocks.

Text analysis

4 Work through a–j, referring to the text (i–viii) and missing paragraphs (A–H).

a Why is the term *compelling evidence* in quotation marks? (i)

b What does the expression *charged with* mean? (v)

c Explain in your own words the expressions *a paradigm shift* and *a mere blip*. (vi)

d Find expressions which mean: in a petty manner; full of bitterness. (vii)

e Why do you think the writer refers to hominids as *an insignificant species*? (A)

f What does the writer mean by the word *epithet*? (E)

g What does the writer mean by the expression *on a par with*? (G)

h Find two idiomatic compound adjectives the writer uses to make his point. (G)

i Why does the writer refer to the plastic bag as *humble*? (B)

j Find a word which means: from this time on. (B)

Vocabulary

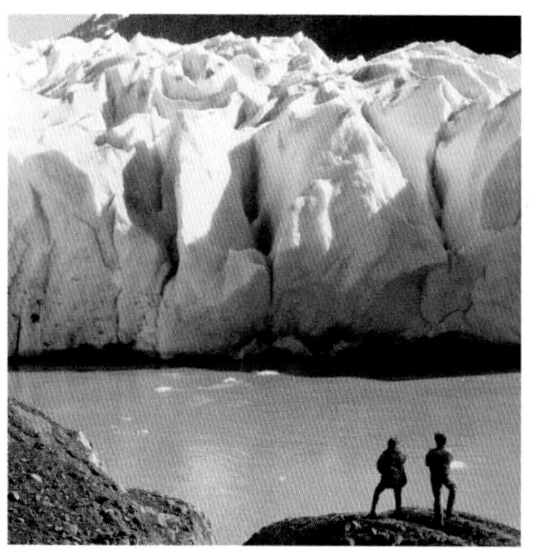

5 **Complete a–j with an adjective from the list. More than one answer may be possible.**

influential compelling accepted catastrophic global geological determining permanent accumulated major

a Geologists study .... layers of rock to find out about previous civilizations.

b Climate change played a(n) .... part in the ultimate demise of the dinosaurs.

c A(n) .... meteor strike could have a huge impact on the Earth as we know it.

d There is .... evidence to suggest that global warming is responsible for the melting of the Earth's glaciers.

e *The Anthropocene* is now a(n) .... term for the new geological epoch.

f Thanks to modern technology, we are living in a(n) .... society nowadays.

g The overuse of plastic can do .... damage to the world around us.

h The scientist is extremely well known and a(n) .... expert in his field.

i Humans are now the .... factor in deciding the fate of the Earth.

j A(n) .... survey revealed the importance of the site in Roman times.

Prepositions

6 **Here is a list of words and phrases taken from the text on pages 24 and 25. What prepositions were used with each one?**

according impact push a par charged fraught term(s) implications responsibility defined shift

7 **Complete sentences a–e with appropriate prepositions.**

a The judge pronounced that the landfill company had demonstrated a cavalier disregard .... regulations and that the damage inflicted .... the environment was substantial.

b The government needs to commit .... imposing tougher sanctions .... corporations who are .... breach .... local and national green policies.

c Congress has approved the establishment .... a revamped wildlife law .... accordance .... its international commitments.

d As the government embarks .... its plans, environmentalists are asking if economic growth really is compatible .... environmental preservation.

e Many of us are resigned .... the fact that we are completely subservient .... fossil fuels despite the fact that this impinges .... the natural world.

8 **Look back at the text on pages 24 and 25. What is the most common preposition? Can you see any patterns in how it is used?**

9 **Use the words below to make sentences of your own. How many can you use together to make one, long coherent sentence?**

the amount of the emergence of all manner of the centre of (at) the end of in terms of the importance of areas of chance of phase of pattern(s) of details of

Compound adjectives

10 **Decide what compound adjectives could be used for these paraphrases.**

a inhabited by many people

b not modern

c not having a closed mind

d attractive / visually appealing

e having a huge effect on

f forgetful

g extremely impressive

h appealing to the taste buds

11 **Use the words below to form compound adjectives.**

eye awe kind mouth mind long far loud ready money

Your views

12 **Who do you think should take responsibility for what happens to our planet? Why?**

Listening Part 2

1 **Which of these statements about wolves are true?**

a They are carnivorous but will eat berries and insects.

b Wolves live in packs of more than twenty.

c They have thick coats consisting of three layers.

d They howl more in the twilight hours.

2 **You are going to hear wolf expert Shaun Ellis talking about his experience of living with wolves. First, read through questions 1–9 and decide what parts of speech or type of information might be needed.**

As a young child, Shaun's knowledge of wolves came from ______ **1**.

In his twenties, Shaun became a ______ **2** in the USA.

Shaun's colleagues considered his method of studying wolves extremely ______ **3**.

After his initial encounter with wolves, Shaun developed ______ **4** for them.

Shaun and the wolves lived mainly on a diet of ______ **5**.

Shaun felt no desire for ______ **6** during his time with the wolves.

One day an incident involving food made Shaun aware that he was in a very ______ **7** position.

On one occasion, a wolf protected Shaun and the pack from a ______ **8**.

After leaving the wolves, Shaun experienced a massive ______ **9**.

Tip

The missing words you need for the answers may be in a different context from the wording in the questions. Do not paraphrase the information.

Exam practice

3 🔊 1·08 **For questions 1–9, listen and complete the sentences with a word or short phrase.**

4 **With a partner, discuss your reactions to Shaun Ellis's experiences.**

Vocabulary

Collocations

5 **Match the adjectives in list A with the nouns in list B to form collocations. More than one answer may be correct. All the adjectives appear in the listening.**

Example: *innate: innate fear, innate behaviour*

A: *innate rugged remote gaunt strict savage ruthless balanced trustworthy*

B: *appearance fear beast behaviour landscape nature spot hierarchy diet*

Animal expressions

6 **Complete a–e with a word from the list below in its correct form. There are two words you do not need. Then explain what the expressions mean.**

fish chicken lion snail rat fly wolf

a Colin's salary isn't great but it's enough to keep the ______ from the door.

b I felt a bit like a ______ out of water when I went on the protest march to ban traffic from the city centre. Everyone else seemed so intense and committed.

c Although this project's beginning to get off the ground, things are still moving at a ______'s pace.

d I'd decided to do some volunteer work on a conservation project in the jungle but at the last minute I ______ out and decided to do something nearer to home.

e I'd love to be a ______ on the wall when governments have those conferences about the environment.

Speaking | Part 2

A

B

C

D

Campaign – improving the environment

1 Your local council is conducting a survey on the local environment. Complete the survey for the area where you live, then discuss your answers with a partner.

Help us to help you! Tell us what you think of your area.

	poor	not bad	OK	good	excellent
litter				✓	
air quality					✓
public transport			✓		
road safety				✓	
noise levels				✓	
green spaces				✓	

Analysing the task

2 🔊 1·09 In the first phase of Part 2, you and your partner will have one minute to answer a question about some of the photos that you are shown. Listen to two students doing the first phase of this part of the test using some of the photos. Answer questions a–c.

a Which photos are the students asked to talk about?

b What does the examiner ask the students to do?

how common this situations were in their countries

c Do you think the students do the task well? Why?/Why not?

3 Listen again and note the expressions the speakers use to make generalizations and exceptions.

Exam practice

Tip

Take up the opportunity to show what you can do but don't forget to give your partner an opportunity to speak, too.

4 Now look again at the two photos that the speakers in 2 talked about. With a partner, discuss how common these situations are in your country. Try to use some of the expressions from 3.

5 🔊 1·10 In the second phase of Part 2, you will be asked to do a task using all the photos. Listen and make a note of what you have to do in this phase of the task.

6 Now work with a partner and do the task. You have about three minutes to do this phase of Part 2.

Suggesting alternatives

7 In the second phase of Part 2, you might be asked to suggest alternatives. With a partner, suggest two other aspects of your local environment that could be improved. Suggest two images for the leaflet to illustrate your ideas.

Writing | Part 1

Understanding the task

1 Read the exam question and answer questions a–f.

> Read the two texts below.
>
> Write an essay summarizing and evaluating the key points from both texts. Use your own words throughout as far as possible, and include your own ideas in your answer.
>
> Write your answer in 240–280 words.

a Is it okay to take ideas from the two texts?

b What two things should you do with the ideas from the texts?

c Is it okay to just use one text?

d Should you give a personal opinion on points in the texts?

e Is it okay to use the exact wording of the texts?

f Should you include all the details from the texts?

Text analysis

2 Read the texts. There are two main points in each. What are they?

Live long and prosper

The announcement by Aubrey de Grey that the first person to reach the age of 1,000 is certainly alive today was instantly shot down by numerous scholars. Undoubtedly, people in the developed world are living longer, but are the dreams of living forever that have been a mainstay of popular culture and science fiction now becoming fact? Only a couple of decades ago, postponing aging would have been seen as a wacky idea. Yet some now argue that, far from being a mere fantasy, the notion that humanity could one day hold the key to eternity is actually a distinct possibility.

Out-living the world

In an overpopulated and under-resourced world, who in their right mind would choose to throw immortality into the mix? Whilst anti-aging crusaders strive to pursue longevity, there are growing numbers of people seeking to ban research into unnaturally prolonging life. In the face of the strain our society is already placed under from a growing population, there is a vast array of ethical, moral and ecological grounds on which to oppose such research. The finite nature of humanity should be seen as a blessing not a challenge to overcome, lest we risk playing god in our own world.

3 Read the sample essay and answer questions a–c.

a Has the writer dealt with all the main ideas in the texts?

b Which views from the text does the writer agree or disagree with?

c Underline parts in each paragraph that paraphrase ideas in the text.

Some people believe that the ability to fulfil the long-held human desire to live forever, or at least for a lot longer than we currently do, is now very likely within our reach. But should we even be considering trying to extend our life expectancy in a world whose resources are already overstretched?

It is said that there are people in existence today whose lives could potentially span a thousand years, or even be prolonged for eternity. Personally, I do not subscribe to this claim and I think that the idea should remain where it belongs – firmly in the realms of fantasy. Otherwise, I fear that we will suffer damaging consequences.

It is blatantly obvious that our planet is already struggling to bear the current burden of human existence. So, is it right then – ethically, morally or ecologically – that while so many people around the world struggle to live from day to day, others are pouring resources into their quest to prolong their lives indefinitely? All creatures, whether man or beast, face the certainty of death, and this is not a battle mankind should choose to fight. Instead, we should be focusing our energies on tackling existing problems like global poverty and global warming, and be trying to improve the standard of living for everyone, rather than trying to change the course of nature.

In conclusion, whilst death is a fact that some people are loathe to accept, it is nevertheless an inevitable consequence of life. In short, we are born to die, and we should be looking to preserve our fragile planet – not pressurizing it to breaking point.

Paraphrasing

4 Tick the elements which can be changed when paraphrasing.

...... word order ...... spelling ...... punctuation
...... vocabulary ...... meaning ...... grammar

5 Read the sentence below and the three paraphrases a–c. Which one do you think is the best paraphrase? Why?

Every country must make a commitment to population stabilization and resource conservation, allowing us to meet the challenges of sustainable development.

a It is of paramount importance that we address the issue of rising population and the exploitation of natural resources to enable us to take sustainable development by the horns.

b For sustainable development to work, it is imperative that nations control population numbers and safeguard their natural resources.

c Every country should make a commitment to population stabilization and resource conservation, allowing us to meet the problems of sustainable development.

6 Paraphrase sentences a–e.

a As we exploit nature to meet present needs, we are destroying resources for the future.

b Climate change can largely be put down to changes in the Sun's activity.

c For the first time since the dinosaurs disappeared, humans are driving animals and plants to extinction faster than new species can evolve.

d If we have unabated man-made climate change, we will go through an absolutely awful period of conflict and migration, until the world's population starts diminishing very rapidly.

e Generating electricity by nuclear reactors does not produce carbon dioxide, the principal greenhouse gas causing global warming and climate change.

7 Use your paraphrases from 6, saying whether you agree or disagree with each view a–e.

Exam practice *See Writing guide page 138*

H.J.

Tip

Remember that there are always two main ideas in each text. Read each text through quickly before you identify these.

8 Follow these stages to write your essay: read, think, plan, write and then check.

Read the two texts below.

Write an essay summarizing and evaluating the key points from both texts. Use your own words throughout as far as possible, and include your own ideas in your answer.

Write your answer in 240–280 words.

Ban the zoo

There is always the risk that those visiting zoos will get the idea that it is acceptable to use these places for their own educational gain without considering how this might impinge on the animals' freedom and quality of life. Whatever the good intentions of zoo-keepers, animals in zoos do suffer, being confined to unnaturally small spaces behind bars where psychological distress and physical pain is the norm. This cruelty exists under the guise of education, despite there being not a scrap of evidence for any educational benefit. How can it be that a visitor can learn anything about animals in such an artificial environment?

The necessity of zoos

Zoos exist to protect species that are struggling in the wild and on the verge of becoming extinct. Increasingly, animals are taken into captivity as they are under threat if they stay in their natural habitat. If human factors have made a species' own habitat a threatening environment, we are morally obliged to intervene. Added to this is the need for zoos to benefit the scientific community: they provide us with an opportunity to study these animals at first hand in a way that is virtually impossible in the wild.

Unit 3 Language & culture

Introduction

1 **Look at the image above. Choose two elements that you think best represent the idea of culture. Discuss your choice. Use some of the words from the list below.**

inseparable from rooted in linked to convey symbolize depict the essence of indicative of at the core of highbrow lowbrow evocative nostalgic cultural identity customs traditions

2 🔊 1·11 **Listen to three people answering the question 'What does culture mean to you?'. For each speaker (1–3), decide which two statements (a–f) best represent their interpretation of culture.**

Speaker 1: ...... and ......

Speaker 2: ...... and ......

Speaker 3: ...... and ......

a Culture exists where there are defined groups of like-minded people but it could exist in a more general sense.

b Culture is what other people teach you it is.

c Culture is what cements society and makes people different from others.

d Culture is how people in a particular place live their everyday lives with their families.

e Culture is a very broad concept and covers many different aspects of life.

f Culture is absorbed during childhood.

3 **Which speaker do you identify with most? Why?**

4 **Discuss these quotes.**

a *A people without the knowledge of their past history, origin and culture is like a tree without roots.* (Marcus Garvey)

b *You don't have to burn books to destroy a culture. Just get people to stop reading them.* (Ray Bradbury)

c *We can learn more about a culture from its art than its literature.*

d *The arts of our time aren't hanging in the 'high art' galleries.* (Ellen Dissanayake)

Listening

Part 3

1 Look at the painting and discuss these questions.

a Which of these adjectives would you use to describe the painting?

timeless contemporary innovative startling arresting compelling

b Who do you think the characters are and what might the relationships between them be?

Exam practice

2 🔊 1·12 You will hear a group of art history students going round an art gallery with their teacher. For questions 1–5, choose the answer (A, B, C or D) which fits best according to what you hear.

1 Burne-Jones believed that a painting
A ought to be true to nature.
B must have a clear moral point.
C should play an instructive role in a modern industrial society.
D need not have any practical value.

2 It appears that the story of the King and the Beggar Maid was
A a well-known Victorian tale.
B popularized by a poet.
C brought to the artist's attention by his wife.
D taken up by novelists at a later stage.

3 According to the student, how did the painter approach the work?
A He wanted to portray the beggar very realistically.
B He copied parts of the painting from an Italian masterpiece.
C He had certain items in the painting made for him.
D He wanted to decorate the clothing with jewels.

4 The student thinks that in some way the painting depicts
A an uncharacteristically personal message.
B the great sadness of the artist.
C the artist's inability to return the girl's love.
D the fulfilment of the artist's hopes and dreams.

5 What was people's reaction to the painting?
A They recognized Frances Graham as the model for the Beggar Maid.
B They realized how personal the painting was for the artist.
C They interpreted the painting without difficulty.
D They did not approve of the subject matter of the painting.

Tip

Don't try to guess what the answers might be. Listen carefully for clues which will lead you to the right answer.

Your views

3 Discuss questions a–e.

a What are your personal reactions to the painting above?

b How relevant do you think this kind of painting is today ?

c What kinds of paintings, pictures or photographs do you have at home?

d Many artists only become famous after they are dead. Why do you think this happens?

e Why do you think people are prepared to pay so much money for some paintings?

Reading & Use of English

Part 3

1 **Read the text below quickly, ignoring the gaps. Then answer questions a–d.**

a What was the initial appraisal of Dickens's ability as a writer?

b What was his enormous success attributed to?

c Who are the most popular novelists in your country? Why?

d What does *unprecedented* mean?

Dickens and his world

It was with the circulation of *Pickwick Papers* in 1836 that young Dickens began to enjoy a truly (0) ***unprecedented*** ascent into the favour of the British reading public. He magnificently (1) .... a theory that his fame would disappear just as quickly as it had come. He remained until his death 34 years later (2) .... the most popular novelist the English-speaking world had ever known. — PRECEDENT, PROVE; DENY

The public displayed an insatiable appetite for his works, and there was also a great diffusion of them through (3) .... dramatic adaptations (nearly all completely (4) ...., the copyright laws being much weaker in those days). — NUMBER, AUTHORITY

His immense popularity was based on the widespread perception of him as a great champion of the poor and the (5) .... against all forms of (6) .... and abuse of power. In his personal life, however, he was (7) .... of achieving the level of fulfilment he enjoyed with the public, and all his close emotional relationships with women (8) .... ended in failure. Yet, he created an extraordinary range and variety of female characters who live on in our minds and culture unlike any others created by Victorian novelists. — POSSESS, JUST; CAPACITY; VARY

Exam practice

Tip

Make sure that you read the sentences through to the end to check that your choices fit in with the overall sense.

2 **For questions 1–8, use the word given in capitals at the end of some of the lines to form a word that fits the space in the same line. Unlike in the exam, this exercise focuses on one specific area: word formation with negative prefixes.**

Vocabulary

Negative prefixes

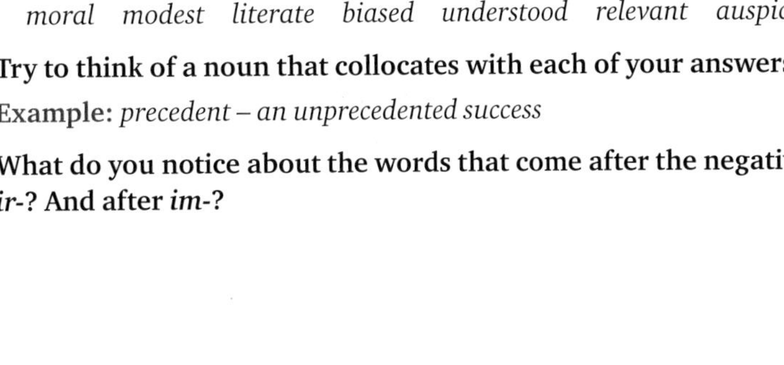

3 **Match the prefixes in list A to the adjectives in list B. Then decide what each one means.**

A: *dis im il in ir mis non- un*

B: *plausible coherent enthusiastic agreeable logical violent reverent moral modest literate biased understood relevant auspicious*

4 **Try to think of a noun that collocates with each of your answers in 3.**

Example: *precedent – an unprecedented success*

5 **What do you notice about the words that come after the negative prefixes *il-* and *ir-*? And after *im-*?**

Reading & Use of English

Part 7

1 1.13 **Listen to four people explaining how the way they speak English affects their lives. Has their experience been positive or negative? Why/Why not?**

2 **Discuss questions a–c.**

a Which accent in 1 did you find the easiest/most difficult to understand?

b Why do some languages become more widespread than others?

c What motivates people to learn another language?

3 **Quickly read the extract from a review of a book about the English language on page 35. Decide what main point the writer of *The Last Lingua Franca* is making, according to the review.**

Exam practice

Tip

Don't just match words in the question with words in the text. Think carefully about the meaning of the words in both the question and the text.

4 **Read the text again. For questions 1–10, choose from the sections A–E. The sections may be chosen more than once.**

In which section are the following mentioned?

- the view that the global influence of a language is nothing new 1
- a return to the global use of not one but many languages 2
- explanations as to what motivates people to learn another language 3
- the view that a language is often spoken in places other than its country of origin 4
- an appreciation of a unique and controversial take on the role of the English language 5
- a query about the extent to which people are attached to their own first language 6
- an optimistic view about the long-term future of the English language 7
- the hostility felt by those forced to learn another language 8
- a derogatory comment about the English language 9
- a shared view about the ultimate demise of English in the future 10

Text analysis

5 **Work through a–l, referring to paragraphs A–E in the text.**

a Which phrase implies that there is no concrete evidence to support a fact? (A)

b Which verb is used to convey a lack of respect for something? (A)

c Which noun could be followed by the phrase 'to the rule'? (A)

d Find a metaphorical reference about the impact of English today. (A)

e Which clause is used to clarify a term of reference? (B)

f Which phrase implies that something was also highly regarded? (B)

g Where is alliteration used in the text? Why might the writer have used this? (C)

h Which two adjectives emphasize the negative aspects of a high-profile lingua franca? (C)

i Which two words and phrase does the writer use as cohesive reference devices? (D)

j What does the word *burden* refer to? (line 63)

k What does the writer mean by his reference to a *state of Babel*? (line 68)

l Find an example of understatement. What does the writer really mean by it? (E)

The Last Lingua Franca by Nicholas Ostler

Deborah Cameron predicts an uncertain future for English

A The Emperor Charles V is supposed to have remarked in the 16th century that he spoke Latin with God, Italian with musicians, Spanish with his troops, German with lackeys, French with ladies and English with his horse. In most books about English, the joke would be turned on Charles, used to preface the observation that the language he dismissed as uncultivated is now a colossus bestriding the world. Nicholas Ostler, however, quotes it to make the point that no language's triumph is permanent and unassailable. Like empires (and often with them), languages rise and fall, and English, Ostler contends, will be no exception.

B English is the first truly global lingua franca, if by 'global' we mean 'used on every inhabited continent'. But in the smaller and less densely interconnected world of the past, many other languages had similar functions and enjoyed comparable prestige. Modern lingua francas include French, German, Latin, Portuguese, Russian and Spanish. Yet these once-mighty languages are now largely confined to those territories where their modern forms are spoken natively. Though at the height of their power some acquired – and have kept – large numbers of native speakers outside their original homelands (as with Spanish and Portuguese in South America), few retain their old status.

C To understand why the mighty fall, Ostler suggests we must look to the factors that enabled them to rise: most commonly these are conquest, commerce and conversion. Conquered or subordinated peoples learn (or are obliged to learn) the languages of their overlords; traders acquire the languages that give them access to markets; converts adopt the languages of their new religion. But these ways of recruiting speakers are not conducive to permanent attachment. The learned language is not valued for its own sake, but only for the benefits that are seen to flow from it, and only for as long as those benefits outweigh the costs. When new conquerors arrive, their subjects switch to new lingua francas. Old empires break up and their lingua francas are abandoned, while the spread of a new religion may advance a language or conversely weaken it. And always there is the resentment generated by dependence on a language which has to be learned, and therefore favours elites over those without access to schooling. Prestigious lingua francas are socially divisive, and therefore unstable.

D English in the global age is often portrayed as an exceptional case. Writers who take this view point out that English differs from previous lingua francas in two important ways: first, it has no serious competition, and second, although it was originally spread by conquest, commerce and missionaries, its influence no longer depends on coercion. Because of this, the argument runs, it will not suffer the fate of its predecessors. But Ostler thinks this argument underplays both the social costs of maintaining a lingua franca (it is not true that English is universally loved) and the deep, enduring loyalty people have to their native tongues. For millennia we have been willing to compromise our linguistic loyalties in exchange for various rewards; but if the rewards could be had without the compromise, we would gladly lay our burden down. Ostler believes that we will soon be able to do that. English, he suggests, will be the last lingua franca. As Anglo-American hegemony withers, the influence of English will decline; but what succeeds it will not be any other single language. Rather we will see a technologically-enabled return to a state of Babel. Thanks to advances in computer translation, 'everyone will speak and write in whatever language they choose, and the world will understand'.

THE LAST
LINGUA
FRANCA
English Until
the Return of Babel
NICHOLAS
OSTLER

E Here it might be objected that Ostler's argument depends on an unrealistic techno-optimism, and puts too much emphasis on the supposed primeval bond between speakers and their mother tongues, which some would say is largely an invention of 19th-century European nationalism. But even if he is wrong to predict the return of Babel, I do not think he is wrong to argue that English's position as the premier medium of global exchange will not be maintained for ever. In the future, as in the past, linguistic landscapes can be expected to change in line with political and economic realities. *The Last Lingua Franca* is not the easiest of reads: Ostler does not have the popularizer's gift for uncluttered storytelling, and is apt to pile up details without much regard for what the non-specialist either needs to know or is capable of retaining. What he does offer, however, is a much-needed challenge to conventional wisdom: informative, thought-provoking and refreshingly free from anglocentric clichés.

From *The Guardian* Review section

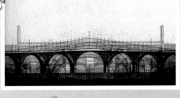

Vocabulary

Style **6** **Choose one of the paragraphs in the text to read again and find examples of formal language. Think of less formal words to replace them.**

Prefixes **7** **Match the prefixes in list A to the words below in list B. The words appear with or without a prefix in the text. There may be more than one answer.**

A: *un-* *im-* *inter-* *dis-* *under-* *in-* *over-*

B: *cultivated* *assailable* *permanent* *inhabited* *connected* *stable* *realistic* *cluttered* *apt* *conventional* *play*

Grammar *See notes page 151*

Focus and emphasis **8** **Look at these two sentences from the text on page 35. Underline the parts of each sentence that the writer is emphasizing. What structures does the writer use to do this?**

a *As Anglo-American hegemony withers, the influence of English will decline; but what succeeds it will not be any other single language.*

b *What he does offer, however, is a much-needed challenge to conventional wisdom: informative, thought-provoking and refreshingly free from anglocentric clichés.*

9 **Now rewrite the two sentences in 8 without any emphasis.**

10 **Choose the best option in *italics* to complete sentences a–j.**

a *All / It / What* is the writer's style that critics have always admired.

b *It / That / What* I have always admired is composers who can perform their own work well.

c *All / All what / What* I bought at the museum was a book of postcards; I couldn't afford anything else.

d He has an unusual job. What he does is *arrange / arranges / arranging* fight scenes in films and plays.

e I don't like ballet; neither *my friends / do my friends / my friends do*.

f Seldom *I have seen / have I seen / have seen I* such a great performance by a film actor.

g Never once *my literary agent managed / did my literary agent manage / my literary agent did manage* to negotiate a reasonable contract for me.

h *In Italy only / In only Italy / Only in Italy* can you see the greatest opera performances.

i I don't like romantic comedies. However, *I like / I do like / what I do like is* a good police drama.

j It's not the hard work *I do mind / what I mind / I mind* – it's the constant pressure of worrying whether the novel will sell.

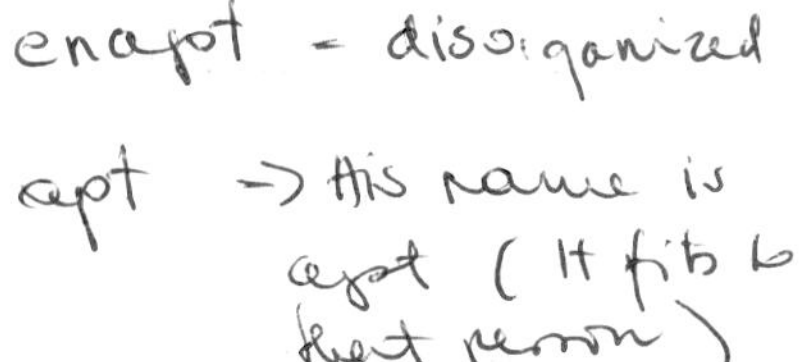

11 **Rewrite sentences a–h to emphasize the information in *italics*. There may be more than one correct answer for each sentence.**

a *His style of acting* really irritates me.

b My friends said that I needed *a better TV*.

c *The bad reviews* put us off seeing the play.

d He hardly ever reads a book because he *works all the time*.

e He knew he'd never be able to afford a ticket to the concert, so he *watched it on TV*.

f She doesn't like novels but *she likes autobiographies*.

g She says that *the programme she saw on TV last night* upset her.

h We were late for the play, but *not because the train drivers were on strike*.

12 **Complete sentences a–d with your own ideas. Then, use emphatic structures to tell a partner how you feel.**

a ______ really upsets me.

b I can't understand why ______.

c I enjoy ______ more than anything else.

d I'm happiest when ______.

Emphasis in speech 13 🔊 1·14 **In speech, we can also use stress to emphasize certain words in a sentence without changing the words or the order in which they are used. Listen to this sentence being said in six different ways. After each one, decide what the speaker's intended meaning is.**

I have read most of Dickens' novels.

14 **Work with a partner. Take it in turns to read out this sentence in six different ways and work out what your partner means.**

I have seen some of Edward Hopper's paintings.

Using idioms for emphasis 15 **Complete sentences a– j with an expression from the list.**

why on earth *way beyond* *no way* *by far* *well and truly* *into the bargain* *ever such a lot* *not just any* *no wonder* *whatsoever*

a Whether a book is written by a well-known author or not makes no difference ______ to me. If it appeals to me, I'll read it.

b There is ______ we can afford to go to that art exhibition in Paris. It would be too expensive.

c Buying a first edition of a book is ______ my budget.

d Dickens was a colourful character and a gifted writer ______.

e When I was younger I used to read ______ of detective stories.

f It's ______ English became so widespread. It was the first language in so many countries.

g We got ______ lost when we were looking for the modern art gallery in Madrid.

h Spanish and Portuguese are ______ the most popular languages in South America.

i This is ______ old painting – it's a Picasso!

j ______ did you drop out of the literature course? I thought it was fascinating.

Writing | Part 2, Review

Understanding the task

1 Read the exam task and answer questions a–c.

A newspaper is running a special feature in its 'Books and Media' section about films and literature that might appeal to both men and women. You have been asked to write a review of a novel for this section. Write your review (280–320 words) explaining why the book might appeal to both male and female readers, and saying whether you would recommend it.

a What main points would you need to cover to answer this question properly?

b Think about the target readers for this review. Will they be literary specialists or general readers? Why will they be reading the review? What will the target readers expect to gain from reading it?

c How formal or informal do you think the review should be?

Text analysis

2 Read the review and answer a–d.

a What is the main topic of each paragraph?

b Where would you read a review like this? Explain why.

c Explain in your own words what the expressions in *italics* in the text mean.

d Identify ways in which the writer creates interest.

One Day

Have you noticed them yet? There they are, all over the country, on trains and in waiting rooms, in cafés and shopping centres, men and women hunched over a novel with a distinctive orange and white cover. There's a good chance they will be chuckling helplessly, or quietly wiping away a tear. The book they are absorbed in is *One Day* by David Nicholls, the highest-selling novel of the year and already translated into 31 languages.

The story opens on July 15, when Dexter and Emma meet just as they are leaving university. The novel revisits them, either separately or together, on the same date for the next 20 years – hence the title. It proves to be a wonderfully effective device, providing a series of *vivid snapshots* of a relationship. At the end of each chapter the reader is left wondering what will happen next, then suddenly a year has gone by and the situation has changed in ways that are often surprising but always believable.

The two main characters are drawn with a *warts-and-all realism* that makes them entirely credible. Dexter is charming and good-looking, but also lazy, arrogant, selfish and deceitful. Emma is more lovable – cleverer and more honest than Dexter, but *prone to stroppiness* and self-doubt. Not *a match made in heaven*, then, but a clearly recognizable *will-they-won't-they relationship* set in equally recognizable modern times.

Yet what has made it *a publishing phenomenon* is not the format, but the fact that it appeals equally to both sexes. There is romance and humour; the comedy lures you in and the romance hits you. But this is not a romantic comedy; there is also *a dark side*, a side about tragedy, grief and loss. As one critic has put it, this is a book for women that makes men cry.

This immensely popular book has already *gone viral*, as deeply affected readers have been urging everyone they know to go out and buy it. If you don't want to be the only person who hasn't read it, hurry.

Vocabulary

Creating interest

3 Improve this extract from a book review. Replace the words and phrases in *italics* with more descriptive or dramatic adjectives. Compare your suggestions with the version of this text on page 163.

'Alex Sharp is a *clever* Cambridge graduate who works for a US research company based in Cairo. During one of his regular weekend visits to the bazaar, he comes across an *old* parchment in hieroglyphics which the stallholder says came from an *old* tomb. At some time in the past someone has tried to decipher the symbols and has written a translation in Arabic underneath. Alex is *very interested in* the parchment and buys it, determined to unravel its mysteries. As he does so, he begins to experience *strange* parallels between the events related in the parchment and his own life and work on genetic engineering. The novel takes us on an *interesting* journey between the *old* and new cities of Cairo. Alex is faced with *difficult* challenges and *big* decisions. We follow him on his journey which lurches from exhilarating breakthroughs to the *horrible* realization of the real message of the parchment.'

Exam practice

See Writing guide page 144

4 Follow stages 1–5 to write your review.

Tip

Take advantage of the opportunity to describe characters and events vividly. Try to avoid being too formal and to involve the reader in the experience as much as possible.

An internet magazine is running a feature on 'Chasing away the winter blues'. You have been invited to write a review about a 'feel good' book or film that you have enjoyed, to share with readers. Write your review (280–320 words), saying who you think the book or film would appeal to, and explaining why reading the book or seeing the film might cheer them up.

Stage 1: Read

Who are your target readers likely to be?
What will they want to get out of your review?
What have you been specifically asked to include?
How formal or informal should the review be?

Stage 2: Think

Decide whether you will write about a book, a film or a film based on a book.
What is special about it?
In what ways does it fit the label of being 'feel good'?
Who are the main characters? What is the basic story? What is special about the themes and settings?
How successful is it? Who would it appeal to?

Stage 3: Plan

Make detailed notes about what to include in each paragraph, using the following outline if you wish:
Introduction – try and grab the reader's attention
The main characters
The basic plot
What gives the book its 'feel good' factor
Your opinions and recommendations

Stage 4: Write

Remember to keep the reader interested in your account of the book/film, but don't give away any unusual twists or surprises.
Use present tenses to talk about elements of the plot and include elements of descriptive or dramatic language. Try to use structures that give emphasis and focus.

Stage 5: Check

Read through the review. Have you answered the question?
Read it again, checking word count and accuracy.

Speaking Part 3

1 **Discuss questions a–d.**

a Are there any words from your language which are used in English?

b Which language do you think the words below originate from: Arabic, German, Spanish, Italian or Hindi?

zero shampoo balcony umbrella assassin hamburger guitar jungle mosquito kindergarten

c Can you think of any English words which are used in your language?

d Why do you think words are 'borrowed' from other languages?

2 **Work in groups of three. Read the three long-turn tasks and brainstorm ideas for each of the prompts in the three tasks.**

How much easier is it to learn a language nowadays than it was in the past?
- technology
- travel
- learning techniques

How has modern technology affected the way we communicate?
- social life
- education
- work

What cultural misunderstandings can arise when someone lives and works in a foreign country?
- body language
- greetings
- customs and habits

3 **1·15 Listen to extracts of two students doing the tasks in 2 and complete a–h.**

Expressions Student A makes to introduce examples supporting his points of view:

a in .... technology ...

b As far as today's students ....

c If you .... visual aids ...

d And when it .... facilities ...

Expressions Student B makes to give herself time to think:

e Well, ... I would say ...

f I suppose you .... – an enormous effect ...

g I .... it's changed the way we arrange our social lives ...

h well, ... – meet up socially ...

Tip

If you find you start a sentence but get stuck or can't finish it, try rephrasing what you were going to say and carry on.

Exam practice

4 **Work in groups of three. You are going to practise a Part 3 task. Student A turn to page 163, Student B turn to page 164, Student C turn to page 165 and follow the instructions. Try to use some of the language in 3.**

Exploring the topic

5 **Discuss questions a–d.**

a If you learn a language, how important is it to also learn about the culture of the people who speak it?

b How important do you think it is for tourists to be able to speak the local language?

c Are there many different ways of speaking your language and is one of them the 'right' way?

d What do you think is the best age to start learning another language? Why?

Unit 4 Family & relationships

Introduction

1 **Divide these behaviours into three categories: positive, neutral and negative.**

a I always try to be as frank as possible.

b I avoid conflict at all costs.

c Sometimes I think one thing but say another.

d I'm quite diplomatic.

e I don't like making waves.

f I'm not at all competitive.

g I'm not terribly assertive.

h I make a lot of rash decisions.

i I'm always sensitive to other people's feelings.

j I can put up with just about anything!

k I tend to be quite antagonistic.

2 **Match these adjectives to the behaviours in 1. There may be more than one possible answer.**

hypocritical upfront tactful impetuous forceful non-confrontational cooperative tolerant passive pugnacious tactless timid sympathetic

3 **Think of one relationship you have had in your life (family, school, work, etc.). Tell a partner about one positive and one negative aspect of that relationship using ideas from 1 and 2.**

4 **How many interpersonal relationships, including family, professional, social, etc., do you think one person can sustain at a time? Compare your ideas.**

5 **1·16 Listen to anthropologist, Professor Robin Dunbar, talking about relationships and answer questions a–d.**

a How many relationships does Dunbar suggest a person can sustain successfully?

b Why is it not possible to sustain more than this number of relationships successfully?

c What, according to Dunbar, are 'relationships'? Why?

d What is special about poets when it comes to relationships?

6 **Do you think face-to-face relationships are better than relationships you form on the internet? Why?**

Reading & Use of English

Part 6

1 Discuss your reactions to this quotation.

You will find as the children grow up that as a rule children are a bitter disappointment – their greatest object being to do precisely what their parents do not wish and have anxiously tried to prevent. (Queen Victoria)

2 Read through the main text below quickly, ignoring gaps 1–7 for the missing paragraphs. What has Lang Lang's relationship with his father been like?

Lang Lang, the virtuoso Chinese pianist

I When Lang Lang was nine, his father told him to kill himself. Four years before, his father had decided that his only son should become the No 1 classical pianist in China. He gave up his job as a policeman and took his son to live in Beijing, leaving Lang Lang's mother behind, planning to get the child into the prestigious Central Conservatory of Music.

1 ______

II Unbelievably, when Lang Lang's father heard the news, he demanded that the boy take his own life. 'It's really hard to talk about. My father went totally nuts,' says Lang Lang quietly. 'He said: "You shouldn't live any more – everything is destroyed." ' The father handed his son a bottle saying, 'Take these pills!' When Lang Lang ran out on to the balcony to get away from him, his father screamed: 'Then jump off and die.'

2 ______

III Now twenty-eight, Lang Lang has surpassed his father's ambition. The musician's recitals and concerts sell out in every major city in the world and he is the first Chinese pianist to be engaged by the Vienna and Berlin philharmonic orchestras. The pianist is now based in New York and lives a rock-star lifestyle, but he began his career in a Beijing slum under a super-strict regime of practice overseen by his unforgiving father, Lang Guoren.

3 ______

IV Lang Lang's parents are from Shenyang, an industrial city north-east of Beijing. They married at the end of the Cultural Revolution. Lang Lang says: 'People were starting to connect with the West, and the piano was becoming an important instrument. My mother had always wanted to be a musician and my father played in the air force orchestra before the budget was cut and he had to become a policeman. My parents bought our piano before I was born – it cost half their annual salary.'

4 ______

V Lang Lang explains: 'My father quit his job as a policeman and off we went. My mother didn't come – she needed to earn money for us.' In Beijing, Lang Lang's father had to be both mother and father. Lang Lang says: 'He didn't like to cook or do the laundry, because my mum had always done it. We couldn't do much, because we only had Mum's salary and had to pay for expensive piano lessons once a week, and if there was a competition, twice a week. It was really hard.' Lang Lang's father does not understand English, but in the past, he has spoken about the way he pushed his son. He said: 'The way I see it is pressure always turns into motivation. Lang Lang is well aware that if he fails to be outstanding at playing the piano, he has nothing.'

5 ______

VI Indeed, the musician has always had as much faith in himself as his father has. But it was after Professor Angry had told Lang Lang some home truths, that the boy's relationship with his father hit an all-time low. But they did not return to Shenyang afterwards. 'For three months, I didn't touch the piano,' says Lang Lang. 'We stayed in Beijing, I don't know why. Probably because having to go home would have resulted in shame for us.'

6 ______

VII So began nineteen months of intensive practice as father and son redoubled their attempts to get Lang Lang into the conservatory. Finally, when Lang Lang was ten, he was admitted on a full scholarship. He and his father remained in their slum until he was fifteen, when they left for America to continue his studies in Philadelphia.

7 ______

VIII Does Lang Lang think he would have succeeded without his father? 'Yes, absolutely,' he says emphatically. 'Over the years I have seen so many different cultures and different ways of bringing up kids. I believe that no matter how you train your kid, you need to give them love. Sometimes my father pushed me too much, but he loved me.'

From *The Guardian*

Tip

For each gap, check each of the options in turn. Make sure that the one you choose fits both before and after the gap.

Exam practice

3 Read the text on page 42 again, then the missing paragraphs. Choose from paragraphs A–H the one which fits each gap (1–7). There is one extra paragraph which you do not need to use.

Missing paragraphs

A Then one day at school, his fellow students hectored Lang Lang into playing some Mozart. He laughs: 'They asked me to play, and I said no, I don't play anymore. Then they just applauded and applauded. They gave me a score and forced me to play. I started and realized that I actually loved to play the piano. So I went home and told my father, "Find me another teacher, I'd like to play again."'

B The 'Lang Lang effect' is credited with inspiring China's forty million classical piano students and, in 2009, he was listed in *Time Magazine*'s 100 Most Influential People in the World. His name, Lang Lang, has even become a trademark.

C Lang Lang says: 'When we came to America, my father could see that the American system was much more relaxed. At that time he said he still believed in the Chinese way. But as we met different musicians from different countries, his opinion changed. He is fifty-eight now and his personality has totally changed, he doesn't push me anymore. When I turned twenty-two, he let go.'

D However, his teacher in Beijing, nicknamed Professor Angry by Lang Lang, had other ideas. 'Professor Angry didn't like me and she always gave me a hard time,' he remembers. 'One afternoon she said that I had no talent, that I shouldn't play the piano and I should go home. She basically fired me before I could even get into the conservatory!'

E Lang Lang explains: 'I started lessons when I was three and a half. In the beginning I just played a little but, when I was five, I played my first recital, and from that point my parents had high hopes for me, especially my father.'

F Born during China's one-child policy, the young musician became his parents' sole focus. When Lang Lang was nine, his father and his piano teacher decided that he must leave Shenyang for Beijing, home of the Central Conservatory of Music. If his father had been strict before, he soon became a lot harder.

G 'I got totally crazy, too,' says Lang Lang. 'I was beating the wall, trying to prevent myself from being a pianist by destroying my hands. I hated everything: my father, the piano, myself. And then somehow, we just stopped. My father went out or I ran out – I can't remember, but somehow we stopped. After that I didn't want to play piano any more. I said, "OK, fine. Let's go home."'

H Lang Lang disagrees. 'I think that attitude is wrong because there are a lot of things you can do in the world,' he says. 'When I was nine, I didn't like my father. I knew he had dedicated his life to me, but I thought it was too much. I found the pressure unnecessary because I was a workaholic from the very beginning. I could understand if I was lazy and didn't care, but I didn't need that kind of push, because I knew what I wanted.'

Text analysis

4 Work through a–e, referring to the text (i–viii) and missing paragraphs (A–H).

a Which word captures the idea of high status? (i)

b Find an example of a euphemism. (ii)

c Find two examples of language used for emphasis. (v)

d Find an expression which means: an unpleasant fact about a person told to him/her by somebody else. (vi)

e Which expression is normally used in a work rather than an academic situation? (D)

Vocabulary

5 In your own words, explain the meaning of these phrases from the text and missing paragraphs.

a *went totally nuts* (ii)

b *surpassed his father's ambition* (iii)

c *the budget was cut* (iv)

d *is well aware* (v)

e *fails to be outstanding* (v)

f *an all-time low* (vi)

g *hectored* (A)

h *a score* (A)

Your views

6 Discuss these questions.

a How would you have reacted if you had been in Lang Lang's position?

b Do children only succeed in life if they have ambitious parents? Why/Why not?

Listening | Part 4

"We like to bring together people from radically different fields and wait for the friction to produce heat, light and magic. Sometimes it takes a while."

Tip

Read through both tasks before you hear the recording. Remember that there are two questions for each speaker and you need to complete both tasks while you listen.

1 **What do you think are the main reasons for problematic relationships at work?**

2 **Read through the exam task and the questions below. Try to imagine what the people might say.**

Exam practice

3 **1·17 You will hear five short extracts in which people are talking about problematic relationships they have had with people at work. While you listen you must complete both tasks.**

TASK ONE: For questions 1–5, choose from the list (A–H) what each speaker says caused the problems.

A a lack of ambition
B a reluctance to pull together as a team
C a highly competitive nature
D a domineering attitude
E an unreasonable increase in workload
F a lack of sensitivity in a tricky situation
G a series of disagreements
H a clash of personalities

Speaker 1		1
Speaker 2		2
Speaker 3		3
Speaker 4		4
Speaker 5		5

TASK TWO: For questions 6–10, choose from the list (A–H) what step each speaker took to solve the problems.

A complained to someone in a higher position
B took compassionate leave
C decided to look for another position elsewhere
D fought back using the same weapons
E accepted the situation but felt bitter about it
F tried to get the message across about how they felt
G decided not to take the problem too seriously
H backed down to avoid unpleasantness

Speaker 1		6
Speaker 2		7
Speaker 3		8
Speaker 4		9
Speaker 5		10

Vocabulary

Expressions connected with communication

4 **Complete expressions a–j using a word from the list. What do they mean?**

miss take have sense chest message say teeth humble fall

a .... what you mean
b eat .... pie
c get your .... across
d lie through your ....
e talk .... into someone
f get something off your ....
g .... something to heart
h .... a heart to heart
i .... out with someone
j .... the point

Your views

5 **Think about a problem you have had, or someone you know has had with a relationship. Then discuss these questions with a partner.**

a What caused the problem?
b How was it dealt with?

Speaking | Part 3

1 Work with a partner. Look at the pictures and discuss these questions.

a Why is it important to have a good relationship with people in these situations?

b What can sometimes make it difficult to achieve this?

Exam practice

Tip

Although you will not be asked a question about what your partner has said, it is a good idea to listen carefully to what they say in their long turn. It might give you some ideas for talking about the further question you will both be asked.

2 Work with a partner. You are going to speak for about 2 minutes about international relations. Student A turn to page 163, Student B turn to page 164 and follow the instructions.

3 1·18 Listen to two students answering an examiner's question. Then discuss the questions a–c.

a What question did the examiner ask?

b Which student gives a better answer? Why?

c How far do the views of the two students you listened to reflect your own views?

Discourse markers

4 Match the pairs of discourse markers a–h to their uses 1–8. Then listen again and note the discourse markers the speakers in 3 use.

a By the way, … / Incidentally, …

b You know, … / Let's see.

c As regards … / As far as … is concerned …

d Actually, … / Well, …

e Mind you … / Still …

f Besides … / What's more …

g In my opinion, … / From my point of view, …

h As a result … / Because of this …

1 as an afterthought contradicting what has already been said

2 to add to or give further information

3 as an afterthought which does not contradict what has already been said

4 as fillers used to give the speaker time to think

5 giving a specific example of what you are talking about

6 giving a relevant response which may contain unexpected information

7 to explain the reason for something

8 to say what you personally think

5 1·19 Now listen to these more general questions about relationships. Discuss your answers with a partner. Try to use some of the discourse markers in 4.

Reading & Use of English | Part 4

1 **Read this extract from a textbook on the history of childhood in Britain. What changes do you think will be mentioned in the rest of the extract?**

For much of the 19th century, childhood was often short and brutish, and the young were treated merely as small adults. Yet some changes have completely transformed expectations for the early years of life.

2 **How do you think children's lives have changed in your country over the last twenty years or so in relation to:**

a family life?
b work and education?
c freedom?
d leisure?

3 **Read the extract below to check your ideas. How far are the changes in Britain reflected in your country?**

Family life

Family size has directly affected children's lives. In the second half of the 19th century, 43% of the population were brought up in a family with seven or more children. By the middle of the 20th century, this proportion had fallen to 2%, and has remained stable ever since.

Changing gender roles have also affected children. The idea of the mother as a sole carer for her children emerged in the mid-20th century. Before then, childcare assistance was common: wealthy classes employed nurses, while humbler families paid a girl to help.

More significantly, the number of stereotypical authoritarian males has been steadily declining. At one time, children encountered the same model across all society – in schools, in the home and elsewhere. Sexual equality gave women more rights and made family relations more flexible. Remarkably, it allowed fathers to become their children's friend.

Work and education

In the 19th century, children from poor families were expected to contribute to the family from an early age. However, various measures since then have gradually marked out childhood as a distinct phase of life. For example, the school-leaving age was gradually raised. Consequently, school work has replaced paid work, and the period of children's total dependency on their parents has correspondingly expanded. Furthermore, until relatively recently, children had expected physical punishment for disobedience at school. If current trends continue, within a very short time, most countries will have outlawed this kind of punishment, even in the home.

Grammar *See notes page 152*

Perfect aspect

4 **Match the tenses below to their uses a–e.**

future perfect past perfect past simple present perfect present perfect continuous

a to describe an action or situation started in the past which connects to the present, or to describe the present result of an earlier action
b to describe a process going on from a point in the past up to the present
c to describe a situation or action that happened before a specified time in the past
d to describe a situation in the past that we think has ended
e to say that something will be completed by a particular time

5 **Find examples from the text for a–e in 4 above. Which expressions helped you decide which category each example belonged to?**

6 **Complete the following extract from the textbook with the correct form of the verbs in brackets. You may need to change the order of the words in brackets.**

Freedom

Up until the end of the 19th century, children (1) .... (be) much more visible. Since then, better quality housing and much more space at home (2) .... (actually/lead) to children spending less time outdoors. More recently, parents' worries about traffic and strangers (3) .... (almost/put) an end to children's street culture. Ironically, children of all classes (4) .... (now/travel) further afield than ever before – including to other countries – yet independent movement is ever more curtailed.

Leisure

In the 1950s, teenage culture (5) .... (begin) to gain an identity of its own, partly due to the influence of the new media. From that time onwards until today, consumerism and mass entertainment (6) .... (sustain) a shared culture for children. They (7) .... (also/create) a generation gap between children and parents even more significant than the gap between different classes. Advertisers (8) .... (be) quick to seize on this as soon as it (9) .... (emerge). Consequently, with higher standards of living, children (10) .... (become) consumers of technical goods, toys, leisure services and much more.

7 **For a–c, which option in *italics* emphasizes that something occurred before now?**

a I feel quite proud of *having written / writing* for the college magazine.

b Hot weather is known to *have caused / cause* many minor illnesses.

c *Having lived / Living* in the town centre, I can tell you exactly what it's like.

Simple and continuous

8 **For a–d, what are the differences in meaning between the sentences in each pair?**

a 1 I'd been playing squash with Jim, so I was exhausted.
2 I'd played squash with Jim, so I knew that he was a terrible cheat.

b 1 My flatmate has been writing her thesis, and she's over half way through.
2 My flatmate has written her thesis, so she's very relieved.

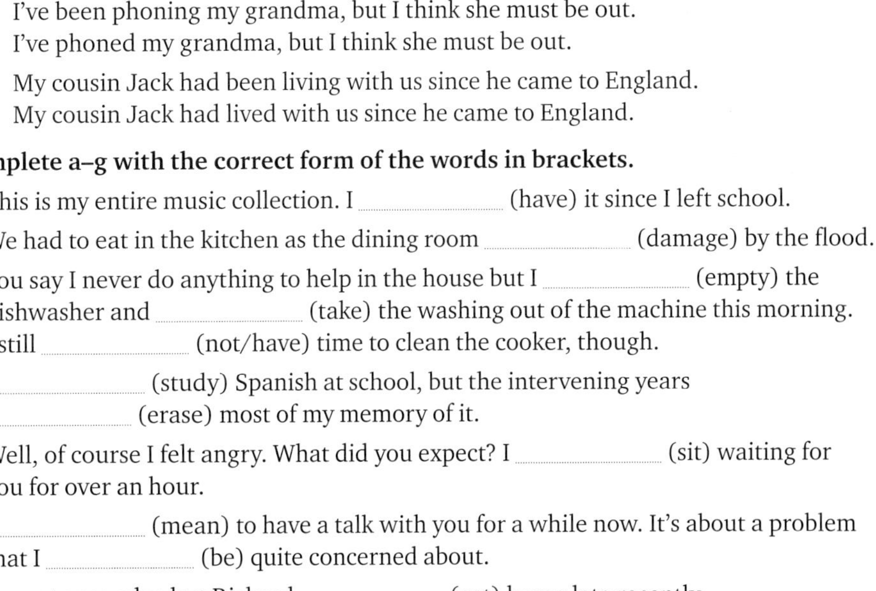

c 1 I've been phoning my grandma, but I think she must be out.
2 I've phoned my grandma, but I think she must be out.

d 1 My cousin Jack had been living with us since he came to England.
2 My cousin Jack had lived with us since he came to England.

9 **Complete a–g with the correct form of the words in brackets.**

a This is my entire music collection. I .... (have) it since I left school.

b We had to eat in the kitchen as the dining room .... (damage) by the flood.

c You say I never do anything to help in the house but I .... (empty) the dishwasher and .... (take) the washing out of the machine this morning. I still .... (not/have) time to clean the cooker, though.

d I .... (study) Spanish at school, but the intervening years .... (erase) most of my memory of it.

e Well, of course I felt angry. What did you expect? I .... (sit) waiting for you for over an hour.

f I .... (mean) to have a talk with you for a while now. It's about a problem that I .... (be) quite concerned about.

g I'm not sure why, but Richard .... (get) home late recently.

10 Complete a–f in an appropriate way.

a The children are excited, because it's the first time they ______________.

b I can't get into these jeans. I / They ______________.

c The film was one of the most ______________.

d Look at all these mistakes! You obviously ______________.

e You look a mess! What on earth ______________?

f I'm sick to death of this weather! It ______________.

11 Read the text below. There are ten mistakes. Find and correct them.

Example: *My friend ~~has come~~ to see me yesterday evening. came*

I've always been holding the view that friendships are one of the most important things in a young person's life. My family and I have being lived in the same area for a very long time, so I'd made a lot of friends here over the years. I'd been having a long chat with a friend last week about just how important my friendships were being to me and he has been in complete agreement with me about the role of friendships in forming our character and personality. Now, I'm not suggesting that my family have not been being influential as well – far from it. I think what I've been tried to say is that if it has not been for my friends, I would had been a different person from the one I am today.

Your views **12 Discuss these statements.**

a *Character, personality and attitudes to life are formed in the first years of our lives.*

b *If you educate a man, you educate one person, but if you educate a woman, you educate a family.* (Ruby Manikan)

Exam practice

Tip

Read the main sentence and think carefully about its meaning, then focus on the word in bold and try to recall phrases and expressions which include it.

13 Reading & Use of English, Part 4: For questions 1–6, complete the second sentence so that it has a similar meaning to the first sentence, using the word given. Do not change the word given. You must use between three and eight words, including the word given.

1 A couple's happiness depends on their frequency of communication.

happier

The more ______________ they will be.

2 Romantic films often lead people to assume that their relationships will be a success.

raise

Romantic films often ______________ their relationships.

3 According to the papers, money had been the cause of the Taylors' marital problems.

run

The newspapers reported that ______________ over money.

4 Mary felt entirely comfortable when her boss was around.

ease

Mary felt entirely ______________ her boss.

5 These days people regard that kind of behaviour as normal.

come

That kind of behaviour ______________ as normal.

6 He said their marriage has been successful as they are tolerant of each other.

put

He ______________ the fact that they are tolerant of each other.

Writing | Part 1

Understanding the task **1 Read two Part 1 texts below. Answer the questions a–c.**

a What do you have to do in a Part 1 essay?
b How many main ideas are there? What are they?
c Are the ideas contradictory or complementary?

Our personality
It is a truth universally acknowledged that we inherit characteristics from our parents. It is pretty obvious that our build, hair colour and eye colour are a direct result of the genetic make-up of our parents. However, if we dwell for a moment on concepts such as intelligence, aggression and personality, who could state definitively whether these stem from our DNA or the environment in which we grow up? One theory that is starting to gain ground is that both play a role, that is to say, that genetics gives us our core abilities and traits and that our environment and upbringing hammer them into shape.

Twins: a case in point
Twins provide an interesting insight into the role of nature and nurture in fostering traits such as intelligence, aggression and personality. Certainly, one would expect identical twins, raised in the same environment, to mirror each other in personality as well as looks. Yet results show similarities to a startling degree between the characters of identical twins even when raised apart. For many, the issue of whether nature or nurture defines who we are is a thorny one. However, it is now a common belief that, although our genes increase the likelihood of certain traits coming to the fore, we cannot escape the influences of the environment in which we find ourselves.

Text analysis **2 Read the sample essay below and answer questions a–c.**

a Find phrases in the sample essay to match these phrases from the texts in 1:
1 *a truth universally acknowledged*
2 *stem from*
3 *hammer them into shape*
4 *to a startling degree*
5 *raised*

b Circle the specific phrases that highlight personal opinion.
c How does the writer present the main idea from the text in their introduction?

What makes one person nice and another one nasty? Were they born that way or did something in their environment create these tendencies? Both texts discuss the relative importance of nature and nurture in the development of individual characteristics such as aggression and intelligence.

While it is commonly accepted that physical characteristics are rooted in our genetic code, the origins of non-physical individual traits are being hotly contested. I agree with the suggestion in the two texts that it is a combination of both genetic and environmental factors that accounts for the development of these traits. The idea expressed in the first text that, although our DNA provides individuals with a simple blueprint for our non-physical characteristics and abilities, it is how and where we are brought up that determine their ultimate shape, seems totally credible to me.

In addition to reiterating points about the impact of nature and nurture, the second text uses the example of twins to explore the issue. It suggests that identical twins are remarkably similar, whether brought up together or apart, because, despite environmental differences, genes have an overriding role in determining who they are. I would dispute this and argue that the role of our environment also plays a significant part, a point expressed in both texts. I would even venture so far as to say that it is ultimately our environment that determines how our genetic inheritance plays out.

In conclusion, although we are born with certain limitations, I believe we have the choice to decide what we do within those limitations. Would you be happy to believe that life was simply fate and no matter what choices we made we would never be able to change the person we are?

Cause and effect

3 Read the texts in 1 and 2 and find the following words. Which ones are followed by a cause and which are followed by an effect?

make   create   develop   determine   stem from   account for   be rooted in

4 Which of the words and phrases below are commonly followed by a cause and which by an effect?

result in   due to   hence   result from   since   mean (that)   thus   provoke   trigger   therefore   as   on account of   as a result (of)   give rise to   consequently   because

5 Write a variety of cause and effect sentences about these subjects.

a Environment

b Personality

c Genetics

Exam practice

See Writing guide page 138

Tip

There are a number of nouns, verbs and conjunctions that can be used to express cause and effect relationships. Try to use a variety of these in your essay.

6 Read this exam task. Use the checklist on page 135 to help you write your answer.

Read the two texts below.

Write an essay summarizing and evaluating the key points from both texts. Use your own words throughout as far as possible, and include your own ideas in your answer.

Write your answer in 240–280 words.

Born criminal

A number of studies have been carried out to try to prove the connection between genetics and criminal behaviour. For example, it has been argued that people are more or less likely to be criminal depending on their body shape. These theories have largely been discredited in recent years, with many arguing that it is preposterous to make such claims. However, the idea that criminals are produced as a result of the environment in which they are raised is rarely disputed. For example, it is a commonly held belief that prison provides an environment in which a criminal is actually able to learn further criminal behaviours.

It's all the parents' fault

Families not only provide the genetic code for their offspring, they also significantly shape the environment in which a child develops. Therefore, it can be particularly challenging to determine the extent to which the environment plays a part in a child's development as opposed to their genes. For example, criminal fathers are much more likely to produce children with a criminal record than a father with no criminal record is. However, to what extent this is due to genetics as opposed to the environment is debatable.

Introduction

1 **Rank the activities above according to the risks they pose to our life expectancy. Begin with the activity you think poses the greatest risk. Then compare your choices with a partner's. Check your answers on page 164.**

2 **Sometimes people are afraid of things which in themselves are not necessarily dangerous. Can you explain what these fears are?**

arachnophobia technophobia agoraphobia acrophobia claustrophobia hydrophobia

3 **1·20 Listen to a clinical psychologist talking about dealing with fears and phobias and make notes under the headings below about what she says. Discuss with a partner how far what she says relates to your own attitudes towards risk taking.**

a influences on our attitudes towards new situations
b the importance of taking risks
c how to approach our fears
d building confidence

4 **Complete sentences a–f to form collocations with *danger* and *risk*.**

grave calculated inherent imminent averse fraught

a I thought I had never been *in* such ______ *danger*.
b A spokesman said last night that neither of the men was *in* ______ *danger*.
c The voyage had been ______ *with danger*; waves swamped the ship and the navigation system broke.
d We live in a *risk*-______ society – everyone just plays it safe.
e Taking this project on was a(n) ______ *risk* – thankfully it's paid off.
f There is always a(n) ______ *risk* in adopting new practices.

5 **Discuss these questions.**

a What do you think is the greatest danger we face?
b What is the most dangerous thing you have ever done?

6 **Apart from those mentioned in 2 above, do you know of any other phobias? Do you suffer from any phobias?**

Reading & Use of English

Part 1

1 **Describe what is happening in the picture on the left.**

a What qualities would people need to be able to do this kind of job?

b What risks would be involved?

c Could you cope with looking down from a height like this? Why/Why not?

2 **Read the text below, ignoring the gaps, to find out what kind of unusual trip the tourists went on.**

Exam practice

3 **Read the text again. For questions 1–8, decide which answer (A, B, C or D) best fits each gap. There is an example at the beginning (0).**

The Bridge *by Peter Michelmore*

Our group (0) ___A___ silent at the base of a narrow steel ladder that rose vertically through the maze of girders at the south-east end of Australia's Sydney Harbour Bridge. We needn't have worried about the first part of the climb. Up to this (1) ____________ our guided tour had been little more than a stroll but now our task was to face the ladder. It must have been at least fifty feet high. There were handrails and our safety belts would be tethered to a cable to (2) ____________ a fall but the water couldn't have been less than 250 feet below us and the (3) ____________ of climbing was daunting.

What lay at the top was stepping out on to the exposed upper arch of the bridge, with blue sky all round and the water almost 262 feet below. We ought to have found this out before embarking on what now seemed a singularly (4) ____________ mission! My own (5) ____________ was extreme, but, on this sparkling morning, I saw no option but to climb to the summit of one of the world's best-loved icons – a miracle of engineering recognized by people everywhere.

As I climbed the tension (6) ____________ out of me; I was driven by an exhilarating feeling of conquest. At the top, I dropped my (7) ____________ to the vast pool of the harbour below. It might just as well have been a mill pond from this height. We stood on a small viewing deck in the warm sunshine, (8) ____________ with excitement and arms raised as our guide took a celebratory photograph.

Tip

Read the text before and after the gap carefully. This will help you to choose the word that fits best.

	A	B	C	D
0	*(A) fell*	*B came*	*C rendered*	*D dropped*
1	A position	B period	C point	D place
2	A hold	B halt	C reduce	D break
3	A perspective	B proposal	C probability	D prospect
4	A negligent	B reckless	C careless	D unthinking
5	A acrophobia	B claustrophobia	C agoraphobia	D arachnophobia
6	A exuded	B drained	C leaked	D came
7	A glare	B glimpse	C gaze	D glance
8	A flushed	B burned	C drenched	D flamed

unit 5 safety & danger

Vocabulary

Ways of looking

4 **Look again at question 7 in exercise 3 on page 52. The words *glare*, *glimpse*, *gaze* and *glance* are used to describe different ways of looking at something. Complete a–g with a word from the list. You can use some words more than once.**

peek glimpse glare peep gaze glance

a As the plane prepared to land, I caught a .... of the lights on the runway below.

b At first .... the list of emergency procedures seems clear and straightforward.

c As long as you don't tell anyone about it, I'll let you have a .... at the plans for the new development.

d When he fixed me with that .... of his, I knew I'd said the wrong thing.

e Let me take a quick .... at the baby.

f She cast a .... over her shoulder to see if anyone was following her.

g It was hard to avoid his .... even though the room was crowded.

5 **Match these adjectives to the words in the list in 4.**

menacing tentative fierce defiant fleeting brief cautious surreptitious unflinching curious furtive dreamy furious steely sneaky intimidating intent

6 **Use the words from the list in 4 as verbs or nouns and appropriate forms of the words in 5 to make sentences of your own.**

Example: *I'm afraid I only caught a brief glimpse of the burglar as he was about to jump from the window.*

Grammar *See notes page 154*

Past modals and meanings

7 **Read the article on page 52 again and underline all the past modal forms. Which of the past modals are used to express these meanings in the text?**

a a comparison

b an obligation that was not fulfilled

c an action which proved to be unnecessary

d a positive deduction

e a negative deduction

Possibility and speculation

8 **Complete the text below about the photo of the bridge using an appropriate modal and the words in brackets. There may be more than one answer.**

When the Sydney Harbour Bridge was built, it (1) .... (be) one of the most famous bridges in the world. It (2) .... (certainly/be) a feature that people ignored. The photographer (3) .... (take) the picture of the bridge with a telescopic lens. On the other hand, the picture (4) .... (take) from an aeroplane. The man on the bridge (5) .... (do) some repairs to it at the time. I don't understand how anyone (6) .... (possibly/work) on a bridge of that height. But it (7) .... (give) you a tremendous feeling of satisfaction although be very nerve-wracking at the same time. If you're ever in Australia, you (8) .... (go) and see the bridge. It's still an amazing sight, even after all these years.

9 **Complete these sentences using *if*, *but* or *because* and your own ideas.**

a Our neighbours could easily have sold their house ....

b Bill might have written to us ....

c Michael could have caught an early train ....

d Ted might have phoned me ....

e Anne would have lent me the money ....

f You should have asked me to the party ....

10 **Complete a–e using the words given and *must have (been)* or *can't/couldn't have (been)* to make deductions about the situations.**

a The bill at the restaurant was astronomical. The meal ....

b I'm sure it wasn't Patrick I saw. He's in America ....

c Look! The pavements are soaking wet! It ....

d I told you about the phone call half an hour ago. You ....

e I'm afraid you only got five out of ten for this homework. You ....

Necessity and obligation

11 **Match a–e with an appropriate ending from 1–7. Sometimes the same ending can be used more than once.**

a They said we needed to have a vaccination, ...

b They said we didn't need to have a vaccination, ...

c They said we needn't have had a vaccination, ...

d They said we should / ought to have had a vaccination, ...

e They said we shouldn't have a vaccination, ...

1 ... because they were now thought to be unsafe.

2 ... so we didn't.

3 ... so they didn't let us into the country.

4 ... but we did anyway.

5 ... but we never got round to it.

6 ... but by then we'd already had one.

7 ... so we did.

12 **Complete sentences a–h in your own words using an appropriate modal and verb.**

a As there were no mosquitoes on that part of the coast, I .... malaria tablets.

b When I went for my first riding lesson, I discovered I .... a riding hat as they were provided by the riding stable.

c When we got to the island, we realized that the water was not safe to drink and that we .... water purification tablets.

d Although we .... insurance, we got it anyway just to be on the safe side.

e I think you ought to apologize – you .... my car without checking that you were covered to drive it.

f George told the ambulance driver that his wife .... hospital as quickly as possible as she was about to have a baby.

g I found out that the operation was a simple, routine process with very little risk to my long-term health, so I .... so much time worrying about it.

h The police officer flagged my car down and pointed out that I .... so fast in a residential area.

Listening

Part 3

1 **Look at these pictures. What are the extreme weather conditions? What problems do they cause?**

Exam practice

2 🔊 1·21 **You will hear an interview with Cindy Talbot on the radio programme, *Young hero or heroine of the week*. For questions 1–5, choose the answer (A, B, C or D) which fits best according to what you hear.**

1 How did Cindy react when she heard the thunder?
- A She decided to take a rest until the storm passed.
- B She was relieved that the storm was so far away.
- C She felt rather worried about what the storm might bring.
- D She was surprised by the closeness of the storm.

2 How did Cindy regard her decision to take shelter from the storm?
- A She thought it was sensible.
- B She admitted it was understandable.
- C She found it incomprehensible.
- D She knew it was inadvisable.

3 What were Rod and Mark doing when they saw Cindy?
- A walking in the woods
- B travelling along a forest path
- C removing a tree blocking the road
- D making their way to a nearby hospital

4 What was Rod and Mark's initial reaction to Cindy's story?
- A They were dubious about its authenticity.
- B They were amazed by her lucky escape.
- C They were worried about the long-term effects on her health.
- D They were curious about the outcome.

5 What effect has the experience had on Cindy?
- A She is more aware of her own limitations.
- B She is wary of hiking long distances alone.
- C She is adamant not to let it stop her pursuing her interests.
- D She is reluctant to venture out in stormy weather.

Tip

In the exam, you will have one minute to read through the questions for Part 3. Use this time to read the questions and all the options quickly. Then read the questions a second time so that you know what to listen for.

Your views

3 **Discuss these questions.**

a What happened to Cindy? What would you have done in her situation?

b Do you have extreme weather conditions in your country? How do they affect you?

c What measures can be taken to protect people from these extreme weather conditions?

Vocabulary

Expressions with *weather* and *storm*

4 **Complete the expressions below using either *weather* or *storm*. Then decide what each one means.**

a *the calm before the* ....

b *make heavy* .... *of sth*

c *ride the* ....

d *under the* ....

e *take somebody/something by* ....

f *keep a* .... *eye on somebody/something*

g *a* .... *of protest*

h *a* .... *in a teacup*

5 **Use some of the expressions to make your own sentences.**

Reading & Use of English | Part 5

1 **If you were in an emergency situation how do you think you would react?**

2 **Now read the text on page 57 about how people react in emergencies. How does it compare with your ideas?**

Exam practice

Tip

Delete the options that you know are incorrect first and then consider the ones you are left with.

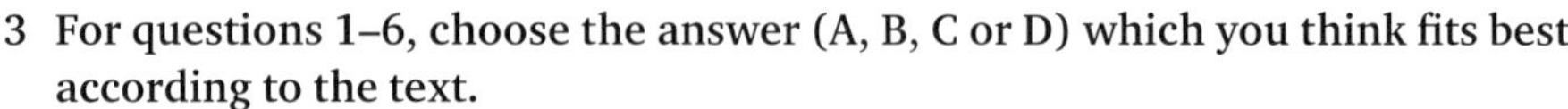

3 **For questions 1–6, choose the answer (A, B, C or D) which you think fits best according to the text.**

1 What is suggested about the reactions of people in emergencies?
- A People are less likely to panic if they are with complete strangers.
- B Being with people we know helps speed up our reactions to danger.
- C People are more determined to escape if they are with family and friends.
- D Our concern for the welfare of others often puts our own lives in danger.

2 The writer compares the notion of affiliation with
- A the attitude of terrorist bombers.
- B the everyday behaviour of ordinary people.
- C the conduct of people towards others they do not know.
- D the change in people's attitudes in an emergency.

3 According to research, how did people behave after the fire broke out?
- A In their desire to escape, they blocked access to many of the emergency exits.
- B They acted more or less as they would have done in a normal situation.
- C Their competitive attitude prevented them from helping those in need.
- D They showed more concern for family and friends than for strangers.

4 What conclusion does the writer draw about people's behaviour in emergencies?
- A People are more likely to reject social norms if they are on their own.
- B People who share a social identity are more hampered in their ability to escape.
- C Identifying with a group in an emergency can be extremely beneficial.
- D It is difficult to predict exactly how a crowd will behave in an emergency.

5 According to the writer, what was exemplary about the case of the miners?
- A their like-mindedness in a critical situation
- B their sticking to their usual routine
- C their determination to be rescued
- D their emphasis on health care

6 What is the writer suggesting happens in an emergency?
- A People respond effectively when they hear sirens and alarms.
- B Issuing adequate information increases the chances of survival.
- C Live public address systems are less effective than they seem.
- D Public warnings prevent danger zones becoming overcrowded.

Text analysis

4 **Work through a–h, referring to paragraphs (A–H) in the text.**
- a Which word is used to explain that something is commonly referred to by the term specified? (A)
- b Which verb is used to conjure up a dramatic picture of catastrophe? (A)
- c Find a phrase which means: if something had not happened. (B)
- d Find a phrase which means: a complete explanation. (B)
- e Why does the writer use the expression *rich insight*? (line 26)
- f Find a word which means: for this reason. (D)
- g Why is the expression *buddy system* in quotation marks? (line 55)
- h Which phrase reflects the writer's criticism of how planners regard the public? (H)

Crowd control

A Perhaps the most obvious explanation for why we help others in emergencies is that we know them. So-called 'affiliation theorists' such as Andrew Mawson, a Professor of Public Health at Jackson State University, say that panic is rare because we are typically in the company of friends or family when disaster strikes. The presence of familiar others soothes us and counteracts our 'fight or flight' instincts.

B Jonathan Sime's study of the 1973 fire at the Summerland leisure centre on the Isle of Man provides poignant support for this view. He showed that many people might have escaped but for the fact that they chose to stay in family groups, going at the pace of the slowest – a pace that was too slow for survival in some cases. Sime argues that people die in emergencies not because they are competing but because they care for one another. But the notion of affiliation cannot be the whole story. In emergencies such as the London terrorist bombings, people were among strangers but were nonetheless orderly, cooperative and even self-sacrificing. Sociologists who study disasters have shown that in an emergency, individuals remain committed to the same rules of conduct that govern everyday behaviour.

C A case in point is the lethal fire at the Beverly Hills Supper Club near Cincinnati in 1977. As the fire spread through the building, the opportunities for exit became more and more restricted. In the end, 165 people lost their lives but there was no mass panic. The 630 witness statements given to the police provide rich insight into how people behaved. Certainly there was evidence of affiliation. People moved in family or friendship groups, and if one died, the others were likely to die as well. But as a number of researchers – particularly sociologist Norris Johnson of the University of Cincinnati – have shown, social norms were observed. The staff continued to look after the customers, with waiters attending to the safety of those at their assigned tables. The customers observed normal courtesies, such as allowing the elderly to go first. As the seriousness of the situation became more evident, there was an increase in competitive behaviours. But Johnson reports that even at the most urgent stages of the evacuation, social bonds remained largely intact; people picked one another up when they fell, for example.

D The conclusion: continuity exists between everyday behaviours and emergencies. Regardless of whether people think of themselves as individuals or as part of a community, they observe social norms. Human beings do not forget themselves, their values or their obligations to others both close and distant. They do not turn into savages desperate to escape. Disasters bring out the best – not the beast – in people. If models of crowd behaviours are to be more psychologically accurate and hence more useful at predicting how people will behave in an emergency, they must include dynamic 'group membership' variables. The shared social identity of any group can be the basis for an efficient and orderly evacuation, rather than a source of pathological 'panic'.

E For example, the social solidarity of the thirty-three Chilean miners trapped half a mile underground in 2010 played an essential role in maintaining their physical and mental health as they awaited rescue. The miners organized their own chapel services and a 'buddy system' of three-person teams, and they began eating each meal only after rations for everyone had been painstakingly lowered through a hole. A miner who had taken a nursing course monitored the group's health and administered tests and vaccinations. The miners aided rescue efforts by preparing a map of their surroundings and clearing rocks.

F Evidence suggests that the single biggest killer in emergencies is lack of information – for example, when people do not evacuate promptly because they do not realize the danger. Live public address systems are more effective than sirens and alarms for providing credible information about the nature and the location of the danger. In places where there is a danger of overcrowding, video monitoring can provide early warning signals.

G Emergency planners should encourage collectivity, not fear of it. Disasters tend to bring people together, but other social forces often divide people. Even the language that is used to address groups in public spaces may make a difference. Addressing people instead as members of a group – 'passengers' or 'citizens', for example – may help prevent them from competing with one another in a rush for the exits.

H Emergency planners need to consider ordinary people their best asset rather than their worst nightmare. Instead of undermining people's natural tendency to organize and help one another, authorities can facilitate it by providing practical information – such as exit routes that are clearly marked with arrows and reflective paint. When ordinary people are asked to take increased responsibility for their own survival and well-being, they can do extraordinary things.

From *Scientific American Mind*

Speaking | Part 3

1 **Discuss your reactions to this quotation.**

Considering how dangerous everything is, nothing is really frightening. (Gertrude Stein)

2 🔊 **1·22 Listen to five people talking about a difficult situation they found themselves in. Match what they say to situations a–f and make a note of how they dealt with the situation. There is one situation you do not need to use.**

a a breakdown

b a delayed flight

c a hotel fire

d a robbery

e got lost

f going through airport security

3 **Compare your notes with a partner's, then decide what you would have done if you'd been faced with the situations in 2.**

Understanding the task

4 **Work with a partner. You are going to speak for about two minutes based on a prompt card. Then you will have to answer a further question. First, read your prompt cards carefully. Underline the key words in the questions.**

A What risks do people face in the modern world?	**B** In what ways are we exposed to fewer dangers than previous generations?
– travelling	– new technology
– environmental problems	– medical breakthroughs
– crime	– rules and regulations

Planning

5 **Think about how to answer. Make notes like those below. For each prompt, use the three perspectives to help you. This will give you ideas to talk about for two minutes.**

Personal: your personal point of view based on experience

Local: the point of view of your local community or surroundings

Global: a global or international point of view

Travelling
personal: feel uneasy when I travel alone
local: some accident black spots in this area
global: air travel increases health risks and environmental problems

> **Tip**
> In the exam, you have up to 10 seconds to think about what you are going to say. As you are talking, use the three points of view (personal, local and global) to help you think up ideas and keep talking.

Exam practice

6 **Work with a partner. You are going to speak for about two minutes. Student A turn to page 164, Student B turn to page 165 and follow the instructions. You can use the notes you made in 5 to help you.**

Exploring the topic

7 🔊 **1·23 Now listen to some more general questions about risks. Discuss your answers with a partner.**

Writing | Part 2, Letter

Understanding the task 1 **Read this exam task and answer questions a–b.**

> You have decided to write a letter to give your views on an article you read in a newspaper about how some rules and regulations, for example anti-smoking laws and traffic control, affect our personal freedoms. You decide to write a letter (280–320 words) in which you briefly describe how you feel about this issue and whether the regulations are justified or not.

a Who is the target audience for the letter?

b What kind of opinions do you think the newspaper would be most interested in?

Text analysis 2 **Read this sample letter and answer questions a–d.**

a What is the main topic or purpose of each paragraph?

b How well does the letter suit the target reader(s)?

c What register has the letter been written in?

d What phrases and expressions does the writer use to express his views?

Dear Editor,

I am writing in response to your recent column about unreasonable rules and would like to share my ideas with you. I would definitely agree that such controls are getting worse, and that it would be infinitely preferable for authorities to spend more time on things such as solving crime.

Having said that, it is also true that the regulations do some good. For example, the anti-smoking campaign has clearly saved lives, and people have also benefited from government advice on sunbathing and skin cancer. As far as road safety goes, the compulsory wearing of seat belts has long been accepted as normal. Accident rates have also fallen, thanks to government initiatives such as drink-driving laws, speed cameras and traffic-calming measures.

However, the main problem is that the controls go too far. Not content with informing people of the dangers of smoking, the government introduces a ban on smoking in pubs and restaurants, on trains and in offices; it introduces high taxation, bans tobacco advertising, and does its best to force people to change their behaviour. This is what tends to irritate people the most. Of course, it is vitally important that we should be given the facts about smoking or sunbathing, but we should also have the right to make up our own mind.

The same applies to road safety. They are continually trying to reduce speed limits on motorways, which is a complete waste of time given that the vast majority of motorway drivers exceed the current speed limit by 10 or 15 miles an hour, and it serves no purpose whatsoever having a law that nobody obeys. The government should accept that there will always be some risk involved in driving a car, and it will never be possible to make the roads completely safe.

To sum up, I think that regulations have gone far enough. There is no evidence of a need for further legislation on health issues and motoring. What we do need is simple information, and we should be allowed to decide for ourselves how we want to lead our lives.

Yours faithfully,

Adverb and adjective collocations

3 Match the adverbs in list A with a suitable adjective in list B. More than one answer may be possible.

A: *drastically vitally gravely wildly wholly vehemently deeply infinitely grossly fully frankly hopelessly*

B: *preferable important offensive inaccurate opposed to unfounded unpopular improved mistaken inefficient ludicrous justified*

Sentence adverbs

4 Rewrite sentences a–l using an adverb from the list below. There are some you do not need to use.

admittedly ultimately apparently theoretically amazingly put simply obviously traditionally typically realistically frankly generally coincidentally as far as … concerned logically financially technically

a I heard that the bus crashed because of faulty brakes.
b I think I should say that there are still some lingering concerns about safety.
c At the end of the day, parents should decide what is best for their children and not the politicians.
d If I have to be honest, I'm not surprised he hurt himself.
e If you use a mobile phone while driving, you are a risk to other motorists.
f They were driving incredibly fast when they crashed, but no one was hurt.
g Smoking is bad for you. Can I make it any clearer?!
h We will never eliminate all risks.
i He took us out for a spin and drove way too fast as he usually does.
j It's possible, but unlikely, that we will be able to rescue them before nightfall.
k The new law will also lead to a reduction in fatalities on our roads.
l Most drivers in my country don't buckle up when driving.

5 Use some of the language in 3 and 4 to write sentences of your own. When you have finished, compare with a partner. Do they agree with you?

Exam practice *Writing guide page 142*

6 Read the exam task below. Use the checklist below to help you write your answer.

A sports magazine has invited its readers to write letters on the topic of dangerous sports. You have decided to write a letter (280–320 words) expressing your views about dangerous sports and what you think the responsibilities of the people who do these sports are.

Stage 1: Read
Who will read your letter?

Stage 2: Think
What is your opinion about dangerous sports? What are the responsibilities of the people who do them?

Stage 3: Plan
Make a detailed plan using this structure if you like:
Introduction – Problems – Risks – Responsibilities – Conclusion

Stage 4: Write
Make your opinions clear, and, where possible, give examples to support your views.

Stage 5: Check
Is the register appropriate?
Have you used a variety of ways to express your opinions?

Tip

Remember that your letter could be read by thousands of newspaper readers. Don't address the editor personally. This is your chance to make your opinions known; express them clearly and intelligently.

Unit 6 Health & lifestyle

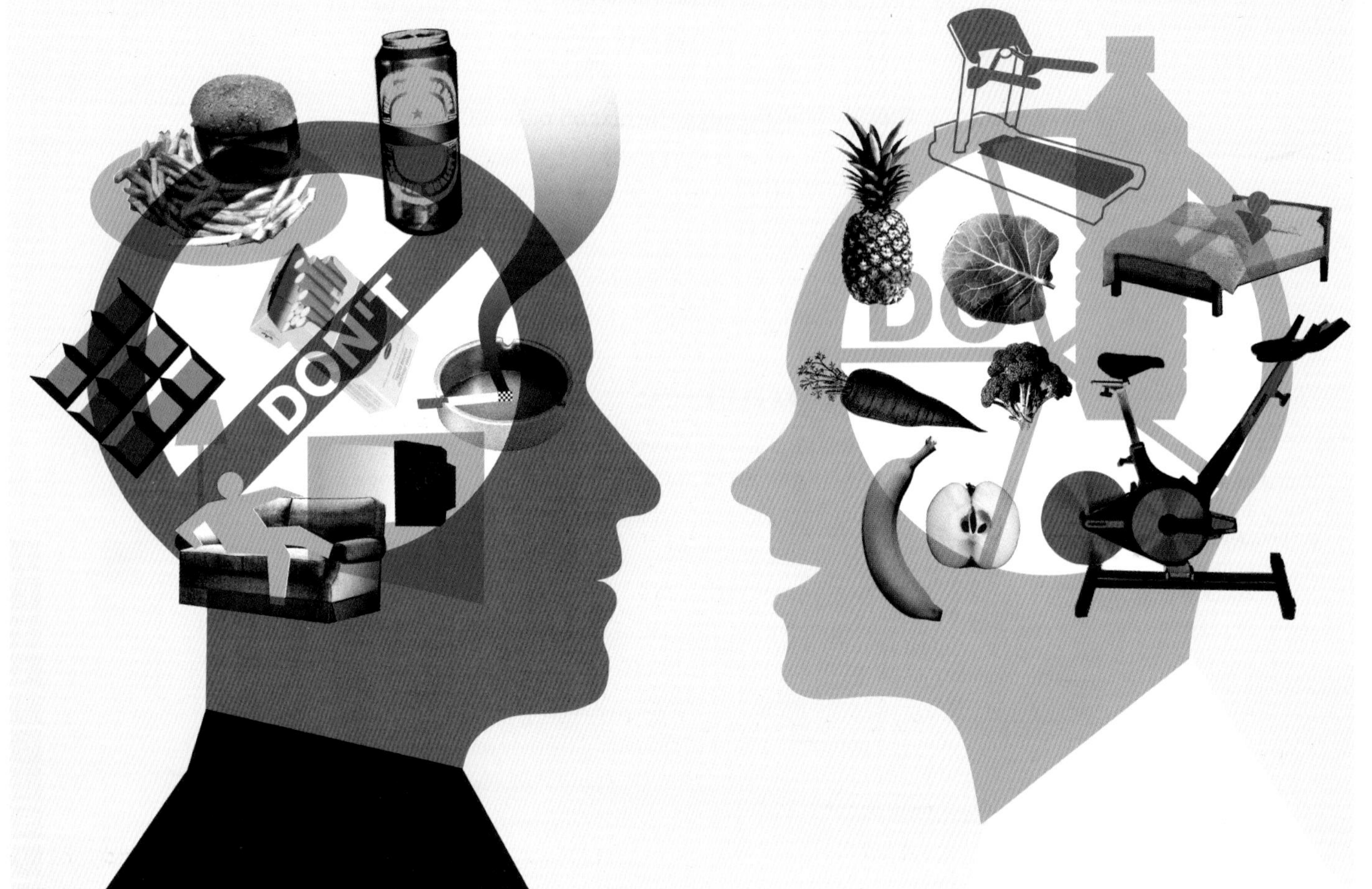

Introduction

1 **Look at the poster about leading a healthy lifestyle. Decide how practical and useful the advice is.**

2 **1·24 Listen to a man expressing his views about taking physical exercise and quickly note down your answers to questions a–e.**

a According to the man, what type of people take physical exercise?

b How does he think people who exercise regularly react to those who don't?

c What does he find rather worrying about exercising?

d What comment does he make about finding out about your true self?

e What other arguments are put forward against exercising?

3 **Listen again and note the phrases the speaker uses to state his opinions and give examples.**

4 **Do you agree with the speaker? Why/Why not?**

5 **Discuss these questions with a partner. Try to give personal examples to illustrate the language.**

a Why would you tell someone to *get a life*?

b Who would you describe as *the life and soul of the party*?

c When would you say an object *has a life of its own*?

d When would you say *life's too short*?

e When would you use *not on your life*?

f When would you say *that's life*?

g When was the last time someone *frightened the life out of you*?

h When would you say *for the life of me*?

i Who would you describe as *the light of your life*?

j How would someone get *a new lease of life*?

6 **With a partner, discuss your *own* attitudes to health and lifestyle. Try to use some of the phrases in 3. The topic areas below might help you.**

video games *dieting* *becoming a vegetarian* *joining a gym*

Reading & Use of English | Part 7

1 **Decide which of these statements applies more to you. Then explain why to a partner.**

a I live to eat. b I eat to live.

Skim reading

2 **Quickly read through the text on page 63. Answer these questions.**

a Which of these is the most suitable heading for the text?
Students' diets healthier than we think
Fast-food fad failure
Male students eschew balanced diet for supplements
New survey reveals full extent of eating disorders

b Would a situation like this happen in your country? Why/Why not?

Exam practice

Tip

Underline the information that helps you to answer the question and put the number of the question beside it. This will help you to locate it when you check your answers.

3 **For questions 1–10 choose from the sections (A–E) in the article about dietary trends. The sections may be chosen more than once.**

In which section are the following mentioned?

– a noticeable gap in existing research 1
– extrinsic motivation 2
– the unimportance of social status 3
– the unwelcome results of a certain dietary regime 4
– a tendency to splash out on things other than food 5
– a potential means of financing further research 6
– a reluctance to take heed of advice given 7
– a sector of the student population with increased awareness of healthy eating 8
– an anecdote about former student days 9
– a discovery which has revealed an unforeseen tendency 10

Text analysis

4 **Work through a–g, referring to paragraphs (A–E) in the text.**

a What does the writer mean by the term *a fair percentage*? (A)
b Why does the writer put the expression *disordered eating patterns* in quotation marks? (A)
c What effect does the use of the construction *The more …, the more…* have on the reader? (C)
d Why does the writer include the three questions? (D)
e Express in your own words what the writer means by a *susceptibility to the blandishments of men's magazines*. (D)
f What is the plural of the word *phenomenon*? (D)
g What does the writer mean by the term *a level playing field*? (E)

Expressions connected with illness and injury

5 **The following list contains eight physical complaints. Unfortunately, the words have been arranged incorrectly. Rearrange them to discover what the complaints are.**

a writer's elbow
b a sprained strain
c a torn disc
d eye cramp
e a splitting infection
f an ear ligament
g a slipped headache
h tennis ankle

6 **Have you ever suffered from any of the complaints in 5? Tell a partner.**

A We didn't need an in-depth research project into students' eating habits to tell us that a fair percentage of the student population eat too few vegetables. Fortunately, the UK's first study of the dietary changes brought about by going to university delves into more wide-ranging issues. And it has already unearthed a less predictable trend. Male students are particularly prone to what Dr Ricardo Costa from Coventry University calls 'disordered eating patterns'. Not to be confused with eating disorders. 'We're not talking about bulimia, anorexia and other psychological conditions,' he stresses. 'That's not my field.'

B Dr Farzad Amirabdollahian, whose field is dietetics and human nutrition, and one of his colleagues have so far carried out around 130 in-depth interviews with undergraduates of both sexes. Between now and next April they hope to talk to another 270. 'That 400 will give us a really strong idea of the trends in one university,' says Costa. 'From there, we hope to apply for a grant and expand the study to two more.'

C One university likely to be chosen for the study is Hertfordshire, where Amirabdollahian used to work; the other is in North Wales, where Costa did research while also working as a dietician elsewhere. 'The more I looked into the obesity epidemic, the more it became clear that there was a lot of evidence about the dietary habits of children and adults, but very little in between,' he explains. 'I knew that my diet changed when I first went to university and colleagues had told me that it was the same for them. I thought it was time we looked at what living the student life is doing to your body.'

D As many as 50% of male students who have taken part in the survey seem to share with contemporaries from all walks of life a susceptibility to the blandishments of men's magazines. 'They're very focused on their body image and not just to meet sporting needs,' says Costa. Does he mean that they want to get rid of the burgeoning paunch and put on muscle to look good for women? 'Yes, that's what the trend suggests. But instead of trying to achieve it through a balanced diet as well as exercise, they're going for disordered eating – outside the norm, in other words. They're spending their money on dietary supplements such as protein powders and amino acids.' Any food to go with that? 'They tend to go for a lot of high-protein, low-fat meat, such as chicken or turkey breast from the economy or frozen ranges. Fish and chips are also one of the fast-food options for students who aren't in the habit of cooking healthy food. Oh yes, and egg whites, without the yolks.' Fruit and veg? 'Very little.' This may, of course, be a phase that many of these young men will grow out of. But if it continues, the consequences for their health could be serious. 'The liver and kidneys eventually struggle to break down an excess of protein,' Costa warns, 'so liver and kidney failure is a distinct possibility in the long term. We've already seen that phenomenon among body builders. They're also going to have a deficiency in good-quality fats. That can ultimately lead to cardiac problems. And don't forget the mental issues that will arise for those who fail to meet this idealized body image.' He would dearly love to involve psychologists as the project expands and spreads. Not only to work with young men worried about their lack of muscle, but also to find new ways of spreading the healthy-eating message across campuses. 'Posters don't seem to work,' he says.

E The research, still in its early stages, already indicates a disinclination to buy what Costa calls 'proper food'. With the exception of mature students, cooking skills are low and consumption of ready meals and takeaways high. Very few respondents are eating anywhere near the 'five-a-day' fruit and vegetable intake recommended, he says. 'Females were better than males in that regard and students in the health professions were well above average. But even among them, the average was only four portions a day.' Admittedly we are talking about flats, bedsits and halls of residence in Coventry rather than a Cambridge college. But the trend seems to be common to students of all social backgrounds. 'Another finding from the early stages of our work is that parents' income and education have no apparent influence on students' dietary choices,' says Costa. 'No matter if you're rich or poor, university is a level playing field.' Well, when it comes to nutritional standards, anyway.

From *The Guardian*

Reading & Use of English | Part 2

1 Look at the images above. Discuss these questions.

a What kind of people do you think enjoy taking part in sports like these?

b What skills and abilities do people need to do these sports well?

c Which of these sports appeals to you most? Why?

2 Read the following extract from a newspaper article, ignoring the gaps. What method of training for sporting activities is suggested.

Working out to music can improve the coordination of your mind and body (1) .... you are football crazy or keen on tennis. The idea of exercise to music is, however, (2) .... new. For years, especially in Eastern Europe, the benefits of having instruction in ballet and classical dance, with their stress (3) .... total body control and balance, have been recognized.

Figure-skating and ice-dance are usually performed to music and can be said to be specialized (4) .... of this type of exercise. But ballet and classical dance can be applied to other sports that are also pleasing to the eye, such as gymnastics and skiing, both of which demand high standards of balance, coordination and suppleness.

In Western Europe and North America, a far (5) .... interest has been shown in working out to classical music. Even participants in sports which seem to demand muscular strength more than (6) .... other physical requirement have taken up exercise to music. Devotees of soccer, rugby and rowing now regularly train to music. Even those who take (7) .... in weightlifting, which demands enormous physical strength, and participants in track and field events, find that exercise to music is beneficial and (8) .... their movements more fluid.

Tip

The words that come before and after each gap can give you valuable clues about the type of word that is missing.

Exam practice

3 Read the article again and, as you read, try to decide which part of speech best fits each gap. Then choose the word you think best completes each gap.

Grammar *See notes page 155*

See notes page 155

Defining and non-defining relative clauses

4 Read through the text in 2 and underline the relative clauses. How many defining and non-defining clauses can you find?

5 Answer the following questions.

a Look at sentences 1 and 2. Which would you use after the following information?
At our annual golf club dinner, we always invite a celebrity to hand out the prizes.

1 The professional golfer who attended the annual club dinner last year had won two previous championships.

2 The professional golfer, who attended the annual club dinner last year, had won two previous championships.

b In which sentence could the relative pronoun be omitted? Why?

1 Ballet and classical dance techniques can be applied to other sports which are also pleasing to the eye.

2 Ballet and classical dance techniques can be applied to other sports which spectators find pleasing to the eye.

c What words are missing from these three sentences?

1 The money, ________ was collected at the entrance to the stadium on Saturday, was stolen.

2 Participants in sports such as gymnastics and skiing, both of ________ demand high standards of coordination, would benefit from dance training.

3 The UK, ________ bid to host the football World Cup failed in 2011, is unlikely to make another bid for some time to come.

d What does the relative pronoun refer to in this sentence?
He resigned as manager of the club, which shocked everybody.

6 Which of the options (1–4) can be used to complete the sentences? More than one option may be correct (– = no relative pronoun).

a The American journalist ________ interviewed the tennis champion reminded me of my brother.
1 who 2 that 3 which 4 –

b The liver, ________ is about 30 centimetres long, helps in the digestion of food.
1 who 2 that 3 which 4 –

c We decided to engage the two young dancers ________ perform on television.
1 whom we had seen 2 who we had seen them 3 which we had seen
4 we had seen

d The new concert hall, ________ was opened yesterday, holds two thousand people.
1 that 2 which 3 which it 4 –

e He had never had any formal education, ________ amazed me.
1 that 2 which 3 which it 4 –

f The new stadium won't be finished for another two years; by ________ it'll be out of date.
1 which 2 which time 3 that 4 then

Reduced clauses

7 We can use reduced relative clauses instead of relative pronouns to make sentences shorter or to vary style and effect. For example:

The cricketer who was found guilty of fixing matches was banned for life.

The cricketer found guilty of fixing matches was banned for life.

Decide whether these sentences are correct or not. If they are wrong, correct them.

a Athletes used these techniques show a marked improvement in performance.

b Competitors trained when they are young stand a greater chance of being successful.

c The stadium having been built for the event is already an architectural talking point.

d Humiliating by their defeat, the losing team trudged towards the dressing rooms.

e Beaming with joy, the swimming champion received her gold medal.

f There was a sudden downpour of rain stopping the tennis match in the final set.

g There are several items needing to buy before your first fencing lesson.

h The first person winning the Tour de France cycling competition was the Frenchman Maurice Garin in 1903.

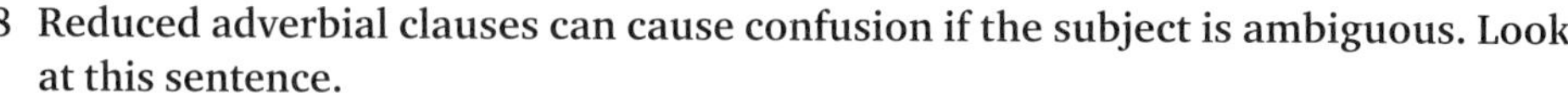

8 Reduced adverbial clauses can cause confusion if the subject is ambiguous. Look at this sentence.

Driven to desperation by hunger, a frog will make a passable meal.

What does it mean?

a A frog will produce a reasonable meal if it's desperately hungry.

b Frogs are only worth eating if they're desperately hungry.

c If you're desperately hungry, a frog might be a good meal for you to have.

9 Decide which of these reduced adverbial clauses might cause confusion. Explain why.

a Opening the door, I began to feel scared.

b Looked after carefully, I can make my car last for years.

c Faced with rising costs, many companies are going out of business.

d Having run half of the race, my T-shirt felt as if it was sticking to my back.

10 Rewrite a–c so that their meaning is clear.

a Dreaming of how their lives would be together, the priest pronounced them man and wife.

b Looking through the binoculars, the distant eagle seemed to be preparing to swoop down on its prey.

c Dressed in her new school uniform, I began to realize Sally was no longer my baby girl.

Vocabulary

Expressions connected with sport

11 Complete expressions a–k using a word from the list. Then decide what the expressions might mean and when you might use them.

towel ropes blow end goal goalposts neck runner stumped square rules

a play by the ______

b back to ______ one

c be thrown in at the deep ______

d move the ______

e be ______ for an idea

f be a front ______

g be on the ______

h deal someone a knock-out ______

i score an own ______

j be neck and ______

k throw in the ______

Listening | Part 1

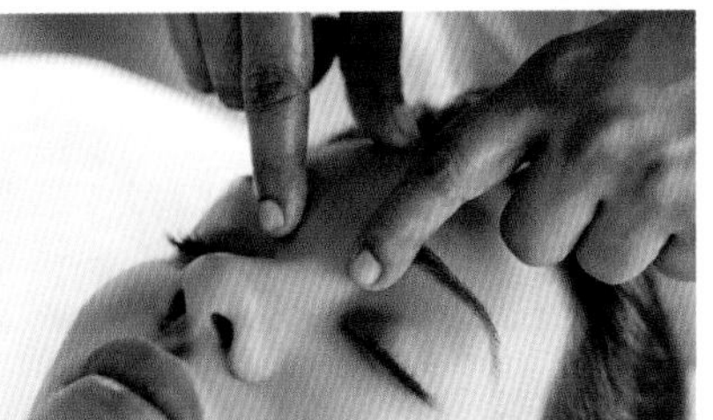

1 **Look at the pictures. What forms of alternative medicine do they represent? Explain what the treatments involve and what problems they might be used to treat.**

acupressure hypnotherapy herbalism acupuncture

Exam practice

2 1·25 **You will hear three different extracts. For questions 1–6, choose the answer (A, B or C) which fits best according to what you hear. There are two questions for each extract.**

Extract 1: You hear part of a conversation about alternative medicine.

1 How did the woman feel before her first session of hypnotherapy?
A distrustful
B enthusiastic
C fearful

2 What do the man and woman agree about?
A the effectiveness of alternative medicine
B the addictive nature of hypnosis
C the hidden powers of the brain

Extract 2: You hear a woman talking on the radio about the power of hypnosis.

3 The woman says people's attempts to give up smoking often fail because of
A the lack of encouragement from friends.
B the desire to retain the freedom of choice.
C their own lack of motivation.

4 She suggests that hypnotherapy can also enable you to
A help others to deal with stress.
B put yourself in a totally hypnotic state.
C cope with your own anxieties.

Extract 3: You hear a journalist talking about diagnosing patients travelling by plane.

5 What comment does the journalist make about people travelling?
A They feel apprehensive about long-distance travel.
B They are terrified of needing medical help when travelling.
C They are prudent enough to take a first-aid kit on a long journey.

6 According to the journalist, on one airline passengers can be reassured by the fact that
A there is always one qualified doctor on board.
B all flight attendants have undergone medical training.
C a patient can be monitored by doctors elsewhere.

Tip

In the exam, the three extracts will all have a completely different theme and style. Read the questions and options carefully in the 15 seconds given before the recording starts.

Talking about feelings

3 **Complete a–e using a word from the list below and a suitable preposition. All the words appear in the listening. More than one answer may be possible.**

craving sceptical suffering addicted apprehensive fascinated

a I was very .... trying hypnosis.
b I thought I was becoming .... sleeping pills.
c I'm .... the human brain.
d Occasionally I have a .... a cigarette.
e I am .... a lot of stress at the moment.

Your views

4 **Discuss these questions.**

a What kinds of cures do you find most effective if you're feeling ill?
b Can alternative medicine ever be a more effective cure than conventional medicine?

Speaking Part 2

A B C D

Promoting a healthy lifestyle

1 List as many words as you can which are connected with the pictures.

Tip

Discuss ideas together and give reasons for your suggestions. Encourage your partner to contribute to the discussion. Don't worry if you disagree but respect your partner's opinions.

Exam practice

2 1·26 Listen and make a note of what you have to do in the first phase of the task.

3 Now work with a partner and do the task. Remember, you have about one minute to do this phase of Part 2.

Being less direct

4 1·27 You will hear eight pairs of sentences. For each pair, decide which is more polite and why.

5 1·28 Listen and make a note of what you have to do in the next phase of the task.

6 Now work with a partner and do the task. Remember, you have about three minutes to do this phase of Part 2. Try and use some of the language in 4.

Useful vocabulary

get the message across	*make an impact*
stand out	*striking/successful image*
attract the attention of the reader	*grab your attention*
makes much more of a statement	

Your views

7 In small groups, discuss the following questions.

a To what extent do you think parents can encourage their children to lead a healthy lifestyle?

b Why do you think governments try to encourage people to be as fit and healthy as possible?

c Should sport be a compulsory part of a school curriculum? Why/Why not?

d Some people say that good health is just a matter of luck. What's your opinion?

Writing | Part 2, Article

Understanding the task

1 **Read this exam task and answer questions a–d.**

A health magazine has invited readers to write an article about significant changes to lifestyles in their own country. Write your article (280–320 words) giving details of changes and your opinion on the positive and negative impacts of these changes.

a Who are the target readers?
b What expectations of the article might readers have?
c What style of writing would be appropriate to this article?
d Write an outline plan of how you would approach this task. Compare your outline with your partner's.

Text analysis

2 **Read the article and answer questions a–d.**

a How is the article different from a formal essay?
b Are the writer's opinions clear? Do they present different perspectives?
c What specific words or phrases make the style informal?
d What persuasive devices does the writer use?

Busy, busy, busy

With obesity having shot up across the globe to dangerously high levels in recent years, it is little wonder that people have started to ask why. True, diets have changed; we all know that we live in a McWorld, hunting and gathering our food from fast-food outlets and supermarket aisles, but it can't all be down to diet, can it?

Technology has changed modern life to such an extent that few aspects of life today bear any resemblance to lives only a couple of generations ago. Just taking jobs as an example, how many of us today spend twelve hours a day on our feet physically slogging ourselves into the ground? Or how many families could you imagine living without a car? Kids walking to school, parents going to half a dozen local shops, on foot, to buy the week's food, family holidays by bus to the nearest seaside town. Take Tina Jameson, a mother of two who has to juggle home and a part-time job. She says 'I haven't got time to walk anywhere. But I'd have even less time without a washing machine or dishwasher.' We now have so many conveniences in our lives that allow us such drastically better lifestyle choices that at times it can be difficult to picture these in a negative way.

Without doubt there are positives to these changes. The number of people who suffer debilitating injuries at work is miniscule in comparison to the past. Fewer hours working and more efficient transport are all to our benefit in allowing us a greater amount of leisure time. At what cost though? We may save a few hours a day travelling and enjoy less physically demanding working conditions, but is this really worth it when the cost to our health and life expectancy is so high? Modern lifestyles have become shockingly sedentary and in combination with the deterioration in diet this is surely creating a ticking time bomb for modern humanity.

Writing skills: exemplification

3 **Read the article again. Underline the examples the writer gives to support each main idea.**

4 **Discuss with a partner how some of the examples are similar in style. How are the examples introduced?**

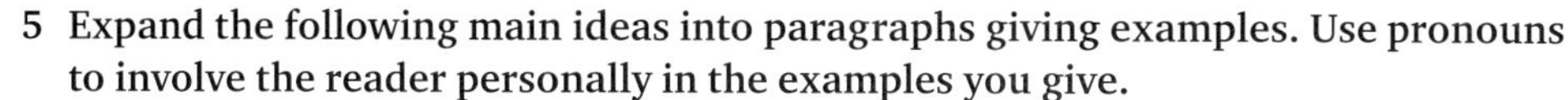

5 Expand the following main ideas into paragraphs giving examples. Use pronouns to involve the reader personally in the examples you give.

a Modern technology means many people can now do a range of things at home that once required them to leave the house.

b Few jobs today require any physical exertion whatsoever.

c Shockingly, in Western countries this is the first generation that is expected to live a shorter life than their parents.

Persuasive devices

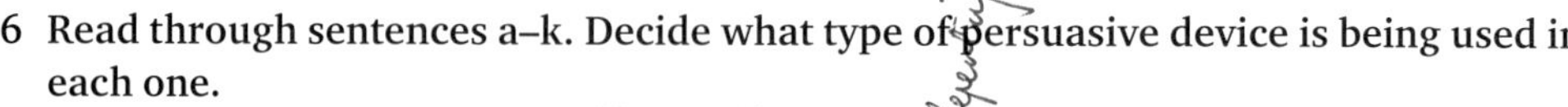

6 Read through sentences a–k. Decide what type of persuasive device is being used in each one.

a That's the truth, the whole truth, and nothing but the truth.

b Can we honestly call ourselves human when we let such injustice go unchallenged?

c I'm sure you will agree that trampling over their rights is simply unfair.

d The fast food industry is responsible for pumping salt and goodness knows what else into our children's bodies.

e For behaviour like this to be taking place today is nothing less than dirty, disgusting, and despicable.

f I despise fitness routines. I despise healthy eating. I despise yoga.

g The economy is on its knees, begging for forgiveness.

h There are a thousand reasons why more research is needed on the dangers of a sedentary lifestyle.

i The argument for a proposed tax on high calorie foods is as flimsy as a philanderer's promise.

j In an age of pressurized happiness, we seem to have grown insensitive to simple pleasures.

k Fame makes men proud; failure makes them wise.

7 Look at the suggested topics below. Write sentences using the persuasive devices above.

dieting *healthy foods* *exercising* *lifestyles*

Exam practice *See Writing guide page 140*

Tip

Providing examples to illustrate the point you are trying to make can help clarify ideas. It also adds interest and personalization to an article.

8 Read the exam task below. Use the checklist below to help you write your answer.

A health magazine has invited readers to write an article about significant changes to diet in their own country. Write your article (280–320 words) giving details of changes and your opinion on the positive and negative impacts of these changes.

Stage 1: Read
Who will read the article?

Stage 2: Think
What are the most significant changes? What have been the positive and negative consequences?

Stage 3: Plan
Make a detailed plan using this structure if you wish:
Main changes – Positive impact – Negative impact – Your opinion

Stage 4: Write
Use language that will capture your reader's interest.

Stage 5: Check
Is the register appropriate?
Will it capture your reader's interest?

Unit 7 Science & technology

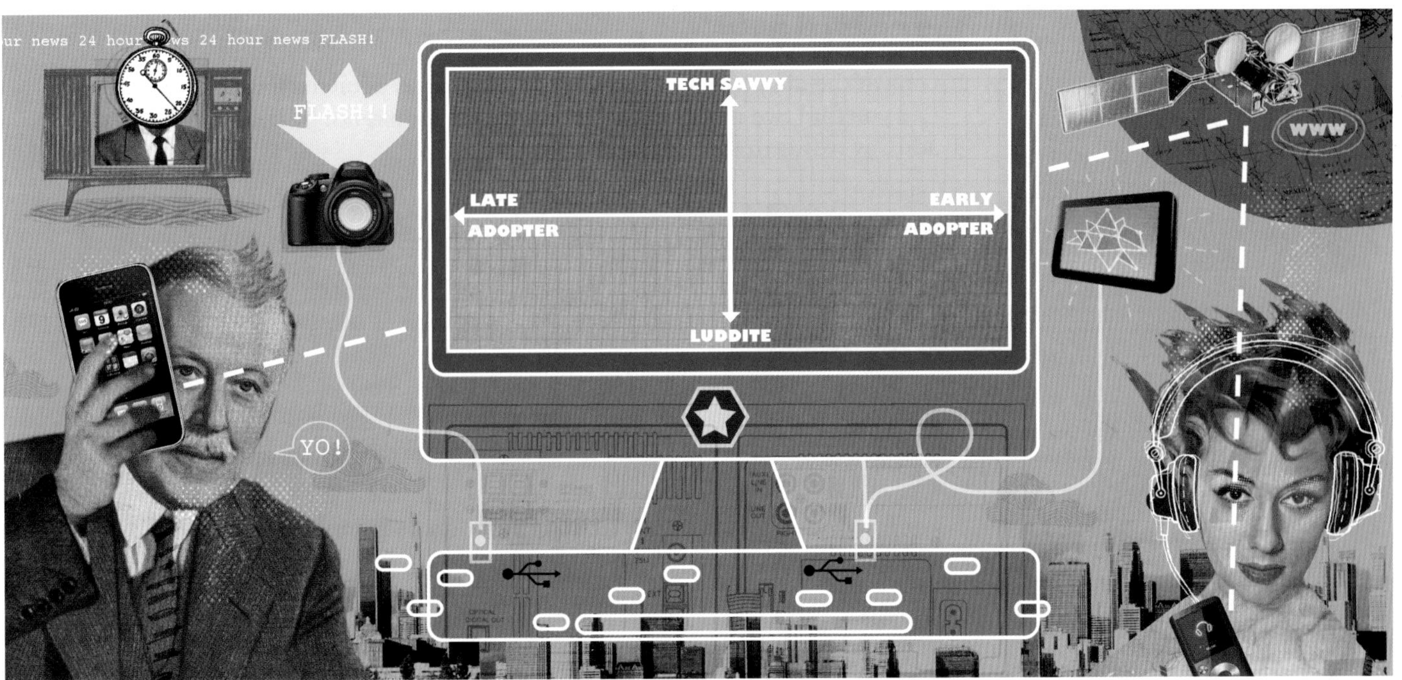

Introduction

1 Discuss these questions.

a What do the expressions *digital native* and *digital immigrant* mean to you?

b Look at the matrix. Mark where you would place yourself in the matrix. Then compare with other students. Which was the most/least popular choice?

2 Which of these statements do you think are true and which are false. Mark them *T* or *F*.

a The composition of the human brain is changing because of exposure to technology.

b Exposure to digital technology has very little effect on our behaviour and feelings.

c The brain has the capacity to focus equally on both technological and social skills.

3 Read the abridged extract from an article below to check your answers.

4 Circle the words in the text that are synonyms of the word *change*. How are they different in meaning? Can you think of any other synonyms for *change*?

5 Discuss these questions.

a How would you define *fundamental social skills*?

b In your view, are people becoming too insular because of technology?

c Do you agree or disagree with this statement? Why?

The need to produce an instant response to online messages has had a damaging effect on the way we communicate with each other.

The current explosion of digital technology is not only changing the way we live and communicate but is also profoundly altering our brains. Daily exposure to high technology – computers, smart phones, video games, search engines (...) – stimulates brain cell alteration and neurotransmitter release, gradually strengthening new neural pathways in our brains while weakening old ones. Because of the current technological revolution, our brains are evolving right now – at a speed like never before.

Besides influencing how we think, digital technology is altering how we feel and how we behave. (...) We rely on the Internet for entertainment, political discussion, and communication with friends and co-workers. As the brain evolves and shifts its focus towards new technical skills, it drifts away from fundamental social skills, such as reading facial expressions during conversation or grasping the emotional context of a subtle gesture.

Extract from *Scientific American Mind*

Reading & Use of English

Part 3

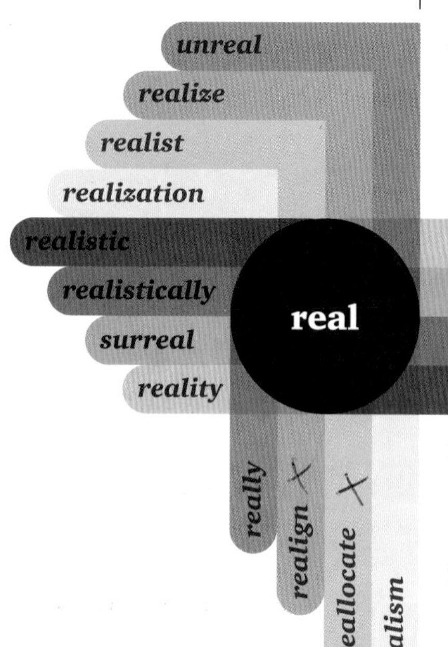

Vocabulary

1 Look at the diagram showing words and phrases connected with the word *real*. Can you find two words in the diagram that should not be there? Why? Can you add any words to the diagram?

2 Work with a partner. Prepare diagrams for the words below. When you have finished, compare your answers with the rest of the class.

legal care appear

3 For each word a–i, write words that can be made by removing the affixes.

Example: *counterrevolutionary – counterrevolution, revolutionary, revolution*

a nonconformity	d misrepresentation	g reconstruction
b disrespectfully	e proportionately	h differentiation
c disentangle	f uncoordinated	i interchangeable

4 Quickly read the text below, ignoring the gaps and the words in capitals. Find out what threat to the world it is focusing on.

Tip

You may need to make one, two or more changes to the word given.

Exam practice

5 Read the text again. For questions 1–8 use the word given in capitals at the end of some of the lines to form a word that fits in the space in the same line.

The cosmic game of darts

'The End of the World is Nigh!' screamed newspaper (0) ***headlines*** recently after astronomers warned	HEAD
that a massive asteroid was heading (1) ______ for Earth. It was predicted that the mile-wide	AVOID
asteroid ZF11 would hit the Earth in 2028 with (2) ______ consequences. It sounded like the stuff	CATASTROPHE
of science fiction, but for a while it seemed (3) ______ threatening. Then suddenly, the danger	ALARM
disappeared. New calculations showed that the asteroid would miss by 600,000 miles – only fairly close in	
astronomical terms, but in practical terms a fairly (4) ______ risk.	SIGNIFY
ZF11 may not pose a danger, but the threat of other strikes still looms, and there is (5) ______	ABOUND
evidence of past asteroid strikes. One of the most (6) ______ of these is the crater in the Yucatan	ORDINARY
Peninsula which measures some 200 km in diameter. It is thought that this is the impact site of an asteroid that struck sixty-five million years ago, wiping out the dinosaurs and leading to the destruction of 70% of the Earth's species.	
Scientists believe that it is only a matter of time before another celestial hulk hits home in this giant game	
of cosmic darts. But what really worries astronomers is the (7) ______ that they have identified very	REAL
few of the asteroids near the Earth. There are (8) ______ thousands more that they do not know about.	FORTUNATE

Grammar *See notes page 156*

Stative verbs

6 Read this extract from the reading text. Then answer the questions below. Give reasons for your answers.

'Scientists *believe* it is only a matter of time before another celestial hulk hits home in this giant game of cosmic darts. But what *really worries* astronomers is the realization that they have identified very few of the asteroids near the Earth.'

a Would it be correct to use 'are believing' instead of 'believe'?

b Would it be correct to use 'is really worrying' instead of 'really worries'?

c Can you find other examples of stative verbs in the text?

7 Look through the list of common stative verbs below and classify them into the following categories: senses, possession, thinking, emotional states, appearance, and others. Then add other examples to each of the categories.

believe involve contain depend on doubt dislike own
belong to mean mind smell seem regard taste

Simple or continuous

8 Complete a–i with the correct form of the words in brackets. Where you think more than one form is correct, write both forms.

a I .... (think) about getting an electric car for some time now, but I'll have to put it off until next year because I can't afford it.

b 'Are you OK? You don't look very well.' 'I .... (feel) fine.'

c It seems to me that you .... (be) too simplistic in your attempt to describe what black holes are.

d You can tell your IT department that you have somehow managed to import a virus into your computer, but I .... (not/imagine) they will be all that sympathetic.

e I .... (mean) to have a chat with you for a while about that fantastic new television series focusing on the planets.

f According to research, there .... (appear) to be a strong link between an asteroid hitting the Earth and the extinction of the dinosaurs.

g '.................... (you/need) the computer tonight? I've got a report to write.'

h At first I found physics very difficult, but now I .... (like) it more and more.

i I used to know lots of formulas by heart when I was studying maths, but as I get older I find I .... (remember) fewer and fewer.

Nouns and *-ing* forms

9 Look at this sentence from the reading text. Would it be correct to use *realizing* instead of *realization*?

But what really worries astronomers is the realization that they have identified very few of the asteroids near the earth.

10 Decide whether a–h are correct or not. Correct the ones that are wrong.

a The threatening of asteroid strikes has been seriously underestimated by scientists.

b Our understanding of how the human brain works has increased hugely over the past ten years.

c The discovering of penicillin was one of the greatest of the 20th century.

d Successful marketing has resulted in increased sales of low-energy light bulbs.

e The increasing in the number of electric cars being sold is an encouraging sign for anti-pollution campaigners.

f One day, space travelling for the masses will be a reality.

g Our ability to predict volcanic eruptions depends on our accurate reporting of seismic activity.

h The nuclear power station undergoes regular health and safety inspecting.

Reading & Use of English

Part 6

1 Quickly read the main text below, ignoring the missing paragraphs. Find out where the place in the photographs on page 75 is located and what goes on there.

Task preparation

2 Now quickly read through the paragraphs on page 75 which have been removed from the main text below. Underline any words you think might help you to find their correct place in the text.

Heavens on Earth

I The white and silver buildings of the VLT or Very Large Telescope at the ESO (European Organisation for Astronomical research in the Southern Hemisphere) stand tall and imposing on top of a mountain shining brightly under the desert sun. At night they come alive, the outer walls open up and silently slide through 360 degrees, allowing an uninterrupted view of the Southern Hemisphere sky. Inside, a giant eye looks deep into the stars and beyond, looking for life, mysteries and making sense out of the darkness.

1

II Getting to the place is a journey of discovery in itself. After leaving the Pacific Ocean, you head south and hook up with the Panamericana Highway and into the desert, the driest on Earth. It's a two-hour drive to the observatory, but it feels longer as the harsh light, the rocky, dusty desert, the complete absence of any form of life, except for the giant trucks plying their trade along the highway, is unsettling.

2

III The reason, we are told, is simple. Astronomers need a clear view of the sky at night. Optimal conditions are to be found in deserts; there are fewer of the negative factors like light pollution that can make the four telescopes which form VLT work less effectively. Here no lights are allowed after dark, all windows are screened, and even the main residence where 108 people sleep, leaks no more than 40W when the lights are turned on.

3

IV These monsters and their smaller auxiliaries bring to mind the set of *Star Wars*. But at sunset, they take on another look. This could be Stonehenge, another magic circle where our forefathers tried to make sense of the stars. Soon after arriving, we are taken to see the inside of one of the telescopes. They have all been named in the indigenous Mapuche language following a competition among Chilean schoolchildren.

4

V Once these have been completed, the telescope is handed over to the team who will operate one or more of the telescopes from a control room. All night long these giants will be moving and pointing to the sky helping the scientists unravel new problems. Fourteen countries contribute around 160 million euros to their joint astronomical cause, and Paranal is allocated 20% of that figure. Standing in the shadow of the VLT, one wonders what all this taxpayers' money buys.

5

VI They all answered with the usual 'finding out where we came from, where we are going, are we alone in the universe...?' And, as the ESO has no commercial use and is a not-for-profit organization, it's easy to imagine these scientists indulging in their research and being cut off from reality.

6

VII One of Paranal's great achievements was the discovery of a planet outside our solar system. It is huge: five times bigger than Jupiter, and the work being done now is aimed at understanding the physical and chemical composition of this, and other, giant Earth-like planets. Truly a quest for life in outer space.

7

VIII 'We needed even sharper images to settle the issue of whether any other configuration is possible and we counted on the ESO VLT to provide those,' says Reinhard Genzel, director at the Max-Planck Institute for Extraterrestrial Physics. 'Now the era of observational physics has truly begun.'

Exam practice

Tip

Check carefully that the missing paragraph not only follows on logically from the one before but also links coherently with the one after it.

3 Choose from paragraphs A–H the one which fits each gap (1–7) in the main text. There is one extra paragraph which you do not need.

Missing paragraphs

A But talking further revealed a simple truth: that having pretty much discovered all there is to know about our world on the Earth, astronomy looks at the vast Terra Incognita which surrounds us. These scientists see themselves very much as a mixture of Renaissance men and women: all questing for further knowledge.

B Every evening an engineer is assigned to one of these telescopes and his or her job is to get it ready so that it can then be taken over at night by a three-person team. The engineer runs through a series of tests in preparation for the work which will be done later that night.

C The central unit inside weighs 450 tonnes and houses the main 8.5 m mirror. A second, smaller mirror is made from beryllium, a rare metal. The external walls can all slide open to allow the telescope to point in any direction as it rotates soundlessly on its base.

D As we drive further into the desert, the road starts to rise gradually, with hills and steep valleys all around us. The environment is harsh in the extreme and it's hard to imagine that a community of European scientists have chosen this place to establish a world-leading laboratory.

E It is a question that many in Paranal find a little difficult to answer. Maybe because scientists, due to the nature of their research and also, maybe, their mindsets, tend to focus on very specific areas of competence and therefore are not required to have a broader 'strategic' view.

F The other big consideration in the desert is the absence of cloud cover and, higher up, the lack of atmospheric dust and all the other interference caused by humans or nature which contributes to partially hiding the secrets of the universe. 'Twinkle, twinkle little star' is just what astronomers do not want to hear, as this means there is debris between the eye, the telescopes and the stars.

G We are in Paranal, in Chile's Atacama Desert, where at 2,600 m above sea level, Europe has its most advanced astronomical observatory. It's a leading site, a joint undertaking by fourteen European countries focused on developing the most advanced scientific tools for observing the universe and enhancing the knowledge base for industry, education and culture.

H Astronomers have also used the data from VLT for another purpose – to attempt to find out how old the universe is. It seems that the oldest star is 13.2 billion years old, which means the universe must be even older. They also use VLT to look into galaxies beyond ours, and where they continue to find evidence of supermassive black holes, where all kinds of violent activity occurs.

Text analysis

4 Work through a–j, referring to the text (i–viii) and missing paragraphs (A–H).

a What literary device does the writer use to successfully create an atmosphere of how impressive the buildings are? (i)

b What does the word *unsettling* refer to? (ii)

c Why does the writer use a semicolon after *deserts*? (iii)

d What is the writer referring to when he mentions *Star Wars* and *Stonehenge*? (iv)

e Why does the writer use the pronoun *one* in the last sentence? (v)

f Why is there no verb in the final sentence of this paragraph? (vii)

g What does the writer mean by *Terra Incognita*? (A)

h Why might the scientists consider themselves *Renaissance men and women*? (A)

i What does the writer mean by the word *mindsets*? (E)

j What might the words *twinkle, twinkle little star* come from? (F)

Vocabulary

5 Match a–h with their definitions 1–8. All the words appear in the text.

a imposing	1 disturbing
b leading	2 searching for
c undertaking	3 improving
d enhancing	4 venture
e plying (their trade)	5 enjoying something that might be considered bad for you
f unsettling	6 most prestigious
g indulging	7 striking
h questing	8 doing your work or business

Words describing light

6 The word *twinkle* is used in the text to describe a light which changes constantly from bright to faint. Match the words on the left with their meanings on the right.

a sparkle	1 shine unsteadily or keep going on and off
b flash	2 shine brightly, especially with reflected light
c glow	3 shine in a bright but brief or sudden way
d shimmer	4 shine with a soft, tremulous light
e gleam	5 give out steady light without a flame
f flicker	6 give out or reflect small flashes of light
g glint	7 shine brightly with flashes of light
h glisten	8 shine with a sparkling light, especially something wet

7 Complete a–h with a word from the list above in its correct form.

a The pavements were ________ after the heavy downpour of rain.

b The window cleaner polished the glass until it ________.

c The candle flame ________ as the wind blew through the open window.

d The diamond rings ________ in the jeweller's window.

e The light from the warning beacon ________ every ten seconds.

f As we sat on the beach, the sea ________ in the sunlight.

g Sally noticed the ________ of excitement in her son's eyes as she mentioned the theme park visit.

h The solar lights look attractive ________ in the garden at night.

8 🔊 2·01 Listen to an extract from a humorous science-fiction novel called *The Hitch-hiker's Guide to the Galaxy*. Then answer these questions.

a What are the two men waiting to hear?

b What does the computer tell them?

c What problem has the computer identified?

d Did you enjoy listening to the extract? Why/Why not?

Listening Part 2

1 **Discuss these questions.**

a What are the most common features of science-fiction TV series, films and books? How have these features changed over the years?

b What possibilities do you think science fiction might explore in the future?

c Why do you think so many people find science fiction interesting?

2 **You will hear a talk about the first science-fiction book written by Mary Shelley. First, read through the questions and decide what type of word or information might be needed.**

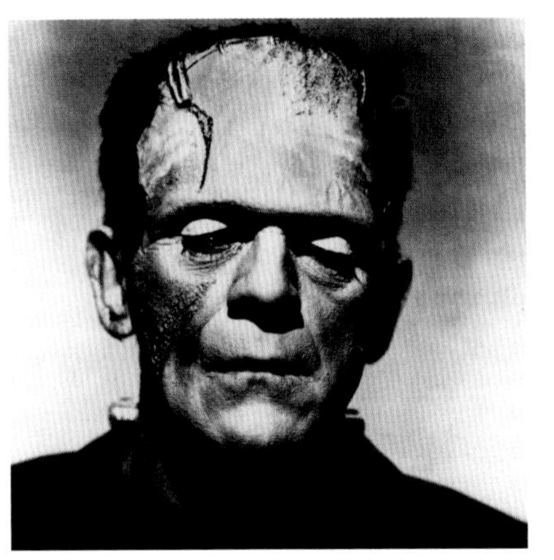

Mary's mother was a high-profile ____ **1** and her father had very high expectations of her.

Her father often took her to see her mother's ____ **2** when Mary was a young child.

One evening, Mary and Shelley stayed with their friend Lord Byron because a ____ **3** prevented them from getting home.

During the course of the evening it was suggested they should each try to come up with a ____ **4**.

It was when Mary had a ____ **5** that she got the idea for the Frankenstein novel.

Victor Frankenstein is a ____ **6** in the story.

The creature only becomes murderous when Victor refuses to create a ____ **7** for him.

Despite the success of her novel, Mary had many ____ **8** in her life.

It was ironic that Mary did not live to see ____ **9**.

Exam practice

Tip

Keep an open mind about what the missing words might be and remember that you will lose marks for incorrect spelling.

3 🔊 2·02 **Now listen and for questions 1–9, complete the sentences with a word or short phrase.**

4 **Were you particularly surprised or impressed by anything you heard about the life of Mary Shelley? Why/Why not?**

Vocabulary

Science and technology expressions

5 **Explain in your own words what the expressions in *italics* mean.**

a Their new car design puts them *light years* ahead of their competitors.

b The Chinese economy has gone into *warp speed*.

c Society is made up of *atomic* individuals pursuing private interests.

d We're all waiting for *the big bang* when the company's taken over next month.

e The government's decision to review funding for schools is *a quantum leap* for education.

f I don't know where the money goes. It just seems to disappear into *a black hole*.

g Most of the cast are unknown to the public, but the famous actor in the lead role brought some Hollywood *stardust* to the play.

h Despite some initial opposition, I think the project has finally got clearance for *lift-off*.

Speaking Part 3

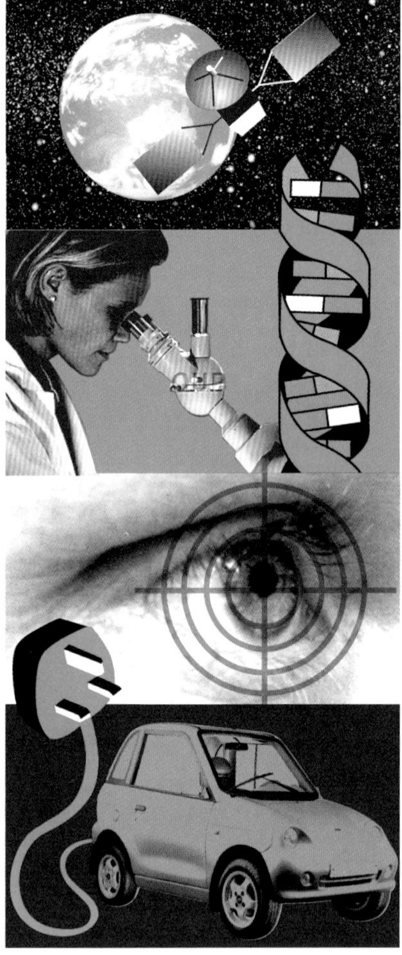

1 **Which two abilities are candidates NOT assessed on in the Speaking test?**

a extending your answers
b avoiding unnecessary hesitations
c understanding what your partner is saying
d speaking clearly enough for others to hear you
e expressing ideas precisely
f collaborating in Part 3
g coming up with the right answer
h being polite and encouraging to your partner
i responding appropriately
j using a range of appropriate vocabulary
k using a range of grammatical structures accurately

2 2·03 **Listen to two students talking about one of the images depicting a technological advance. Which image are they talking about?**

3 2·03 **Listen again. Tick the expressions they use to talk about its consequences and effects.**

...... It's led to ...	...... It's had very little impact on ...
...... It's resulted in ...	...... That's been a very positive step.
...... It has a rather negative effect.	...... have a knock-on effect
...... And as a consequence ...	

4 **Work with a partner. Look at the images depicting three other technological advances. Decide if their use has had largely positive or negative results. Try to use some of the expressions in 3.**

5 **Compare your ideas with another pair of students. Did you agree on whether the effects were beneficial or not?**

Exam practice

Tip

In the exam, you will not have the time or opportunity to make notes so you will have to think quickly about what you are going to say.

6 **Work with a partner. Make a short list of other recent technological advances. Then each choose one of the ideas from your list. You are going to give a short talk about it. First, make notes about:**

the positive effects it has had on our lives
the negative effects it has had on our lives
how it might develop in the future

7 **Using your notes, take it in turns to tell your partner about the technological advance you have chosen. Try to speak for about two minutes.**

Responding

8 **After your partner has finished speaking, say whether you agree or disagree with what they have said. Give reasons for your opinions.**

Exploring the topic

9 2·04 **Now listen to some more general questions about technology. Discuss your answers with a partner.**

Writing | Part 1

Understanding the task

1 Read the two Part 1 texts. What are the two main points in each text?

The changing world of work
Technology has dramatically altered the world of work in the last century. Previously, many tasks that were undertaken by hand are now carried out by machine and many processes are now fully automated. In recent years, many of these changes have resulted from improvements in telecommunications that allow for remote working. These mean that companies can save money as they do not need to accommodate so many staff in one location or pay their employees to travel around the country or abroad. In addition, companies can make savings by being more flexible about where their offices are based.

Work-life balance
Whilst technological changes have clearly had a number of benefits for companies, the same could perhaps not be said for families. More and more people are working from home, which is causing a blur between the boundaries of the home environment and the work environment. It also means that people are starting to work longer and more irregular hours, especially as more and more business is done internationally. Consequently, many families are feeling an additional and unwelcome strain.

Text analysis

2 Read the sample essay and answer questions a–c.

a What is the main topic of each paragraph?

b Underline the parts in each paragraph that paraphrase ideas from the texts.

c Circle examples of evaluative language that the writer has used.

Both texts highlight how technology now plays a significant part in many people's lives at both home and work. The first text discusses how, for companies, technology has brought a number of cost-saving benefits. However, according to the second passage, the increasing number of people who work remotely is having a detrimental impact on family life that needs to be addressed.

The first text explains that technology has transformed the world of work over the last century. In recent times, telecommunications advances have helped companies to cut their costs, specifically by enabling staff to work off-site. Not only have these developments involved a reduction in office space, they also mean that people working for large companies do not have to travel so much.

However, whilst the benefits of these changes to firms are obvious, text two questions whether they benefit families. In my view, unless an individual working from home is fortunate enough to own a large property, their work space is often the same room where the family relax. Also, home workers are less likely to finish their work at a set time, meaning that the home and work environments are merged. As a result, employees may work more hours and at inconvenient times, placing pressure on themselves and their family.

In conclusion, like other periods such as the Industrial Revolution, I would argue that technological advances bring both positive and negative changes for everyone. In this case, however, it could be said that the positives are firmly on the side of the employer and the negatives on that of the employee. I feel that until companies acknowledge the significance of this, the situation is likely to get worse.

Evaluative language

3 Complete sentences a–e with a suitable word.

a His argument .... on the premise that all technology is good.

b While I .... with the claim that technology has some drawbacks, I would not .... so far as to say that technology is useless.

c In .... that readers cannot live without mobile phones, the writer fails to .... into account the fact that many readers rely on such devices.

d This argument does not fully .... the question of whether technology really provides us with more free time.

e There is no evidence to .... the claim that exposure to too much technology is detrimental to our health.

4 **Look at a–i. Decide if the words in *italics* have a similar or different meaning. If the two words are different, how are they different?**

a The first text *focuses on* / *broaches* the subject of whether …

b The author *touches on* / *argues* the need for increased …

c The writer *maintains* / *asserts* that the teaching of …

d The second text *claims* / *asserts* that we must set aside …

e The writer *states* / *argues* that there is no correlation between …

f The author rightly *highlights* / *emphasizes* the risks of …

g The writer *purports* / *professes* to have a doctorate in …

h The writer *addresses* / *explores* the issue of …

i Text one *contends* / *maintains* that there are no …

5 **Rearrange the words in a–e to make sentences.**

a first text's basic assumption the author of the that technology is inherently evil is wrong had on healthcare impact it has considering the positive

b the positive impact evil technology is having dismissed of technology on our explain how inherently lives, the first text goes on to

c are now irreversible the author argues not only that technology is corrupting our young but also that its effects

d second text, in reading the one may well all society's ills be the saviour of be convinced that technology will

e of the first text what the writer science to save lives people depend on fails to consider is the fact that a large number of

Exam practice *See Writing guide p138*

Tip

Try to use a range of evaluative language in your answers.

6 **Read the exam task below. Use the checklist on page 135 to help you write your answer.**

Read the two texts below.

Write an essay summarizing and evaluating the key points from both texts. Use your own words throughout as far as possible, and include your own ideas in your answer.

Write your answer in 240–280 words.

An end to commuting?

Cars and better transport infrastructure have created a society in which very few people live near their place of work. Consequently, numerous people spend around two hours every day commuting to work. For many people a daily commute can take up to six hours, while others choose to live in one location Monday to Friday and another at the weekend to avoid this. Advances in telecommunications could result in these commutes no longer being necessary as people are able to work from home. Ultimately, this could significantly save people time and reduce the levels of stress associated with commuting.

Office life

Telecommunications technology permits a greater number of people to work from home or to work in locations remote from other staff of the same company. Many people now do not have one fixed location for work and often work on the move. Unfortunately, this can have a negative impact on staff motivation. The sense of team spirit with a common purpose is something many people find pleasurable. This camaraderie and positive atmosphere helps companies to recruit and retain good members of staff and by underestimating this factor companies could be losing out on the best employees.

Unit 8 Law & order

Introduction

1 **Complete the definitions of human rights using these words.**

entitled freedoms status ethnic basic human virtue race

Human rights are (1) ________ rights and (2) ________ that all people are (3) ________ to regardless of nationality, sex, age, national or (4) ________ origin, (5) ________, religion, language, or other (6) ________. (Amnesty International)

These rights are conceived as universal and egalitarian, with all people having equal rights by (7) ________ of being (8) ________. (Universal Charter)

2 **What do you think are the three most important human rights? Discuss your ideas in pairs or small groups.**

3 **2·05 Listen to someone talking about human rights. Decide whether these statements are true or false according to what you hear.**

a The concept of human rights was conceived a very long time ago.

b Human rights abuse is less of a problem now than it was in the past.

4 **What is the grim reality that the speaker refers to in 3?**

5 **Were you surprised by any of the information you heard in 3? Why/Why not?**

6 **Brainstorm as many words as you can that collocate with the words in this list.**

crime punishment rights rules

Example: *equal rights, violate rights, human rights abuse*

7 **Now use some of the collocations you found to form questions to ask other students.**

Example: *Can you think of a situation in which people do not have equal rights?*

1 Discuss these questions.

a What kinds of punishments would be suitable for these crimes?

blackmail	arson	computer hacking
manslaughter	shoplifting	fraud
libel	reckless driving	tax evasion

b Are there any crimes in your country that are currently receiving a great deal of attention from the media?

c Can you think of any crimes that are seen as less serious now than they were in the past?

2 Read the text below and answer these questions.

a What was Owen accused of?

b Do you think his actions were justified? Why/Why not?

c What do you think the jury decided? Turn to page 164 to see if you were right.

A crime of passion

Reaching a verdict can be an extremely difficult and complicated process, and juries sometimes have to balance a sense of justice against knowledge of the law.

Take the case of Stephen Owen, whose twelve-year-old son Darren had been killed after being knocked off his bicycle and crushed by a lorry. Mr Taylor, the lorry driver, left the scene without reporting the accident. The police tracked him down, only to discover that he had never had a driving licence. Mr Taylor showed no remorse for what he had done, which greatly distressed the family. He was banned from driving and sentenced to eighteen months in prison for reckless driving, but served only twelve months.

Stephen Owen could not get over the death of his son. He was shaken by how quickly Taylor had been released from prison. When he discovered that Taylor had not stopped driving after his release, he wrote a letter to the Queen to ensure that the ban was enforced. Owen let the event take over his life entirely, becoming unable to lead a normal existence. He traced Taylor to his home in Kent, and confronted him in the street. With a sawn-off shotgun he fired twice at Taylor at point blank range, hitting him in the back and his common-law wife, Alison Barratt, in the arm. They survived, but Owen was charged with attempted murder.

At his trial, the prosecution said that his shooting of Taylor had been premeditated, but Owen claimed to have fired the gun in a moment of near insanity. At the end of the trial, the judge told the jury: 'Any parent must feel sympathy, understanding and compassion for a father or mother who receives a phone call only to hear of the death of a child.' But he warned the jury not to be swayed by understandable sympathy for Owen, and advised them to concentrate on whether Owen had any intent to kill at the time of the shooting, regardless of what had happened beforehand.

Grammar *See notes page 157*

See notes page 157

Gerunds and infinitives

3 Read the text and underline examples of gerunds and infinitives. Can you see any patterns in how they are used?

4 Write sentences of your own using the same gerund or infinitive constructions that you underlined in 3.

Purpose or result?

5 What is the difference between the use of the infinitive in these two sentences from the text? How does *only* change the meaning of a?

a *The police tracked him down, only to discover that he had never had a driving licence.*

b *He wrote a letter to the Queen to ensure that the ban was enforced.*

6 Complete a–e using *to* or *only to* and a suitable word.

a Rod arrived at the airport check-in desk .... that his passport had expired.

b The customs officer waved the car over to the inspection shed .... the contents of the car boot.

c The judge adjourned the trial .... the defence more time to prepare.

d The prosecuting barrister arrived in court .... that an important witness in the case had not turned up.

e In order .... your safety, the wearing of seat belts on the coach is compulsory.

7 In the following pairs of sentences, decide whether the verb should be in the infinitive or the gerund. Is there a difference in meaning between each pair of sentences?

a 1 I regret (say) that we have had no success in tracing a witness to the accident.
  2 I regret (not/study) the instructions for evacuating the building more carefully.

b 1 Don't worry about losing the game. We tried our best (play) by the rules and that's all anyone can ask.
  2 I tried (learn) the Highway Code last night but there was too much to take in.

c 1 Brad distinctly remembered (see) someone suspicious prowling around the streets last night.
  2 Remember (fill in) your passport application and send the correct fee when you post it.

d 1 The solicitor mentioned the existence of a will, then went on (outline) what it contained.
  2 The lecturer in law went on (talk) for ages. In the end, nobody was actually listening to a word she said.

e 1 The council does not permit (cycle) in this park.
  2 A visa permits tourists (enter) the country for a certain period of time only.

f 1 I dread (think) what Alan's going to say when he sees his motorbike has been vandalized. You know how proud he is of it.
  2 Clare dreaded (have to) see her ex-husband again in court because she knew there was a danger of his becoming abusive.

g 1 I meant (put) my warning triangle in the car, but I never got round to it.
  2 If you do join the police force, it'll mean (work) unsocial hours.

h 1 Many restaurants now stop people (smoke) even if they are eating outside.
  2 The security guard stopped (check) that the front entrance was securely locked before carrying out his routine inspection of the building.

8 Make sentences of your own beginning with these words.

I've always regretted … *I've tried …* *I remember …* *I went on …*
I dread … *I meant …* *I'm going to stop …*

Vocabulary

Crime

9 **Complete a–j with the correct form of a verb from the list and an appropriate preposition. There may be more than one possible answer.**

accuse release acquit charge appear crack lodge find sentence defraud ban remand arrest

a Four men have been ______ ______ smuggling and will ______ ______ a magistrate tomorrow.

b The 58-year-old man ______ ______ blackmail has been ______ ______ bail.

c The gangster was ______ guilty ______ money laundering.

d The computer hacker was ______ ______ ten years behind bars.

e After several motoring offences, Paul was ______ ______ driving for two years.

f Two teenagers have been ______ ______ custody in connection with the recent spate of burglaries.

g The defendants said they will ______ an appeal ______ the court's decision which ordered them to pay $5 million in fines.

h A man was ______ late last night ______ being in possession of an illegal firearm with intent to commit robbery.

i She was relieved when the jury ______ her ______ attempting to ______ the bank ______ $10,000.

j The police are ______ ______ ______ anti-social behaviour to curb the rising number of street gangs.

Exam practice

Tip

Gerund and infinitive forms are sometimes focused on in Part 4. Bear this in mind when you look through the questions.

10 **Reading & Use of English, Part 4: For questions 1–6, complete the second sentence so that it has a similar meaning to the first sentence, using the word given. Do not change the word given. You must use between three and eight words, including the word given. Here is an example (0).**

Example:

0 *Ignoring the brutal nature of the crime was not easy for me.*
swayed
I tried ***not to be swayed by*** *the brutal nature of the crime but it wasn't easy.*

1 It's futile to appeal against your prison sentence.
point
There ______ against your prison sentence.

2 Burglary in the home is not something most people recover from quickly.
get
Most people do not find ______ a burglary in their home.

3 The visitor ignored the no-entry sign and walked straight into the Director's office.
attention
The visitor ______ the no-entry sign and walked straight into the Director's office.

4 The jury couldn't reach a verdict because of the complexity of the case.
prevented
The complexity of the case ______ a verdict.

5 The accused was very unapologetic about the crimes he had committed.
showed
The accused ______ the crimes he had committed.

6 The local authority stopped the children from playing games in the road.
end
The local authority ______ were playing in the road.

Listening | Part 3

1 **Look at this statue which stands above a famous court of law in London. What is the symbolic significance of the sword and the scales?**

2 **Explain in your own words what *forensic science* means.**

Tip

If you don't manage to get the answer the first time you hear the recording, don't get distracted. You will hear the recording a second time.

Exam practice

3 **2·06 You will hear an interview with Dr Lafford, a leading expert in the field of forensic science. For questions 1–5, choose the answer (A, B, C or D) which fits best according to what you hear.**

1 According to Dr Lafford, Sherlock Holmes was a good forensic scientist because of his
 A psychological insight.
 B unbiased approach.
 C detailed observations.
 D medical knowledge.

2 Forensic scientists pay particular attention to
 A evidence of mutual contact.
 B items criminals have touched.
 C a suspect's clothing.
 D carpet fibres and human hair.

3 Dr Lafford mentions the broken headlight to show that forensic science nowadays is
 A more complex than it used to be.
 B just as reliable as it was in the past.
 C not as time-consuming as it once was.
 D more straightforward than it was in the past.

4 According to Dr Lafford, electron microscopes can
 A produce conflicting results.
 B sometimes damage evidence.
 C provide a chemical analysis.
 D guarantee total accuracy.

5 Dr Lafford feels that the value of forensic science lies in
 A how its significance to a case is explained.
 B the use of advanced genetic fingerprinting.
 C the possibility of eliminating human error.
 D reducing the number of possible suspects.

Vocabulary

Word knowledge: *law*

4 **What do the phrases in *italics* mean?**

a She takes absolutely no notice of anything I say. She's *a law unto herself*!
b Ministers seem to regard themselves as *above the law*.
c By sticking to *the letter of the law*, the spirit of the law could be lost.
d If politics reflects *the law of the jungle*, beware of the tigers!
e She could have at least waited until tomorrow to *lay down the law* so heavily.
f When we *take the law into our own hands* we become little better than criminals.

Your views

5 **Discuss these questions.**

a Give a brief description of the system of justice that operates in your country.
b How confident are you that you would be acquitted if you were charged with a crime that you had not committed?

Reading & Use of English

Part 7

1 **You are going to read a text on the history of human rights. Before you read, answer the questions below.**

a What do you know about the history of human rights?

b What do you think you might learn from the text?

2 **Now read the text. What did you learn?**

Exam practice

Tip

Remember that the text may use different words from those in the questions. If you spot the same words, this does not necessarily mean that the question refers to that particular extract.

3 **Read the text again. For questions 1–10, choose from the sections (A–F). The sections may be chosen more than once.**

In which section are the following mentioned?

- the view that a situation which had wreaked widespread havoc could not be repeated **1**
- a recent consensus that an event had far-reaching global repercussions **2**
- treating all sides equally during military conflicts **3**
- the view that a protest against the flagrant injustice of a despotic monarch had far-reaching consequences **4**
- surprise that widespread change came about in a relatively short space of time **5**
- the suggestion that the unusual actions of a monarch were far ahead of their time **6**
- an acknowledgement that a leader was prepared to justify his actions **7**
- an expression of regret for mistakes made in the past **8**
- the importance of something which officially tried to prevent a certain type of gender discrimination **9**
- the idea that everyone should have the same opportunities for advancement **10**

Text analysis

4 **Work through a–e, referring to the paragraphs (A–F) in the text.**

a Find an example of a cleft sentence. Why does the writer use this? (A)

b Which two words appear together but seem to be a contradiction in terms? Why? (B)

c Why does the writer use a colon after the word *themes*? (line 36)

d Find a metaphorical expression. What does it mean? (D)

e Which expressions suggest an emotional reaction on the part of the writer? What do the expressions mean? (F)

5 **Think of a recent human rights abuse story. Use the questions and language below to tell a partner about it.**

campaign petition lobby boycott sanction
demonstrate rally hunger strike march

a Were any of the methods above used to tackle the problem?

b How effective were they?

c Are there any other methods which you think should have been used?

A history of human rights

A In 539 BC, the armies of Cyrus the Great, the first King of ancient Persia, conquered the city of Babylon. But it was his next actions that marked a major advance for the human race. He freed the slaves, declared that all people had a right to choose their own religion, and established racial equality. These and other decrees were recorded on a baked-clay cylinder in the Akkadian language with cuneiform script. Known today as the Cyrus Cylinder, this ancient record has now been recognized as the world's first charter of human rights. It is translated into all six official languages of the United Nations and its provisions parallel the first four Articles of the Universal Declaration of Human Rights.

B The Magna Carta, or 'Great Charter', was arguably the most significant early influence on the extensive historical process that led to the rule of constitutional law in the English-speaking world. In 1215, after King John violated a number of ancient laws and customs by which England had been governed, his subjects forced him to sign the Magna Carta, which enumerates what later came to be thought of as human rights. Among them was the right of the church to be free from governmental interference, the rights of all free citizens to own and inherit property and to be protected from excessive taxes. It established the rights of widows who owned property to choose not to remarry, and established principles of due process and equality before the law. It also contained provisions for forbidding bribery and official misconduct.

C On 4 July 1776, the United States Congress approved the Declaration of Independence. Its primary author, Thomas Jefferson, wrote the Declaration as a formal explanation of why Congress had voted on 2 July to declare independence from Great Britain, more than a year after the outbreak of the American Revolutionary War, as a statement announcing that the thirteen American Colonies were no longer a part of the British Empire. Congress issued the Declaration in several forms. It was initially published as a printed broadsheet that was widely distributed and read to the public. Philosophically, it stressed two themes: individual rights and the rights of revolution. These ideas spread internationally as well, influencing in particular the French Revolution.

D In 1789, the people of France brought about the abolition of the absolute monarchy and set the stage for the establishment of the first French Republic. Just six weeks after the storming of the Bastille, and barely three weeks after the abolition of feudalism, the Declaration of the Rights of Man and of the Citizen was adopted by the National Constituent Assembly as the first step towards writing a constitution for the Republic of France. The Declaration proclaims that all citizens are to be guaranteed the rights of liberty and equality. Liberty was defined as 'being able to do anything that does not harm others'. Equality, on the other hand, was defined as judicial equality, which 'must be the same for all, whether it protects or punishes. All citizens, being equal in its eyes, shall be equally eligible to all high offices, public positions and employments, according to their ability, and without other distinction than that of their virtues and talents.'

E In 1864, sixteen European countries and several American states attended a conference in Geneva on the initiative of the Geneva Committee. The diplomatic conference was held for the purpose of adopting a convention for the treatment of wounded soldiers in combat. The main principles laid down and adopted by the later Geneva Conventions provided for the obligation to extend care without discrimination to wounded and sick military personnel and respect for the marking of medical personnel transports and equipment with the distinctive sign of the red cross on a white background.

F World War II had raged from 1939 to 1945, and as the end drew near, cities throughout Europe and Asia lay in smouldering ruins. Millions of people were dead, millions more were homeless or starving. In April 1945, delegates from fifty countries met in San Francisco full of optimism and hope. The goal of the United Nations Conference was to fashion an international body to promote peace and prevent future war. Its ideals were stated in the preamble to the proposed charter: 'We the peoples of the United Nations are determined to save succeeding generations from the scourge of war, which twice in our lifetime has brought untold sorrow to mankind.' The Charter of the New United Nations organization went into effect on 24 October 1945, a date that is celebrated each year as United Nations Day.

Speaking | Part 2

A

B

C

D

E

F

Magazine report: Civil liberties

1 **Discuss these questions.**

a If you could change any laws on civil liberties in your country, which would you change? Why? How would you change them?

b If you could make new laws affecting people's freedom of action and speech, what would you introduce? Why?

Speculating

2 **2·07 Listen to two students talking about pictures B and D and make a note of the expressions they use to speculate about the pictures. Then compare your notes.**

Exam practice

Tip

The second phase of Part 2 consists of two stages. Make sure you deal with the first stage before you move on to deal with the second stage.

3 **With your partner, look at pictures A–F and discuss what aspects of personal safety and freedom you think they show. Use some of the expressions you made a note of in 2.**

4 **2·08 Listen and make a note of what you have to do in the next phase of the task.**

5 **Now work with a partner and do the task. Remember, you have about three minutes to do this phase of Part 2.**

Exploring the topic

6 **Discuss whether you agree or disagree with these statements.**

a All governments have the right to prevent people from doing things they enjoy but might not be very good for them, e.g. smoking and drinking.

b The more you try to stop people doing something, the more they will want to do it.

c Things like protest marches are not the most effective way to ensure that everyone has the same rights and privileges.

Writing

Part 2, Report

Understanding the task

1 Read this exam question and answer questions a–c.

> You recently took part in a project which aimed to reduce juvenile crime by providing a programme of voluntary education and training courses for young offenders. You have been asked to write a **report** (280–320 words) for the local government on the impact of this programme based on feedback from questionnaires completed by course participants. In your report you should describe the strengths and weaknesses of the programme and make recommendations.

a What solutions have been implemented to tackle the problem of juvenile crime?

b What ideas do you think you would find in the report and how might they be organized?

c What style do you think would be appropriate?

Text analysis

2 Read this sample report and answer questions a–e.

Introduction

This report evaluates the effectiveness of a recent training and education programme aimed at tackling the problem of juvenile crime. Teenagers with a history of offending were actively encouraged to attend free courses in disciplines ranging from IT to mechanics. Participants completed a questionnaire and the findings discussed in this report are based on their feedback.

Strengths

Attempts were made to increase the level of self-esteem of attendees. Notwithstanding some obstacles, the majority felt that their self-esteem had improved. A further aim was to equip the participants with the skills needed for employment. A number of attendees have managed to secure employment as a result of the course. In view of many of the participants' prior experience of education, attention was paid to fostering an interest in learning. 87% of those surveyed expressed a desire to further their studies.

Weaknesses

There was the perennial problem of truancy. A number of attendees, albeit a minority, were continually absent or late for the sessions. The voluntary nature of the course and the lack of any deterrent for such behaviour were the principle reasons. Overall, the majority of attendees completed the course. However, 5% failed to do so. With no provision for income, they had resorted to criminal activity for monetary gain.

Conclusions

The consensus of opinion was that the course was a positive approach, giving attendees the skills to break the criminal cycle rather than simply punishing their actions. For those candidates who did not feel the need to engage in criminal activity for financial rewards, this scheme has been successful. However, the course does not tackle a fundamental poverty issue that forces many of these candidates into a life of crime.

Recommendations

The best solution would be for the government to consider giving financial support to participants. This should lead to an improvement in student retention. We would also advise adopting more punitive measures for participants who are absent or late for courses.

a Are any of your ideas from 1 mentioned?

b How are the ideas organized?

c How does the writer avoid repetition when presenting their findings?

d What is the function of the modal verbs in the recommendations?

e What formal linking words does the writer use?

Hedging

3 Look at sentences a–e. How does using each of the modal verbs affect the sentence?

a A comprehensive ban on handguns would / could reduce crime levels.

b Increasing jail sentences could / will act as more of a deterrent.

c Targeting drink drivers should / could see a drastic reduction in road accidents.

d CCTV cameras may / might make the streets safer.

e Tackling truancy at school can / will reduce the number of young offenders.

4 Complete sentences a–e with a suitable word. There may be more than one possible answer.

a As a general ...., criminals tend to go for easy targets.

b Hate crimes are, in a ...., akin to terrorism in that their effects are far more widespread than a simple assault.

c Gang youths often compare their gangs to family, and in some .... gangs resemble families.

d It is .... that repeated exposure to real-life and to entertainment violence .... alter cognitive, affective and behavioural processes.

e It is tacitly .... that the perpetrators of knife crime are representative of an alienated working-class youth.

Vocabulary

Problems and solutions

5 Complete the words in sentences a–g.

a The possibility of eradicating crime seems *in*............ .

b The recent riots have revealed *sh*............ in our country's criminal justice system.

c The *un*............ problem is that the legislation only *t*............ the surface of the disadvantages that women face in society.

d The government is to inject $3 million into deprived areas to *a*............ poverty.

e Corporal punishment in school tended to *ex*............ rather than *di*............ misbehaviour.

f His mother was asked to remove him because the staff never managed to get to *g*............ with his behaviour.

g There seems to be a lack of *v*............ solutions on offer to *gr*............ with the *on*............ problem of car theft.

Exam practice *See Writing guide page 146*

Tip

When giving an opinion it can sometimes be a good idea to soften it by using hedges.

6 Follow these stages to write your report: read, think, plan, write and then check.

The local government has recently installed CCTV cameras in your neighbourhood. You have been asked to write a **report** (280–320 words) of local people's feelings about the installation. In your report you should describe the positive and negative effects of the introduction of the CCTV cameras and suggest any other measures that could be taken.

Unit 9 Psychology & employment

Introduction

1 **Imagine you are selecting people to fill vacancies for each of the jobs shown in the pictures. What selection criteria would you use in each case? Why?**

2 **People can be divided into two categories: 'divergent thinkers' and 'convergent thinkers'. Which of these descriptions do you think matches these two terms?**

a They work towards something finite and need specific instructions before they do something. They are logical and systematic.

b They are creative, extroverted and intuitive. They are not particularly systematic or dependable.

3 **Which category of thinker do you think you belong in?**

4 **Try this test and find out if you were right about what kind of thinker you are. Look at the shapes below and choose which one appeals to you most, then decide which one would be your second choice.**

5 **Which of these descriptions do you think might apply to people who have a preference for one of the shapes in 4? Match descriptions a–e to the shapes.**

a individual and creative but not particularly systematic or dependable

b logical and systematic but possibly lacking in creativity

c sociable and good with people, extrovert and intuitive, but against rigid plans and systems

d conservative and happy when things are regular and orderly

e goal-orientated, logical and systematic and fond of planning and succeeding

6 **2·09 Listen and check your answers to 5. How accurate do you think the test was for you?**

7 **Which of the descriptions do you think might apply to the people in the pictures above?**

8 **Discuss these questions.**

a Do you agree or disagree that our personality remains the same for life?

b Which do you think affects our personality more: genetic make-up or our experiences and environment?

Reading & Use of English

Part 3

1 Read these headlines and decide what you think the newspaper articles would be about.

Unfair dismissal laws spur claims

Computer sacks 'star' employee over quiz failure

Overlooked executive gets compensation

2 Read the text below, ignoring the gaps and the words in capitals. Find out what happened to Mr Filer. Which of the headlines in 1 would be most suitable for this article?

A newly-employed sales assistant at a DIY store was (0) *unexpectedly* sacked after failing a computerized	EXPECT
test, despite having performed so well that he was offered a promotion. However, Mr Filer had been	
promoted before the results of the company's psychometric test had come through.	
The ten-minute test presents (1) .... with statements including things like 'I prefer to have	APPLY
close relationships outside work rather than with fellow employees,' and 'My (2) .... is higher	PRODUCE
than others I work with.'	
Unfortunately, after accepting the promotion, he received (3) .... that his efforts in the	NOTIFY
psychometric test had been unsuccessful. Although his manager had given him (4) .... that	ASSURE
there would not be a problem, he was (5) .... by the head office who insisted on Mr Filer's	RULE
dismissal. A company spokesperson insisted that their procedures were fair and '(6)	SURE
consistency and (7) ....' Mr Filer was eventually escorted off the premises by security guards.	OBJECT
'It is an (8) .... strange way to run a company,' he commented.	ORDINARY

3 Use one of these suffixes in list A to make a noun from each of the verbs in list B.

A: *-ency -ication -ance -ment -tion -ure -al -ant -ee*

B: *modify develop assist dismiss indicate assail employ announce legislate preside proceed nominate gratify reiterate resemble embarrass renew*

Exam practice

4 Read the text in 2 again. Decide what part of speech the missing words might be. Then use the word given in capitals at the end of some of the lines to form a word that fits in the space in the same line.

5 Do you think Mr Filer was unfairly treated?

6 Now read the continuation of the text on page 93 and make notes to answer the following questions. Then compare your notes with a partner's.

a What arguments are put forward in favour of psychometric tests?

b What arguments are put forward against psychometric tests?

Tip

Try to imagine what the word you have made sounds like in context. This might help you to decide if it is correct or not.

Despite the negative publicity of a case such as that of Carl Filer, psychometric testing is big business. Applicants to 40% of large British companies will have their future prospects at least partially determined by personality tests – and intelligence testing may sometimes be used as well.

Enthusiasts argue that there is plenty of predictive validity in such tests. Only by carrying them out can one predict the rates of absenteeism and productivity. Cynics would say it is a case of dissonance reduction – of employers wanting passionately to believe in tests for which they have parted with a large amount of money.

It is Sir Francis Galton who must bear some responsibility for this, as it was he who first introduced the concept of the personality test in the 1880s. This concept was taken forward and refined in 1917 by the US Army, who were anxious not to have their efficiency undermined by the recruitment of unsuitable soldiers. From the 1950s onwards, the test as lucrative business began to sweep across America. In Britain, what made the difference were the mass layoffs of the 1980s. To firms whose personnel departments were inundated by applicants, testing seemed a cheap, reliable and sensible alternative to the expensive, time-consuming interview.

The sacking of Carl Filer will bring the critics out of the woodwork again, rehearsing the same old arguments. They point out that not only can applicants lie, but also the tests themselves are invalid. Most people agree that ability, personality and motivation are the most important predictors of work success or failure. But what is really controversial – and as yet undecided – is whether a simple test can reliably measure a quantity as vague and shifting as personality in the first place.

Grammar *See notes page 158*

Passives with *have something done*

7 Read these sentences and answer the questions that follow.

a *Applicants to 40% of large British companies will have their future prospects at least partially determined by personality tests.*

b *This concept was taken forward ... by the US Army, who were anxious not to have their efficiency undermined by the recruitment of unsuitable soldiers.*

c Our company has all job applicants take a psychometric test.

d We had them all tested by a leading recruitment company during a two-week period.

1 Which pair of sentences describes what is caused by the subject of the sentence and which pair describes what is experienced by the subject of the sentence?

2 What is the grammatical difference between c and d?

Uses of *have* and *get*

8 Explain the difference in form and meaning in the use of *have* and *get* in these sentences.

a We had the office broken into last night.

b After being with the company a year, she got asked to work in their Tokyo office.

c I didn't think the interview went well, but I got myself invited back for a second one.

d He argued with his manager so much that he got himself fired.

e I'm afraid your application form seems to have got lost in the post.

f My manager is running the meeting, but I'll try to get you invited.

g I had the recruitment agency check my CV before I sent it off.

h I got myself locked out of the office last night.

i After an hour or so, we had everyone at the office party dancing.

Using passives

9 Look at this extract from the text. Why is the passive used here?

This concept was taken forward and refined in 1917 by the US Army, ...

10 Write short introductions (3–4 sentences), using the passive, for a news article on each of the following topics:

unfair dismissal *rise in (un)employment* *training scheme* *working abroad*

Listening

Part 4

Tip

While listening for the first time, put a dot beside the option you think is correct in each task. Check that the options are correct on the second listening.

1 **Do you think you are a good listener? Why / Why not?**

Exam practice

2 🔊 2·10 **You will hear five short extracts in which different people are talking about their listening skills.**

TASK ONE: For questions 1–5, choose from the list (A–H) how each speaker reacts while listening.

A gets bored listening to facts and figures
B switches off if the content seems irrelevant
C needs to be able to relate to the person talking
D is very quick on the uptake when someone is speaking
E is very sensitive to the tone people adopt
F gets annoyed if their train of thought is interrupted
G doesn't maintain eye contact with people
H gets irritated when a speaker stops mid-sentence

Speaker 1		1
Speaker 2		2
Speaker 3		3
Speaker 4		4
Speaker 5		5

TASK TWO: For questions 6–10, choose from the list (A–H) what strategy each speaker adopts to process what they are hearing.

A needs to identify exactly what the speaker is trying to say
B never interrupts when someone is talking to them
C likes to interact initially with the speaker
D discards the details they hear and focuses on the main points
E gives the impression they're interested in listening
F connects what they're hearing with their own circumstances
G makes a mental note of what the speaker has said
H tries to visualize what the speaker is saying to them

Speaker 1		6
Speaker 2		7
Speaker 3		8
Speaker 4		9
Speaker 5		10

Your views

3 **Discuss these questions.**

a Which of the speakers has a similar listening style to you?
b What methods do you use to try and remember what you have heard?

Vocabulary

Expressions with *listen*, *hear* and *ear*

4 **Complete the phrases in *italics* in a–i with one word. Explain what the phrases mean.**

a Why were you *listening* .... on our conversation?
b If we don't do it, we'll *never hear the* .... *of it*.
c You can stop right there! *I've heard it* .... *before*.
d You could at least *hear him* ....
e Let's see what happens and .... *it by ear*.
f He has credit cards .... *out of his ears*.
g I'm .... *to my ears* in work at the moment.
h I thought that would make *your ears* .... *up*.
i He .... *me an earful* for not getting the report in on time.

Speaking | Part 3

1 How would you define a 'good speaker' of another language?

Exam skills

2 🔈 2·11 Listen to a student doing his long turn based on the prompt card below. As you listen, answer questions a–g below.

> How is the role of work in our lives changing?
> - demography
> - technology
> - health

a What discourse markers does the student use?
b How does he develop his contributions?
c How does he put forward his opinions?
d How does he avoid repetition?
e Does he show range and accuracy of vocabulary?
f Does he show accuracy and a range of grammatical forms?
g How does he avoid long pauses or silences?

Exam practice

Tip

Remember that you are not being examined on your ideas, only on your ability to express them. Take full advantage of the opportunity to show the examiners what you can do.

3 Work with a partner. Choose one of the prompt cards each. Take turns to speak for two minutes using the prompts. Using the criteria in 2, make a note of how your partner manages their long turn.

> **A** To what extent does a successful career depend on a good education?
> - aptitude
> - qualifications
> - economic conditions
>
> **Follow-up question:** Which is more important in a career, a high salary or an interesting job?

> **B** How important is it to choose the right career?
> - job satisfaction
> - financial considerations
> - lifestyle
>
> **Follow-up question:** Do you think that staying in the same job all your life is a good or a bad thing?

4 🔈 2·12 Now listen to some more general questions. Make a note of the questions and then discuss your answers with a partner.

Reading & Use of English

Part 5

1 **Which of the following quotations about success do you identify with? Why?**
Whenever a friend succeeds, a little something in me dies. (Gore Vidal 1925–)
Is it possible to succeed without any act of betrayal? (Jean Renoir 1894–1979)

2 **Read the abridged extract from an article on page 97 and think of a suitable title for it.**

Exam practice

Tip

Questions sometimes focus on the writer's opinions and implied meaning. Read the text carefully before trying to identify the correct option.

3 **Read the article again. For questions 1–6, choose the answer (A, B, C or D) which you think fits best according to the text.**

1 What comment does the writer make in the first paragraph about rivalry?
A Its effects are always harmful.
B It makes us feel that we understand our opponents better.
C It has a greater influence on us than our body chemistry does.
D It creates opportunities that can't be derived from normal competition.

2 What did Gavin J. Kilduff's research show?
A Contestants performed better when up against unknown rivals.
B Competing against those with comparable abilities improved performance.
C Athletes ran faster when competing against more than one rival.
D Athletes' performance improves during a race once they realize that their opponents are capable of beating them.

3 What happened during Deepak Malhotra's simulated auction?
A Those told that they were bidding against just one person became more determined to succeed.
B Those who thought that they were bidding against a group never bid higher than the agreed price limit.
C All the participants behaved in a highly competitive manner.
D All those who thought that they were bidding against a group had no sense of rivalry.

4 What did the research carried out on basketball fans prove?
A Participants remembered more when watching the match with other fans of their team.
B Fans watching with rivals were unable to remember any positive aspects of the opposing team's performance.
C Participants felt more rivalry towards opponents when watching the match with other fans of their team.
D Fans were more likely to recall positive features of their own team's performance.

5 What does the writer imply that Kilduff believes in paragraph E?
A Being made aware of the achievements of others can be disorientating.
B Comparing our own achievements with a rival's can motivate us.
C People who seek out information about their rivals on Facebook are likely to behave badly.
D Feeling envious of the achievements of others is a natural reaction.

6 What conclusion does Kilduff come to about rivalry?
A The margins between victory and defeat are bigger between rivals than between ordinary competitors.
B In a competition situation, participants behaved in an unethical fashion.
C Students who had confronted a rival showed more unscrupulous character traits.
D There was no evidence to show that students who competed against a rival exhibited worse behaviour than those who did not.

A (...) Rivalry differs from other kinds of competition in its intimacy. It offers contenders a psychological prize people cannot win in other contexts: the chance to beat someone obnoxiously familiar, someone whose abilities and traits are frustratingly matched with their own. Whether on the field, in a classroom or at work, rivalry changes more than our body chemistry. Researchers are now finding that it also sways our minds, changing how we think and behave during competition – and outside of it. Rivalry not only boosts motivation but can also disrupt rational thinking, bias memories and encourage unethical behaviour.

B Although competition has long interested social psychologists, only recently have scientists looked at situations involving true rivals. They are discovering that the psychology of rivalry differs in important ways from that of ordinary competition. On the positive side, rivalry can be highly motivating. In unpublished work, social psychologist Gavin J. Kilduff of New York University's Stern Schools of Business analysed six years' worth of race results achieved by a running club in New York to identify rival racers – runners who were evenly matched, similar to one another in race and gender, and who frequently competed against one another. Kilduff found that runners consistently ran faster when competing against rivals. The mere presence of a rival could trim between 20 and 30 seconds off a runner's total race time in a five-kilometre race. (...)

C Rivalry can often hamper performance, however, especially when it comes to decision-making. In a 2005 study, negotiations expert Deepak Malhotra of Harvard Business School and his colleagues asked participants to imagine themselves at an auction for a one-of-a-kind item for which they agreed to pay no more than $150. In the final round of bidding, some of the participants were told there were eight other contenders for the item, whereas others were told they were up against only one, to simulate a type of rivalry. Then the researchers told all participants that a competitor had bid $150 and that they had to decide whether to bid higher. Participants facing a single bidder rated their excitement and anxiety as much higher than those bidding against a group and were far more likely to exceed the preset bidding limit. This behaviour is economically irrational, because the more bidders remaining in the final round, the more the contested object is likely to be worth. (...)

D Rivalry impairs not only our judgment but also people's memories. In a study published in February, psychologist Kevin S. LaBar of Duke University invited male fans of the Duke men's basketball team and of the Duke's rival University of North Carolina at Chapel Hill to watch their teams face each other on a big screen TV. Each participant watched the game with two or three other fans of the same team. Later LaBar asked the fans to view segments of the game while lying in a functional MRI machine. Each segment focused on a single play whose outcome clearly benefited either Duke or U.N.C. – but the clip always ended just before the play did, at which point the fan tried to recall how the play ended. LaBar found that fans remembered outcomes that favoured their team far more accurately than those benefiting the rival team. (...)

E Because we encounter people we consider rivals quite often – both in and outside direct competition – rivalries may alter our motivation and moral code on a regular basis, Kilduff believes. Logging onto Facebook in the morning and scrolling through your newsfeed only to stumble on a personal rival's obnoxious status update or vain photos could influence your behaviour and decisions throughout the day. You may be more likely to, say, run that red light, cut in line at the movie theatre, claim a co-worker's idea as your own or tell a white lie to excuse a transgression against someone you love.

F In related work, also unpublished, Kilduff tested the relationship between rivalry and unethical behaviour by simulating rivalries in the laboratory. He set up two contests. In the rival condition, students repeatedly faced the same opponent and experienced narrow margins of victory and defeat; in the ordinary competition situation, participants faced different opponents and experienced lopsided margins. The students who faced a rival later scored higher on a test of Machiavellian attitudes, which measures whether people endorse selfish, devious and manipulative behaviour. High scores on this scale are correlated with unethical actions such as cheating, lying and exploitation. Competing against a rival, Kilduff says, may bring out the inner Machiavelli in people. 'Rivalry opens up the possibility you might behave irrationally or unethically based solely on the relationship you have with your competitor. It just changes everything.'

From *Scientific American Mind*

'Machiavellian' derives from the Italian statesman and political philosopher Machiavelli (1469–1527). His best-known work *The Prince* advises rulers that the acquisition and effective use of power may necessitate unethical methods and acknowledges that an individual can become cunning, scheming and unscrupulous.

Text analysis

4 Work through a–g, referring to the paragraphs (A–F) in the text.

a Which words capture the feelings of resentment people have towards their rivals? (A)

b Why does the writer use a colon after the word *contexts*? (line 3)

c What stylistic device does the writer use at the beginning of the paragraph to emphasize the point he is making? (B)

d Why does the writer use the verb *trim* instead of *cut*? (line 23)

e What impression is the writer trying to create by using the word *stumble*? (line 59)

f What does the writer mean by *lopsided margins*? (line 71)

g What does the writer mean by *the inner Machiavelli*? (line 77)

Reacting to the text

5 Discuss these questions.

a Do the results of the research surprise you? Why/Why not?

b Some people say that we all have an inner Machiavelli. What's your opinion?

c To what extent do you think that competitive events like the Olympic Games encourage international cooperation and understanding?

Vocabulary

Verbs and meanings

6 Explain the meaning of the verbs in *italics*. Then divide them into three groups:

a those used to describe something positive

b those used to describe something negative

c those used to describe something neutral

Some verbs may be used in more than one category

1 *sways* our minds
2 *boosts* motivation
3 *disrupt* rational thinking
4 *bias* memories
5 *hamper* performance
6 *rated* their excitement
7 *impairs* our judgement
8 *encounter* people
9 *endorse* selfishness
10 *exploited* others

Word knowledge: *face*

7 Complete a–g using the phrases below. You may need to make other changes.

face facts   *face the music*   *lose face*   *on the face of it*   *save face*
throw it back in someone's face   *put a brave face on it*

a ________, psychometric tests seem to be a useful way of recruiting staff but they can often be inconclusive.

b Let's ________! A computer will never be as powerful as the human brain.

c Sam's exam results weren't as good as he'd expected but he decided to ________ and re-sit the paper he had failed.

d If your boss has discovered that you've keyed in the wrong figures for the report, the only thing you can do is ________ then try not to make the same mistake again.

e The results of the survey showed that the local council's decision to reduce funding for education had been unpopular, so to ________, they reversed their decision.

f I was only trying to help when I made you the offer, so please don't ________.

g When the information about the cover-up leaked out, the Managing Director ________ so he handed in his resignation.

Writing | Part 2, Letter

Understanding the task **1 Read the exam question and answer questions a–c.**

A friend of yours has applied for a job as a Regional Manager. The company has asked you to write a **letter** (280–320 words) of recommendation for your friend. In your letter you should refer to the characteristics of your friend that would make them suitable for this role and describe any relevant experience your friend has.

a Who is the letter about and who is it written to?
b What specific things should you mention in your letter?
c What register will you need to write in?

Text analysis **2 Read this sample letter and answer questions a–d.**

a How does the writer support their opinion?
b How does the writer soften their opinion?
c What formal expressions do they use to recommend their friend?
d Is it positive, negative, or neutral? Give reasons for your choice.

Dear Ms Powell,

I am writing to you regarding your request for a reference for Daphne Varnava, with respect to her application for the position of Regional Manager. I have had the pleasure of knowing Daphne for ten years in both a social and professional capacity.

As well as being a joy to work with, Daphne is also a highly motivated individual who has demonstrated an inordinate amount of initiative on numerous projects. As a result she works well autonomously and constantly strives to achieve an optimum level of performance in all tasks she undertakes. Whilst being highly adept at working independently, she occasionally finds it hard to collaborate with members of her team on account of her ambition. Having said this, she has been instrumental in ensuring that a strong work ethic is fostered within the group.

Daphne embraces the task of rectifying errors and never shies away from the situation. For this reason, whenever Daphne has encountered a setback in her work, she has swiftly identified the most appropriate and effective solution. Even when faced with particularly arduous challenges, she has the drive and tenacity to successfully cope with the situation.

During her time here, she has consistently commanded the respect of her colleagues, drawing on leadership skills that have enabled many projects to keep on track against the odds. On account of her effective delegation and her assertiveness, she has regularly formed and managed a number of high performing teams. She is clearly ready to take the next step up the managerial ladder.

It is for the above reasons that I highly recommend her for employment. Without doubt Daphne will be a tremendous asset to your organization.

Should you require any further information, please do not hesitate to contact me.

Yours sincerely,
Elena Tofini

Supporting and giving reasons

3 Complete sentences a–f using an appropriate word or phrase. There may be more than one possible answer.

a She is a highly effective employee .... her efficient organization skills.

b He is a valued member of the team .... his organizational ability.

c He shows great attention to detail and .... he does so at speed he is highly respected.

d She is an excellent motivator and .... makes a great leader.

e He has a caring nature .... he is ideally suited to the role.

f He makes an excellent salesman .... his professional communication skills.

4 Write sentences giving reasons why you would be suited to a particular job.

Vocabulary

Personal qualities

5 Match a–j with 1–10 to make phrases to describe personal qualities. Then, decide what each one means and when you might use them.

a get carried	1 someone's throat
b jump down	2 an inch
c throw something	3 away
d not give	4 together
e get up	5 meal of something
f make a	6 someone's nose
g too big	7 weight around
h wriggle	8 out of something
i pull	9 for your boots
j throw your	10 your socks up

6 Think of synonyms for each of the phrases in 5.

Being tactful

7 Choose some of the phrases in 5. Rewrite them to make them sound more positive. The language below might help you.

Get carried away: Whilst Peter is very hard-working, he sometimes finds it difficult to control his enthusiasm for new projects.

while/whilst   tend   tendency   although   when it comes to   find
not always   yet to   known to   a certain   at times   not exactly

Exam practice *See Writing guide p142*

Tip

Most genres of writing require you to give a balanced view. Try to include positive and negative opinions in your writing.

8 Follow these stages to write your letter: read, think, plan, write and then check.

A friend of yours has applied for a job as a project manager in an office. The company has asked you to write a **letter** (280–320 words) of recommendation for your friend. In your letter you should refer to the duties and responsibilities your friend has had in their previous job and any admiral personal qualities that would make them suitable for the role.

Unit 10 Entertainment & leisure

Introduction

1 **Look at the pie chart above showing the amount that people in Britain spend on different kinds of entertainment and leisure activities. Try to match the percentages with what you think people spend their money on.**

sport film eating out mobile music video games

2 **Now check your answers on page 164. How different were the results from yours?**

3 **Besides those mentioned in 1, what forms of entertainment do you and your friends enjoy?**

4 **Read the text and discuss questions a–c.**

a What main points is the writer making?

b Which forms of entertainment would you describe as 'active' and which as 'passive'?

c Do you agree with what the writer is saying? Why/Why not?

The word 'entertainment' and the word 'activity' may seem to have different meanings for us. But there are *reams* of social data to show that as we have adopted more forms of passive entertainment, the most *ubiquitous* being television, our level of activity has steadily dropped.

This, however, is not the only *fallout* of our addiction to TV. This expectation to be passively entertained has *spilled into* other areas of our society as well. How we perceive our world may have changed from an environment we interact with to a parade that we simply sit back and watch go by. We have become a society of attention *deficit* watchers that have high expectations of being passively entertained, no matter where we are.

5 **What do the words in *italics* mean?**

6 **Can you make sentences of your own using the words in italics?**

Reading & Use of English

Part 1

1 Discuss these questions in pairs or small groups.

a Why do you think young people often consider celebrities as role models?

b How influential do you think celebrity role models are?

c What might be the advantages or dangers of viewing celebrities as role models?

2 Read the text, ignoring the gaps. Decide what its main point is.

Celebrity role-models

Research in the University of Leicester Department of Media and Communication examined interest in celebrities and gossip about them. It was carried out by Dr Charlotte De Backer who sought in her study to explain interest in celebrity culture.

According to Dr De Backer: 'Life is about learning and (0) ....*B*.......... experience, and in that process we have a tendency to observe and mimic the actions of others. Ideally we mimic what makes others successful and (1) .... unsuccessful actions others have trialled and paid for. In reality, humans seem to have the tendency to mimic the overall behaviour pattern of the higher status of those more successful than themselves. This explains why celebrities act as role models for broad (2) .... of behaviour they display – whether good or bad.'

Dr De Backer also examined another theory for interest in celebrity, known as the Parasocial Hypothesis. In this (3) ...., the bonds are parasocial, or one-way, because the celebrity reveals private information, often involuntarily. The audience members respond emotionally to this information, although there is hardly ever any feedback on the private life of the audience going to the celebrity, nor do celebrities (4) .... emotions towards their audience.

Her study of 800 respondents and over 100 interviews (5) .... that younger participants showed greater interest in celebrity gossip, even if it was about celebrities who were much older than them and even when they did not know who the celebrities were. They showed greatest interest in internationally-known celebrities, because they considered those as more (6) ....

Her study also found that older people were interested in celebrity gossip not because they wanted to learn from the celebrities, but because it helped them to form social networks with other people. 'We found in the interviews that older people do not gossip about celebrities because they want to learn from them or feel (7) .... by them, but because they use celebrity gossip to (8) .... with real-life friends and acquaintances. As we live in scattered societies, celebrities can act as our mutual friends and acquaintances.'

Tip

The word may fit grammatically, but it might not be the best meaning of the word for this particular context.

Exam practice

3 For questions 1–8, read the text again and decide which answer (A, B, C or D) best fits each gap. There is an example at the beginning (0).

	A	B	C	D
0	*A winning*	*(B) gaining*	*C achieving*	*D capturing*
1	A escape	B avoid	C prevent	D evade
2	A reaches	B domains	C ranges	D spheres
3	A case	B instance	C state	D position
4	A exhibit	B present	C display	D expose
5	A reinforced	B assured	C validated	D confirmed
6	A reputable	B honourable	C prestigious	D illustrious
7	A befriended	B sustained	C patronized	D upheld
8	A tie	B link	C cement	D bond

4 Do you agree with the points the writer is making in the text in 2? Why/Why not?

Grammar *See notes page 159*

Contrast clauses

5 Look at this extract from the text. Identify the contrast clauses. How are they introduced? What information might you expect to find in a contrast clause?

... younger participants showed greater interest in celebrity gossip, even if it was about celebrities who were much older than them and even when they did not know who the celebrities were.

6 Which words or phrases can you use to complete these contrast clauses? More than one answer may be correct.

a I hate TV talent shows .... my children love them and never miss a show.
1 even 2 even when 3 even though 4 even if

b .... I like watching films at home, you can't compare the experience with seeing them on the big screen.
1 Although 2 Though 3 Much 4 Much as

c Eating out in restaurants is still very popular in my country, ... it has become increasingly expensive in recent years.
1 although 2 even 3 even though 4 even although

d Expensive .... the tickets are, I go to the opera at least twice a year.
1 although 2 though 3 even though 4 that

e I can't find many programmes that I want to watch on TV, ... there are a lot more TV channels now than there were five years ago.
1 although 2 but 3 despite 4 despite the fact that

f .... we love classical music, we don't go to concerts very often.
1 Although 2 Despite 3 In spite of 4 While

g We try to go to the theatre as often as we can .... not living near a big city.
1 despite 2 in spite 3 in spite of 4 despite the fact that

h Tickets for musicals are expensive .... tickets for plays are cheaper.
1 while 2 whereas 3 even if 4 much as

i The play was wonderful, ... a little too long at over three hours.
1 if 2 while 3 even though 4 whereas

j I'll be at the concert tomorrow .... it means queuing for tickets all night.
1 while 2 despite 3 if 4 even if

Reason clauses

7 Look at this extract from the text. What words could you use instead of *as* without changing the meaning?

As we live in scattered societies, celebrities can act as our mutual friends and acquaintances.

8 Complete a–f using a word from the list below. There may be more than one possible answer.

as since while now for in

a We can see whatever films we want at home .... that we get on-demand TV.

b Sales of audio CDs have decreased sharply .... it's now so easy to download music directly from the internet.

c .... it was very late, all the restaurants had closed so we got a takeaway.

d Watching TV is a very different experience from what it was ten years ago, ... that there are now so many channels to choose from.

e .... we're on the subject of comedians, have you been to the new comedy club opposite the station?

f People may spend even more of their free time at home in the future, ... there are likely to be further advances in technology over the next decade.

Adverb clauses of manner

9 Circle the correct option in *italics* to complete sentences a–g.

a When you watch a film in 3D, it's so realistic that it feels *though / as if / just as* you're really there.

b The film depicts life *as / as if / so* it was in 1900.

c I programmed the recorder *like as / just as / just so* you told me, but it didn't record the programme.

d The speakers on his sound system are so good it's *as if / as like / just as* you are actually there in the concert hall.

e Some celebrities get so much publicity that it sometimes feels *as / if / like* you know them personally.

f When we moved here, we discovered that there weren't as many restaurants in the town centre *as / like / than* we'd expected.

g There's a long queue at the box office so it looks *as / as though / though* there won't be any spare seats.

10 Complete these sentences in your own words.

a Although I'm quite interested in ……………, I …………… .

b I always try to …………… despite …………… .

c Even if it's raining, I …………… .

d Much as I love ……………, I …………… .

e Even though I've never ……………, I …………… .

f Since I'm not very keen on ……………, I …………… .

g While I can see the advantages of ……………, I …………… .

Word knowledge: *make*

11 Complete sentences a–j with one or two words. What do the phrases with *make* mean?

a He made …………… the woods, then disappeared.

b We were late for the party and had to make …………… some leftover sandwiches.

c The actress promised to make …………… the damage caused to the photographer's camera.

d It's make or …………… for the singer with his new single.

e Her energy on stage goes some way towards making …………… her lack of singing ability.

f The singer's manager has been accused of being …………… make.

g His first film has all the makings …………… becoming a cult classic.

h I find him really hard to make …………… .

i He makes …………… he's this rock legend.

j The thieves made …………… all the band's equipment.

Writing | Part 1

Text analysis

1 Read the two Part 1 texts. There are two main points in each. What are they?

Fame and fortune

It is a poor reflection on the development and progress of our society when the primary aim of many people is simply to get rich. A survey of nine-year-old children showed that above and beyond other goals such as happiness is the desire for obscene levels of wealth. Furthermore, and perhaps even more shockingly, is how most kids believe that they can choose to attain this goal. Not through determination and perseverance, but through becoming famous. Not even through the grotesquely rewarded ability to kick a ball or hold a tune but through simply being famous for the sake of who they are.

I want to be a footballer

Not so long ago, the aspirations of youngsters were directed at admirable or at least achievable careers. Professions such as nursing, firefighting and teaching were high on the agenda, perhaps a reflection on a society that functioned as a community. How sad then that today most ambitions are purely self-serving. Number one on the list is sports star, with pop star/celebrity hot on its heels. It is worrying that so many children want to be fast-tracked to super-stardom with minimal effort. It is all well and good to dream, but I fear too many of today's youth are lining themselves up for a long hard fall.

2 Read the sample essay and answer questions a–b.

a Underline the expressions that the writer uses to compare the texts.

b What does the author reveal by using the phrases *purports to* and *the underlying assumption*?

Are the unrealistic ambitions and aspirations of today's youth a cause for concern? What is the impact of this on our society? These are questions which are reflected on in the texts.

Both writers bemoan the fact that young people today only seem to aspire to fame and fortune, which they expect to be handed to them on a plate. While I am sure it is true that many young people do think this way, I do not believe this is anything new. The writer of the second text purports to prove that this trend amongst children is a recent phenomenon. However, I believe that people always have and always will desire wealth. The perception that this desire is more prevalent now could probably be put down to the fact that society today, as a whole, is wealthier and therefore our aspirations are perhaps just higher than they used to be. That said, I do think that, given the choice, many young people would still put happiness at the top of their agenda.

The underlying assumption about the youth of today in both texts, is that they are inherently lazy and individualistic. The second text points out that they don't have any sense of contributing to their communities through their career aspirations. While this is undoubtedly true of some, I feel it is a bit of a gross generalisation. In a similar vein, I am sure that not all young people just want to be propelled effortlessly into fame, something that the writers of the texts seem to feel is the case. Of course, those who do are indeed setting themselves up for bitter disappointment when they realise that attaining anything in life generally involves hard work. Although it is fine for younger children to contemplate these idealistic goals, they will need a reality check as they move into adulthood.

In summary, even though some people do not agree with the way in which children wish to acquire riches, it is unsurprising that wealth, so central to our society, is the aspiration of so many of them. And, while I agree that ambitions may have changed, I feel it is an exaggeration to suggest that this reflects the demise of our society; it simply represents a shift in the dreams of children.

Complex sentences

3 **Combine the sentences from each set 1–4 to make one complex sentence. Use the words below to help you.**

which not only but also while and nevertheless as well as during

Set 1

Traditional professions such as firefighting and teaching are realistically obtainable.
These professions remain admirable in many people's eyes.
Few children aspire to these professions.

Set 2

Fame is seen as a career by many young children.
Fame is seen as a realistic way of making vast sums of money.
Fame is unattainable for the vast majority of people.

Set 3

Popular reality television shows now take up much more air time on TV than dramas.
Popular reality television shows have given ordinary people aspirations to simply be famous.
Popular reality television shows created a reduced number of acting roles available to many aspiring actors.

Set 4

The food industry has helped to transform our diet.
It has also transformed our workforce, landscape, economy and popular culture.
It has done it in a relatively short period of time.

Exam practice *See Writing guide page 138*

4 **Use the checklist on page 135 to help you write your answer.**

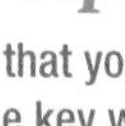

Tip

Remember that you don't have to paraphrase key words such as technical terminology. Similarly, you should not leave out key words in order to be concise.

Read the two texts below.

Write an essay summarizing and evaluating the key points from both texts. Use your own words throughout as far as possible, and include your own ideas in your answer.

Write your answer in 240–280 words.

Positive role model?

No matter whether it was a politician, singer or someone closer to home, as children each and every one of us had people we aspired to be. Whoever we chose as our role models will have had a significant bearing on some of the life choices we made. It is little wonder then, that some fear for the moral development of children who base their ambitions around the culture of celebrity. Few would criticize a child idolizing someone in the media spotlight with a blatantly obvious talent. What many abhor is the clearly discernible lack of talent that is spread across our media twenty-four seven.

Celebrities and the media

The very same people who thrust celebrity culture down our throats on a daily basis are at the same time the ones quickest to knock celebrity culture. As quickly as a new media darling is put on a pedestal, they are knocked down for some minor indiscretion in their past or an unfortunate incident in the glare of the media spotlight. Whilst there are clearly celebrities who bring little benefit, or even for that matter a vague resemblance of entertainment to our society, there are a great number who are positive role models. Not all of them live in dream palaces; some do in fact have very worthwhile charity institutions that they run.

Speaking

Part 3

1 Discuss questions a–c.

a Approximately how much TV do you watch per week?

b What are your opinions of TV programmes like these:
crime reconstructions?
home video 'disasters'?
reality TV programmes?

c Computer games are popular with people of different ages nowadays. Do you think they are a good or a bad thing? Give reasons for your opinions.

2 🔊 2·13 At the end of Part 3, the examiner will ask both candidates questions related to the topic on the prompt card. Listen to two students, Jan and Silvia, answering a question related to the topic on the question card below. Then answer questions a–h below.

What effects has TV had on our lives?
- access to information
- family relationships
- outside activities

a What question does the examiner ask?

b What does Jan ask the examiner to do?

c How does Jan expand on his initial response?

d How does the examiner invite Silvia to join in the conversation?

e Has Silvia listened to Jan's answer? (How do you know?)

f How does Jan interrupt his partner the first time?

g How does Silvia suggest that he may be mistaken?

h How does Silvia end the conversation?

Exploring the topic

3 Look at the useful language below. What function does each set a–c have? Can you add further examples to each set? Then, decide when each of the expressions would be appropriate.

a ....
What do you reckon?
What are your thoughts on this?

b ....
If I could just come in here …
I'm sorry but …
Can I just add …

c ....
Just a moment, please.
Don't butt in!
Let me finish!

Exam practice

4 🔊 2·14 Now listen to some more general questions about television. Make a note of the questions. Then, discuss your answers with a partner. Try to use some of the language from 3.

Tip

Listen carefully to what your partner is saying because you will be asked to join in answering the related question.

Part 6

1 **Discuss how strongly you agree or disagree with the following statements.**

a The cinema was the single greatest influence on people's lives in the 20th century.

b Home cinema has usurped the role of the more traditional movie theatre.

c The growth of the Hollywood film industry has replaced quality with quantity.

2 **What do you think the film director Alfred Hitchcock meant when he said:**

For me the cinema is not a slice of life, but a piece of cake?

Hollywood

I In the years after the Second World War, the Hollywood film industry underwent a major transformation. Increased competition from foreign films, falling numbers of cinema audiences, and attacks on the studio structure by government agencies led to a loss of revenue which crippled the American industry, and forced it into rapid and profound change.

[1]

II This phenomenon cannot simply be blamed on the rise of television, as it began five years before television existed as a viable alternative to movie-going. After the Second World War, there was a demographic and cultural shift in urban America that profoundly altered the leisure patterns of US society.

[2]

III The Hollywood studios were not oblivious to these population shifts. They saw the need to provide new theatres, and, once the necessary building materials became available, they began the process of constructing 4,000 drive-ins throughout the USA. The drive-in theatre offered a pleasant, open space where movie fans in parked cars could watch double features on a massive screen. By June 1956, at the very height of the drift away from the urban environment to green belt areas, and of the baby-boom, more people in the USA went to the drive-ins than to the traditional 'hard-top' theatres.

[3]

IV Meanwhile, the shift of movie houses to where the audience was now located created another problem for the shaking foundations of the Hollywood studios. The disappearance of the division between 'first-run' houses in town centres showing prestige pictures, and local neighbourhood cinemas, changed the pattern of film demand, necessitating a major change in the organization of film production.

[4]

V Even before the war, Hollywood studios had been up in arms about attempts to break up their vertically integrated systems of production, distribution and exhibition. They appealed the case all the way to the Supreme Court; but 1948 proved to be the end of the road, and, in what became known as the 'Paramount decision', the court ruled for the divorce of production and exhibition, and the elimination of unfair booking practices.

[5]

VI However, the studios still retained a significant measure of direct control through international distribution. The 'Paramount decision' wounded Hollywood, but did not break it. Although the major companies would have adjusted far better to the new conditions had they retained their theatres, they still held sway as long as they produced what exhibitors and audiences wanted.

[6]

VII In 1939, Technicolor had lit up the screen in *Gone with the Wind*, but throughout its early years had only been employed for a select group of features, principally historical epics and lavish musicals. Just over a decade later, Technicolor lost its market monopoly as a result of antitrust laws, and the giant Eastman Kodak soon surged into the market, introducing Eastman Color, which required only one, not three, separate negatives. The studios brought out Eastman Color under a variety of names, and by the early 1960s virtually all Hollywood movies were being made in colour.

[7]

VIII However, theatres which contracted for the new process were required to employ three full-time projectionists and invest thousands of dollars in new equipment, and this financial outlay proved too much for most.

Tip

Try to visualize the paragraph you have chosen written in the space between the other two paragraphs. This might help you decide.

Exam practice

3 Read the article on page 108 about the Hollywood film industry. Seven paragraphs have been removed from the article. Choose from the paragraphs A–H below the one which fits each gap (1–7). There is one extra paragraph which you do not need to use.

Missing paragraphs

A A further blow to the stability of the studio system was delivered by the government. The years immediately after the war saw the culmination of federal antitrust action against the Hollywood studios: a campaign that had started in the 1930s, but had been temporarily halted by the war.

B So Hollywood looked to innovation and new technology to tempt patrons back to the theatres. Films were designed on a spectacular scale, clearly superior to the black and white video images broadcast into the home. The first of the 'new' film technologies, colour, had long been available to the movie industry.

C People were cashing in the savings bonds accumulated during the war and buying houses in the suburbs, accelerating a trend which had begun at the turn of the century. This took away the heart of the film-going audience. Suburbanization also raised the cost of going out to the movies; upon relocation it became inconvenient and expensive to travel to the centre of town simply to see a film.

D A more permanent solution arrived with the shopping centre theatre. As new malls opened in record numbers, the locus of movie attendance permanently shifted. With acres of free parking and ideal access for the car, shopping centres generally included a multiplex with five or more screens.

E In 1952, the Hollywood studios went one step further, and made their movies bigger. Cinemas offered spectacular widescreen effects by melding images from three synchronized projectors on a vast curved screen. To add to the sense of overwhelming reality, it also included multi-track stereo sound.

F What the Hollywood studios needed was a widescreen process without the added complications of 3-D, or the prohibitive investment of Cinerama. Fox's CinemaScope seemed to be the answer: a widescreen process which used an anamorphic lens to expand the size of the image.

G Perhaps the most important watershed in the Hollywood system began in the middle of the last century. Certainly, by the early 1960s, attendances at US movie houses were half what they had been during the glory days, and thousands of flourishing theatres had closed forever.

H During Hollywood's 'golden age', the major studios had directly controlled their own destinies by owning the most important theatres. Now they were legally obliged to sell these off, and split their companies in two; the 'golden age' was over and a new age loomed.

Text analysis

4 Work through a–k, referring to the text (i–viii) and missing paragraphs (A–H).

a Which two words does the writer use to create a sense of drama and suffering? (i)

b Which word is used to describe a remarkable thing or event? (ii)

c Which expressions capture a) the precarious state of the Hollywood film industry and b) the high regard in which some of its productions were held? (iv)

d Which expression captures the militant nature of people who worked in the film industry? (v)

e Find an expression which conveys the power of film companies. (vi)

f Find an expression which conveys the initial impact of a new development in the cinema and the later success of its rival. (vii)

g Which word is used to describe the attack on the film industry by the government? (A)

h What does the phrase *upon relocation* refer to? (C)

i Which phrase indicates an unprecedented increase? (D)

j Find a phrase which means: do something to a greater degree or extent. (E)

k Explain in your own words what *watershed* means. (G)

Your views

5 Discuss these questions with a partner.

a How would you describe the state of the film industry in your country?

b How do you think technology will change the film industry in the future?

Listening | Part 2

1 **Read the extract below from a restaurant guide to London. Then discuss these questions.**

Although it may be a cliché to state that there are more curry restaurants in London than you are likely to find in many other capital cities, it's true. And now it seems, with its growing plethora of international cuisines, that London has usurped New York to become the food capital of the world.

a What is rather surprising about the information?

b How varied is the cuisine in restaurants in your country?

c How authentic do you think the food is in restaurants which serve dishes from other countries. Why?

Exam practice

Tip

Read what comes before and after the gap carefully. This will help you to decide what part of speech and what kind of information might be missing.

2 🔊 2·15 **You will hear part of a radio programme presented by author and foodie, Pat Chapman. For questions 1–9, complete the sentences with a word or short phrase.**

Pat says that the British were a ______ **1** according to Napoleon.

Pat likens curry in Britain nowadays to a ______ **2**.

Britain suffered from a ______ **3** in the period after the Second World War.

Immigrants to Britain had to arrange for their prized ______ **4** to be imported.

Eating curry became compulsive as the dish was ______ **5** for most people.

The majority of curry restaurants in the UK are not ______ **6**.

Indian dishes prepared in their own containers need ______ **7** to be authentic.

Nowadays, additional ______ **8** are added to pre-cooked ingredients.

A ______ **9** is responsible for cooking breads and tandoori items.

Vocabulary

Food and drink

3 **Match the words in list A to words in list B to describe different kinds of food and drink. Then decide what type of food and drink a–g they are used to describe. More than one answer may be correct.**

A:	B:	
oven	*fed*	a meat
pan	*aged*	b fruit
hand	*roasted*	c vegetables
organically	*squeezed*	d fish
charcoal	*grown*	e soup
heavily	*picked*	f chicken
corn	*caught*	g wine
line	*grilled*	
oak	*fried*	
freshly	*spiced*	

Your views

4 **In small groups, discuss these questions.**

a What different types of food and drink do you like most/least?

b How important is it to you to eat food which is ethically sourced, organic or free-range?

Unit 11 Money matters

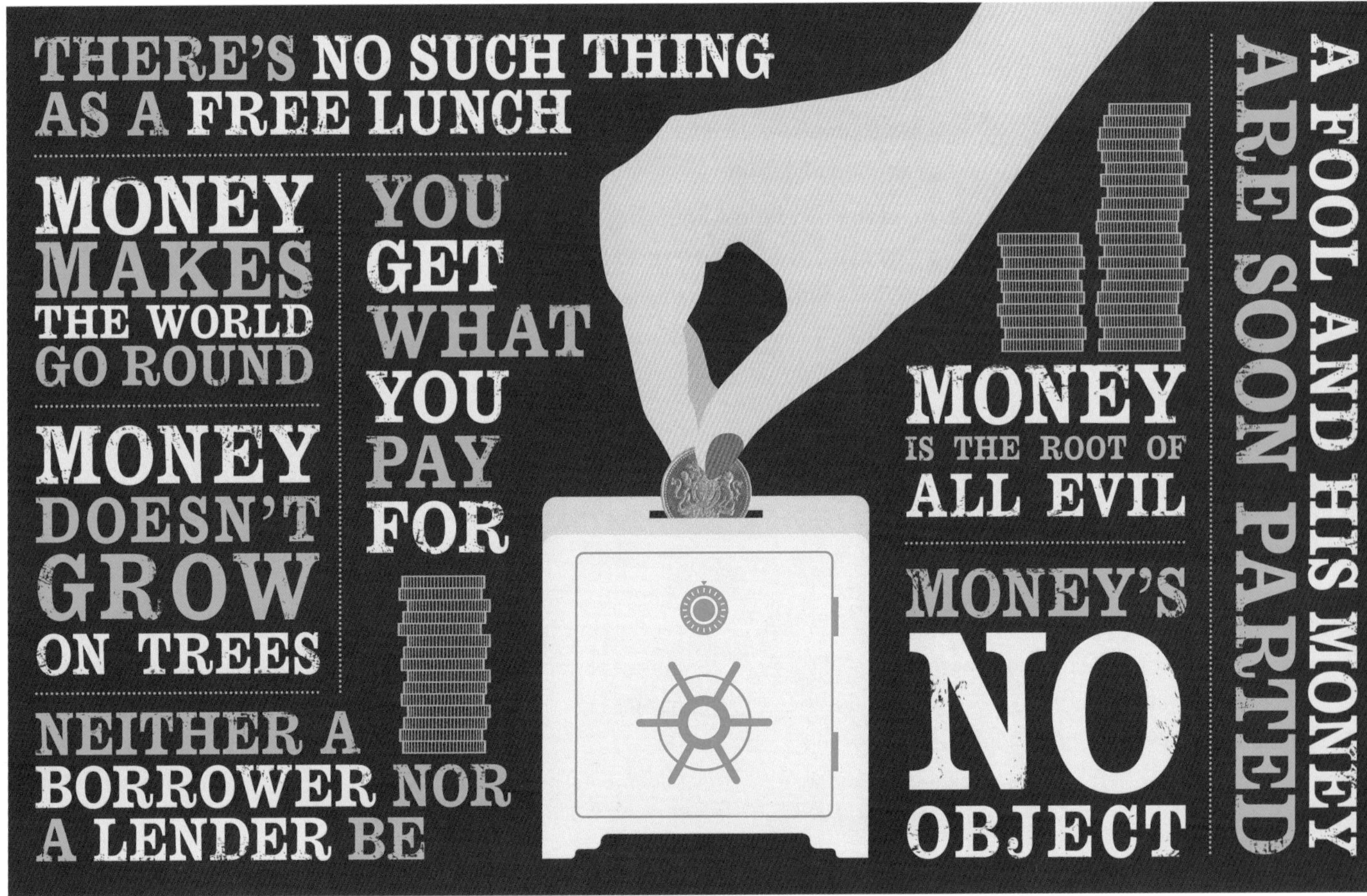

THERE'S NO SUCH THING AS A FREE LUNCH
MONEY MAKES THE WORLD GO ROUND
YOU GET WHAT YOU PAY FOR
MONEY DOESN'T GROW ON TREES
NEITHER A BORROWER NOR A LENDER BE
MONEY IS THE ROOT OF ALL EVIL
MONEY'S NO OBJECT
A FOOL AND HIS MONEY ARE SOON PARTED

Introduction

1 **Read the sayings above connected with money. Decide what is meant by each one.**

2 **Now, decide on what type of situation you might need to use each one in.**

3 **2·16 Listen to three people talking about their attitude to money. Which speaker do you identify with most?**

4 **The speakers mentioned *splash out, fritter away, not have a penny to rub together*. What do these expressions mean?**

5 **Divide the words below into the three groups that follow.**

fork out prosperous hard up squander sink (into) be on the breadline loaded shell out be rolling in it be strapped for cash well off deprived funnel affluent siphon off broke hoard penniless privileged needy

a synonyms of *poor*

b synonyms of *rich*

c collocations with the word *money*

6 **Look back at the words in 5. What is the difference in meaning and use between each word in the group?**

7 **Read the text below. Then answer the questions that follow.**

The English find 'doing business' awkward and embarrassing at least partly because of a deep-seated but utterly irrational distaste for money-talk of any kind. When it comes to what we call 'the sordid subject of money', we tend to become tongue-tied and uncomfortable. Some cover their embarrassment by joking, some by adopting a blustering, forthright, even aggressive manner; some become flustered and hurried, others may be over-polite and apologetic, or prickly and defensive. You will not often see an English person entirely at ease when obliged to engage in money-talk.

a To what extent is this true where you are from?

b What is your attitude to money?

Reading & Use of English | Part 2

1 **Which of these descriptions best sums up your attitude to shopping? Why?**

I like to shop around. I can never decide what to buy.
I'm a window shopper. I buy things on impulse.
I'm a compulsive shopper. I'm a reluctant shopper.
I can shop till I drop. I'm a bargain hunter.

2 **Read the text below, ignoring the gaps. Then answer these questions.**

a What myth does the text explode?

b What solution to the effects of retail therapy is put forward?

Retail therapy

For many people, 'retail therapy' offers the ultimate salvation (0) ___*from*___ the stresses of modern living. But a major new study now suggests that for millions of people, binge shopping is (1) __________ longer an emotional cure-all. (2) __________ anything, it may make you feel worse. 'For significant numbers, dissatisfaction is now part of the shopping process,' said Lucy Purdy of analysts Publicis, which (3) __________ out the nationwide study. 'Shopping offers a short-term buzz, and, (4) __________ a society, we now recognize this and we're getting fed (5) __________ with short-term emotions.' The Publicis researchers said retailers should tailor their marketing more carefully so that shoppers don't feel that they are being tricked (6) __________ making unnecessary purchases.

The psychologist Oliver James said: 'We're now seeing a generation which has been brought up to believe that the pursuit of status and wealth is the route to fulfilment, which has (7) __________ out to be manifestly not true. In fact, (8) __________ rich you are has no bearing whatsoever on your mental health or well-being.'

Tip

Make sure you read the whole sentence to give you a better idea of what word will fit the gap.

Exam practice

3 **Read the text again. For questions 1–8, think of the word which best fits each space. Use only one word in each space. There is an example at the beginning.**

4 **To what extent do you agree with Oliver James' comments?**

Grammar *See notes page 160*

Reported speech

5 **Look at sentences a–c which report what was said in the text in 2. Is one of the options in *italics* in each sentence more appropriate than the other, or are both possible? Give reasons for your choices.**

a Lucy Purdy said that, for significant numbers, dissatisfaction *was / is* now a part of the shopping process.

b The Publicis researchers actually said that shopping *was / is* a short-term buzz, and, as a society, we now *recognize / recognized* this.

c Oliver James said that we *were / are* now seeing a generation which *had / has* been brought up to believe that the pursuit of status and wealth *was / is* the route to fulfilment.

Reporting questions

6 **How would you report the following questions?**

a 'Have you ever bought something and then regretted it?' Bella asked me.

b 'How many T-shirts did you buy yesterday?' Tom asked me.

c 'Who is the man in the grey suit?' Paul asked me. 'Is he your bank manager?'

d 'When should I start a savings account at your bank and why should I do it?' I asked the bank manager.

e 'Have you been given a pay rise or not?' I asked Pat.

Reporting verb patterns

7 **Divide the reporting verbs below into groups according to the patterns in a–e.**

encourage explain promise whisper agree tell refuse ask suggest boast

a *to* + infinitive

b object + *to* + infinitive

c *that*

d *-ing*

e *to* + object + *that*

Synonyms

8 **Match the words below to their synonyms above in 7. How are the words different in meaning and use?**

acquiesce blab brag clamour clarify demand egg on
fill in go along with gloat moot mouth mumble pledge
propose rebuff spell out swear turn down urge

9 🔊 2·17 **Listen to conversations a–k. Report the conversations using appropriate verbs from 7 and 8.**

Vocabulary

Describing voice

10 **Look at these adjectives. Decide which ones describe the quality of a voice and which describe emotion in a voice.**

husky stern gravelly shrill slurred velvety grating
high-pitched booming whiny hushed matter-of-fact
mellifluous tremulous gruff plummy taut

11 **Can you use any of the adjectives in 10 together, e.g.** ***a gruff, matter-of-fact voice*****?**

Reading & Use of English | Part 5

1 **Discuss these questions.**

a What does it take to be an entrepreneur?

b Would you consider moving abroad to find a job?

2 **Read the text quickly and answer these questions.**

a How did Doctor Brandreth earn a living?

b What methods did he use to sell his wares?

c How successful was he as an entrepreneur?

Exam practice

Tip

Read each option carefully and scan the relevant section of the text to find whether it is correct or not.

3 **Read the text again. For questions 1–6, choose the answer (A, B, C or D) which you think fits best according to the text.**

1 What is suggested in the first two paragraphs about Doctor Brandreth?
A He began his life in rather privileged circumstances.
B His claims about his medicine were grossly exaggerated.
C His family background was somewhat complicated.
D He had a strictly limited knowledge of medicine.

2 The writer portrays the British medical establishment as
A involved in a variety of innovative cures.
B susceptible to the criticism of others.
C competitive in its own ranks.
D dismissive of outsiders.

3 What comment does the writer make about the many people emigrating to the USA from Liverpool in the 19th century?
A They had to pay over the odds for their tickets on a ship.
B They had great difficulty purchasing tickets to get on board a ship.
C They risked losing their assets before they even got on a ship.
D They often had to wait a long time to find an available ship.

4 The writer uses the phrase 'a small alphabet soup' to illustrate
A the difficulties of validating academic qualifications in another country.
B the willingness with which academic qualifications were handed out.
C how academic qualifications varied from one country to another.
D what types of academic qualifications were considered important.

5 In paragraphs F and G, what does the writer imply about Brandreth's success?
A It relied on selling a product which far outshone its market rivals.
B It stemmed from exceedingly aggressive marketing techniques.
C It was helped by having contacts like the showman P. T. Barnum.
D It relied on shock tactics which people found hard to resist.

6 What does the writer imply about the newspaper industry?
A Brandreth's involvement changed the nature of the entire newspaper industry.
B Advertising in newspapers was not the best way to reach a large number of potential buyers.
C The ethics of people in the newspaper industry were no better than those in other businesses.
D Brandreth's reputation was damaged by his connection with the newspaper industry.

A nose for business

A The year 1809 was a year to reckon with, a year to remember. It was the year of Beethoven's Emperor Concerto, and of the birth of great men like Charles Darwin and Abraham Lincoln. In that same year my great-great-grandfather was born in Yorkshire. Benjamin Brandreth started life as a nobody but he ended it seventy-one years later, 3,000 miles away in very different circumstances.

B Doctor Brandreth was a patent medicine man*. He claimed his pills were lifesavers and they made him a fortune. They were a mixture of gums and aloes*, sarsaparilla*, bitter apple, peppers and white Castile soap*. They were laxatives. So was he a confidence trickster? Well, he called himself a doctor when he wasn't one, and he called himself Brandreth when his father's name was Daubeney. But that's perhaps forgivable. His father, William Daubeney, was a Catholic, and his mother, Anne Brandreth, a Quaker. They were married but it was a union neither welcomed nor recognized by the Daubeneys. When Mr Daubeney disappeared from the scene, Anne married a second time, a Mr Holmes. My great-great-grandfather was brought up using his stepfather's surname. He spent part of his childhood with his maternal grandfather, another so-called Doctor Brandreth, and it is this gentleman who is said to have first formulated a little vegetable pill with amazing curative powers. So, young Benjamin apparently learned pill-making at his grandfather's knee.

C The boy had a nose for business and an eye for the ladies. He married his first wife, Harriet, when he was just eighteen. Benjamin and Harriet had four children in quick succession and the family pill business was proving fruitful, too. But pill-peddling in the early years of the 19th century wasn't a pushover. There was competition – and hostility. The British medical establishment, more used to prescribing bloodletting*, mercury and arsenic, regarded the unqualified patent-pill men as quacks. Benjamin decided to leave the country.

D In 1835, aged only twenty-five, and equipped with nothing more than ambition and the recipe for his grandfather's medicine, the young man set out from Liverpool for the New World. When Benjamin Holmes set sail, he would have been considered lucky to have actually got on board the ship because Liverpool was notorious for its 'sharpers' – undesirables who tried to rip the tens of thousands of passengers off before they even boarded.

E But Benjamin was a risk-taker and when he got off the ship, he had reinvented himself as Doctor Brandreth of New York. The youthful entrepreneur presented himself to the learned elders of the Eclectic Medical College of New York City, who, after due examination, awarded him a small alphabet soup* of academic distinctions. Within weeks of disembarkation, a notice appeared on the front page of *The Sun*, New York's leading daily newspaper, advertising his services for those requiring medical aid for an extensive list of complaints, and outlining his consultation hours. You name it, Doctor Brandreth cured it.

F There were already many competing patent medicines on the market but Brandreth's advertising was very unique and very forceful. He more or less invented the concept of the 'brand'. Everything he owned carried his name and his signature. He was the pioneer of getting your name across. He took to the road, touring with his pills and his props, including an enormous tapeworm that he kept in a gigantic jar. It was proof positive of the efficacy of his potent little pills.

G He even taught the greatest showman of the day a thing or two. P. T. Barnum visited Benjamin, and across the top of the building he noticed an enormous billboard, with gold letters advertising 'Brandreth's universal vegetable pills'. Barnum was fascinated because billboards in New York were never that size and this was really an eye-catcher. It was the advertising hoarding of its day. Barnum decided that advertising was like learning; a little was a dangerous thing.

H But perhaps the key business relationship of Brandreth's life was with the Gordon Bennetts: the founders of the *New York Herald*. The family was having trouble financing the paper and up turned Doctor Brandreth with his pills and poured money into advertising in the paper – keeping it afloat and funding the birth of popular journalism. However, nine months later, when Brandreth withdrew his advertising, James Gordon Bennett, with an amazing show of principle, immediately exposed him as a charlatan. Despite this, in his first year in America, Brandreth sold pills to the tune of $90,000. He was giving people what they wanted. Why risk going to the doctor when you could be cured with a pill? In his day, doctors were expensive, and conventional medicine didn't amount to much. Most Americans ate rich and starchy foods which they consumed at great speed so people needed laxatives as never before. Brandreth was the right man, in the right place, with the right product, at the right time. He was a pioneer with energy and focus, and a prince among marketeers. He became a New York State Senator, a multi-millionaire and a household name.

patent medicine man someone who sells medicines of dubious quality they make themselves

aloes a strong laxative obtained from bitter juices of various species of aloe

sarsaparilla the dried roots of various plants used to flavour some drinks and medicines

Castile soap a hard white or mottle soap made with olive oil and soda

bloodletting the surgical removal of some of the patient's blood

alphabet soup soup containing pasta in the shape of letters of the alphabet

Text analysis

4 Work through a–n, referring to the paragraphs (A–H).

a Find an example of a rhetorical question. Why does the writer use this device? (B)
b Find an example of a euphemism. What phrase could the writer have used instead? (B)
c Which adjective is used with a double meaning? (C)
d Find an example of understatement. What does the writer really mean? (C)
e What is the writer implying by using the word *quacks*? (line 31)
f Which phrase is used in a rather 'tongue in cheek' fashion to refer to people in the New York medical profession? (E)
g What effect is the writer trying to create with the last sentence in this paragraph? (E)
h What does the writer mean by the phrase: *he took to the road*? (line 54–55)
i What effect does the use of alliteration have in the last sentence of this paragraph? (F)
j Find an example of a witticism related to a well-known saying. (G)
k Find an inversion which emphasizes the intervention of Doctor Brandreth. (H)
l Which two words are used metaphorically when referring to the association between Brandreth and the *New York Herald*? (H)
m Which phrase is used sarcastically when referring to Gordon Bennet? (H)
n What stylistic device does the writer use to emphasize the reasons for the extraordinary success of Brandreth? (H)

Vocabulary

Words or expressions connected with trade and money

5 Find words in the text which mean the same as the following.

a someone who makes money by gaining his victim's trust (B)
b an ability to make a profit (C)
c selling goods by going from one place to another (C)
d cheat someone financially (D)
e invested large sums in (H)
f to the considerable sum or amount of (H)
g people who favour a particular way of advertising or offering something for sale (H)
h a well-known person or product (H)

Word knowledge: *market*

6 Complete the missing words in a–g.

Example: *a small number of customers who want a particular type of product or service:* ***niche*** .... *market*

a study customer needs and preferences: market r........
b create a monopoly by squeezing out the competition: f........ out of the market
c a product that is the most successful of its kind: market l........
d fill or suffuse the market completely: f........ the market
e wish to buy something: be i........ the market for something
f be available for sale: be o........ the market
g economic factors affecting the price, demand and availability of a commodity: market f........

Discussion

7 Discuss these questions in small groups.

a What types of products are market leaders in your country?
b How useful do you think market research is?
c How easy do you think it is for an individual to make a fortune selling a product nowadays?

Listening | Part 1

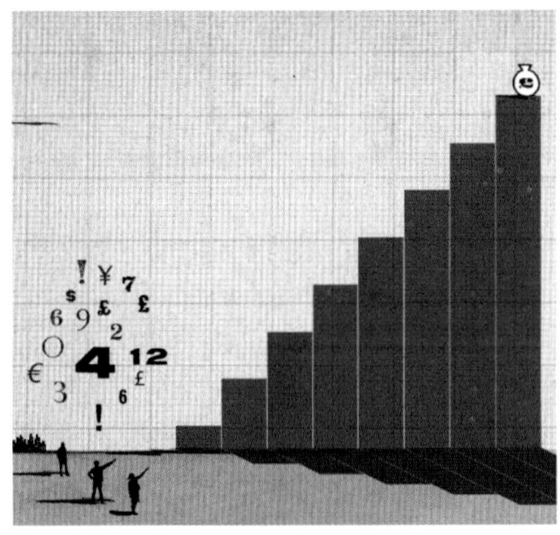

Tip

On the first listening, put a dot beside the answer you think is correct. On the second listening, check that the other options can be eliminated.

1 What does success mean to you? How would you go about achieving it? How difficult might it be to achieve your aims?

Exam practice

2 2·18 **You will hear three different speakers. For questions 1–6, choose the answer (A, B or C) which fits best according to what you hear. There are two questions for each extract.**

Extract One: You hear a woman training a new recruit to a firm selling water purifiers.

1 What is the woman's view of the ten-point plan approach to selling?
A It helps to identify potential customers.
B It comes complete with all the necessary paperwork.
C It is likely to succeed within a specific time period.

2 What does she emphasize as a particularly important factor in door-to-door selling?
A being extremely well dressed
B interacting socially with potential customers
C dealing with objections at the door

Extract Two: You hear a fashion designer talking about footwear.

3 In the speaker's opinion, fashions in shoes are now becoming
A more sport-orientated.
B less formal.
C more versatile.

4 He feels that the main sports shoe manufacturers should
A be wary of competition.
B employ more adventurous designers.
C take advice from traditional specialists.

Extract Three: You hear a pop star talking about his sudden rise to fame.

5 What does the man put his initial success down to?
A experience gained touring with a group
B setting up in business on his own
C working in the film industry

6 What is his attitude towards his potential wealth?
A He thinks he'll find it hard to cope with.
B He's afraid it will be short-lived.
C He won't let it change him.

3 How different were the aspirations and achievements the speakers mentioned from the ones you talked about in 1?

Vocabulary

Success and failure

4 Which of the words below describe success, and which failure? Which are formal and which are less formal? Decide what situations they can be used in.

take off   flunk   bomb   go down a storm   go to pieces   breakthrough   lapse   on the rocks   out of your depth   go under   buoyant   blow it   come unstuck   flop   miss the boat   cut your losses   sail through   rest on your laurels

5 Use the language from 4 to talk about success and failure. Think about:

products   companies   yourself   friends   family

Speaking Part 2

1 **Work with a partner to discuss these questions.**
   a What kinds of advertisements are popular in your country?
   b What is your favourite advertisement?
   c To what extent are you as an individual influenced by advertisements?

2 **2·19 Listen to part of a classroom discussion about the statement below. Make notes about how the students structure their responses, their range of grammar and vocabulary, and any mistakes they make.**

Advertising should be banned as it persuades people to buy goods they don't want or need with money they don't possess.

Student 1 ....

Student 2 ....

Student 3 ....

Tip

Remember that you will not see the tasks written down. You only see the heading above the visuals, so you need to listen carefully to what you have to do.

Exam practice

3 **Look at these advertising images, and talk with a partner about what you think pictures A and B might be promoting. Give reasons for your opinions.**

A

B

C

Advertising campaign

4 **2·20 Listen and make a note of what you have to do in the next phase of the task.**

5 **Now work with a partner and do the task. Remember, you have about three minutes to do this phase of Part 2.**

Further discussion

6 **You would like to use a slogan to accompany the image you have chosen. Decide what these expressions mean, then choose the best one to accompany your image.**

Time flies!
The time has come!
The time is ripe!
Time is on your side!
Time for a change.
Time and tide wait for no man.
Times are changing.

Your views

7 **Now, in pairs, explain to each other why you agree or disagree with this statement.**

Advertising provides information and stimulates trade.

Writing | Part 2, Report

Understanding the task

1 Read this exam task and answer a–c.

> You recently took part in a project to find out how employees in a company think costs can best be cut. You have been asked to write a report (280–320 words) for the company on the employees' ideas for cost-cutting. In your report you should describe the advantages and disadvantages of the employees' suggestions and your evaluation of these.

a Underline the main information your report must include.

b Brainstorm with a partner ideas you might include.

c Think about who the report is for and the style you will need to write in.

Text analysis

2 Read the sample report and answer a–c.

a Does it include all the points you would expect?

b How are the ideas organized?

c How does the report include personal opinion?

Introduction

This report sets out to analyse employees' perspectives on ways in which ACA Ltd could reduce costs. The findings are based on focus groups and interviews with key members of staff.

Background

The company is currently facing a challenging economic environment and needs to explore every avenue in order to avoid closure. A variety of approaches to meet these goals are being taken, of which this is one.

Employees' Suggestions

The employees were very forthcoming with a range of creative and innovative suggestions. The three main suggestions that recurred throughout are related to cutting advertising budgets, staff training and relocating offices.

Advantages

Advertising makes up a significant proportion of company spending and consequently is an obvious area to cut; furthermore, savings would be instantaneous. Likewise, ACA has a highly trained body of staff. Whilst this does give the company a competitive edge, a temporary reduction in spending may allow resources to be allocated elsewhere. Finally, and obviously a decision that cannot be taken quickly, was the suggestion to relocate. Staff felt that running and rental costs of a large traditional building far outweighed the advantages of such a location.

Disadvantages

Advertising and staff development are often two of the first areas under threat during a recession, however, cutting both clearly could have negative consequences. Should competitor companies not make such cuts to advertising then there is the potential that their profile could be raised above ACA's. Equally, if these companies continue to invest in staff development there is a danger that some of ACA's top employees could be attracted to these organizations. Lastly, relocating offices is a strategic long-term decision. Whilst annual costs would be reduced and, in the long term, savings made, short-term expenditure would increase.

Conclusions

In conclusion, staff were very positive about helping the company reduce costs. Based on the need for immediate savings, and the limited negative impact, a reduction in staff training is potentially the best path to follow.

Nominalization

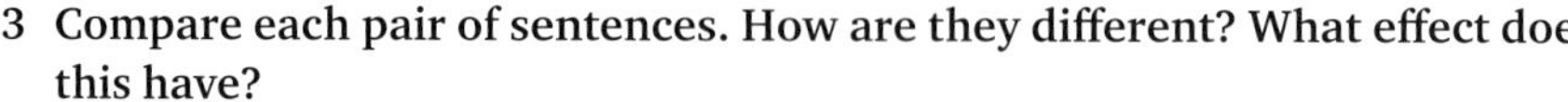

3 Compare each pair of sentences. How are they different? What effect does this have?

a 1 ... a temporary reduction in outgoings may allow resources to be allocated elsewhere.
  2 ... if we reduce outgoings, we could allocate the money elsewhere.

b 1 Finally, and obviously a decision that cannot be taken quickly, was the suggestion to relocate.
  2 Finally, staff suggested that we should relocate. This obviously can't be decided quickly.

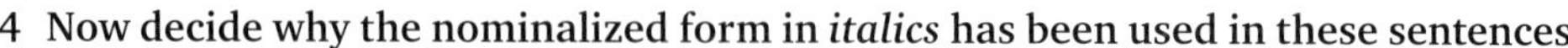

4 Now decide why the nominalized form in *italics* has been used in these sentences.

a The *sacking* of Mr Phillips was grossly unfair.
b The company is cutting back on staff. These *cuts* were instigated as a result of declining sales.
c A *decision* has been reached over pensions.
d Your *flight* is at half past eight in the evening.
e There are a number of *discrepancies* in his expenses.
f The *commitment* to ring-fence frontline services was welcomed by campaigners and opposition leaders.

5 Rewrite a–h using a nominalized form.

a The government will *expand* the tax-relief scheme to include small businesses.
b Tax payers are *demanding* lower taxes.
c The board of directors *restructured* the organisation and profits *increased*.
d Government ministers *condemned* the banks for reckless practices.
e The CEO *announced* that the company is *planning* to *relocate*, and this *shocked* people.
f It is very *important* that we *reduce* budgetary spending.
g The *rising* cost of living is *slowing down* and this has been welcomed by investment banks.
h Prices of oil have *risen* suddenly in recent weeks.

Vocabulary

Work problems

6 Complete a–f with a suitable word.

a Union leaders have urged all their members to vote in the upcoming ______.
b The current ______ crisis has forced many employees to take voluntary ______.
c After the merger, a number of employees were ______ off.
d The number of firms going ______ has increased in recent months.
e The city came to a grinding halt as transport workers went on ______.
f A former employee is taking the firm to an industrial ______ accusing them of unfair ______.

Exam practice

See Writing guide page 146

Tip

When writing a report, make sure that you haven't allowed your personal opinion to come across, especially if the topic is one you feel strongly about.

7 Follow these stages to write your report: read, think, plan, write and then check.

You work for a large company. The company is considering ways to reduce its carbon footprint. Your manager has asked you to write a **report** (280–320 words). In your report you should describe the positive and negative things the company is doing in relation to its carbon footprint and add your own suggestions on how it could improve.

Unit 12 Travel & tourism

Introduction

1 **Look at the image above. What do you think it would be like to visit a city like this?**

2 **Now read this extract from a text about the city and complete 1–7 with the most appropriate word from the list.**

hooked ultimate abominable vibrant extreme overwhelmed improvised

'Mumbai is the (1)............ Asian city — big, (2)............, brash, unequal. You can love a city in a way you don't love a village or a nation. It can get under your skin and have you (3)............, for its energy, its buildings, its markets, its bustle, its scamsters, even its yellow and black taxis, which buzz up and down like bees. So it was with Mumbai when I first swooped in over the (4)............ slum shelters and landed at the airport near Juhu on my first visit to India, aged 19. At once I was (5)............ by the magnificence of this (6)............ city, the most (7)............ place I had ever seen.'

3 **How different is the description of the city from what you expected?**

4 **What rhetorical devices does the author use to evoke his memories of the city?**

5 **2·21 Listen to someone remembering the sights, sounds, smells and tastes of a place they once visited. Make a note of the words they use to describe these things. Then, answer these questions.**

a What place is the person describing?

b What do you think attracts tourists to visit a place like this?

6 **Divide the words in the list into five groups: smell, taste, sound, feeling and sight. Some words might fit in more than one group.**

spicy clatter fascinating rugged delectable hum impressive imposing acrid buzz heady bitter tart fragrant creamy odorous roar rumble sharp tender thriving musty screech heaving stench sweltering clammy nippy crisp

7 **Think of a town or city you know well or would like to visit. Imagine you are there.**

a Write a list of the things you can hear, see, smell and taste and think of adjectives to describe those things.

b Now describe the place to a partner using your ideas. See if your partner can guess which city or country you are thinking about.

Reading & Use of English | Part 7

1 **Discuss these questions.**
   a What do you think motivates people to become travel writers?
   b What qualities do you think you need to become a successful travel writer?
   c Why do you think there are more well-known male than female travel writers?

2 **Read the text about how to become a successful travel writer and think of a heading for each section.**

Successful travel writing

A One of the biggest temptations for someone new to the travel game is to look at everything through rose-tinted glasses, and this typically comes out in their writing. They paint everything to be magical and perfect, and their stories are laid out in romantic, flowery language. But the reality is that over time the road will lose its lustre, and any reader who knows that is going to see right through your prose. Not to mention that the harsh realities of a place are often just as interesting as the poetry used to describe it – probably even more interesting. Look over what you've written, and if it seems as if you've just written a brochure, you might want to have another look. It might be your limited perspective that is causing the issue – perhaps you're still caught up in the magic of the road. Or perhaps you are too caught up in selling the romance of travel.

B Although getting off the beaten track is always a good idea when travelling, travel writers nonetheless feel they need to capture the biggest sites that everyone comes to a specific country to see. So, even if they are the more adventurous type, they end up going to the same places that everyone else goes to. It may depend on what audience you're writing for, but the best advice is always to head in the opposite direction to everyone else and just see what happens. In another country, the seemingly mundane often creates the most interesting, humorous and exciting moments. If you are stuck to the biggest attractions by assignment, always look for another angle and point out things that others miss. Rolf Potts' story about trying (and failing) to crash the set of *The Beach* when it was being filmed in Thailand (featured in his book *Marco Polo Didn't Go There*) was far better than many other travel stories I've ever read.

C An extremely valuable habit for a writer to form, especially in this genre, is the habit of taking notes. Travel is exciting, and while you are caught up in the moment, it is easy to think to yourself that there is no way it will slip from the forefront of your mind. But as the day winds down, you will find yourself sitting in front of your laptop screen, trying your hardest to grasp the best details out of what happened. Carry a small notebook on you at all times.

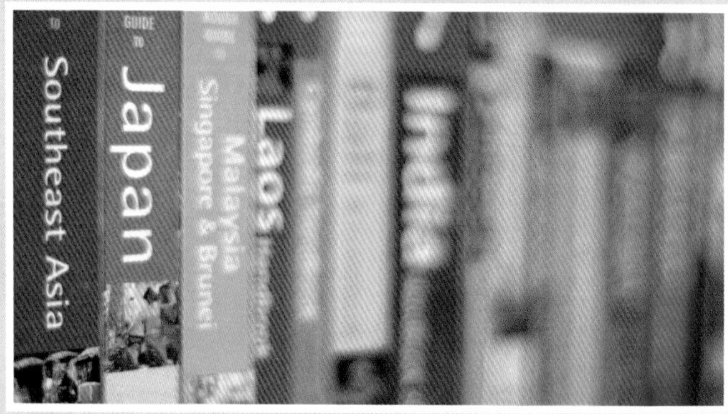

And don't only take it out when you think you are going to do something worthy of a story, because you never know when good fodder for a story will jump out of nowhere.

D Writers always want to seem like an authority on their subject, but when you are a travel writer, always experiencing new places and new things, you will never be the complete authority on anything. Don't be afraid to reveal your awkward moments, your embarrassments and your mishaps. These are the things that other readers who have travelled can relate to and it makes you seem more human.

E Finally, if you want to produce good content on the road, you should be willing to take risks – if your idea of world travel is sitting in world-class resorts with a bottle of sunblock in one hand and a cold ice tea in the other, you will be waiting a long time for anything interesting to happen. Hop on the backs of motorbike taxis where death on the road seems a certainty. Eat eyeballs, barbecued rats, giant fried beetles and anything else they throw on your plate. Sample that home-made whisky from the dusty bottle some farmer hands you while touring through the middle of nowhere. Go hang-gliding in the Swiss Alps. In short, get out there and live the road. Bad things will happen here and there, but the same would be true if you never left your home. And all the other adventures you have in between, well, those are the dreams that good travel writing (and life) are made of.

Exam practice

Tip

If you can't answer a particular question, leave it and go onto others, then look at it again at the end as you may have missed something.

3 For questions 1–10, choose from the sections (A–E). The sections may be chosen more than once.

In which section are the following mentioned?

- the desirability of conveying a more personal message 1
- the danger of writing in too transparent a fashion 2
- the downside of subjecting yourself to an uneventful travel experience 3
- the idea of being restricted by work commitments 4
- the need to adopt a more reckless approach 5
- the advantages of being prepared for an idea to pop up 6
- the dangers of writers getting carried away by their own enthusiasm 7
- the technique of trying to see things from a different perspective 8
- the need to earmark something significant 9
- the realization that writers are not infallible 10

Text analysis

4 Work through a–h, referring to the paragraphs.

a What does the writer mean by *the travel game*? (A)

b What does the writer mean by the phrase *look at everything through rose-tinted glasses*? (A)

c What does the writer mean by *flowery language*? (A)

d Which phrase means 'become less appealing'? (A)

e Which word does the writer use to describe something which is apparently not very interesting or dynamic? (B)

f What does the writer mean by the word *genre*? (C)

g Which word is used metaphorically to refer to source material or ideas? (C)

h Which phrase does the writer use to refer to a remote place? (E)

Word knowledge: *road*, *path* and *track*

5 Use the correct form of *road*, *path* and *track* to complete the expressions in *italics*. Then explain what the expressions mean.

a This piece of travel writing's not great but you're certainly *on the right* ....

b When I discovered that my boss at the travel agency was fiddling the books, I knew it was *the end of the* .... for me.

c I hadn't seen Martin for years then one day our .... *crossed* while I was on a daytrip to London.

d I love my job but it does mean that I'm *on the* .... four days a week.

e I'm sure there will be more opportunities *further down the* ....

f It's getting late. I think we'd better *make* .... back to the hotel.

g It's a fantastic holiday spot even though it's slightly *off the beaten* ....

h If we want to get to the beach before noon, we ought to *hit the* .... now.

i I completely *lost* .... of time when I was on holiday in Spain this summer.

j When James told me he was going to sail round the world on his own, I stopped *dead in my* ....

6 Discuss these questions.

a Would you rely on a piece of travel writing to inspire you to travel to certain places. Why/Why not?

b How reliable do you think travel reviews on the internet are?

Writing | Part 2, Article

Understanding the task

1 Read this exam task and answer the questions below.

A travel magazine has invited readers to write an article about a memorable journey that was spoiled by a travelling companion. Write your article (280–320 words) giving details of the journey and why it went wrong.

a Who are the target readers?

b What register should the article be written in?

c What aspect of the question means that this article should not just be a description of a journey?

d Write an outline plan of how you would approach this task. Compare your outline with a partner.

Text analysis

2 Read the sample article. Then answer questions a–d.

a What would cause the article to lose marks in the exam?

b How could the article be improved?

c What are some of the good features about the article?

d What verbs and other devices does the writer use to describe the movements of the train?

Twelve hours of talking

There had been rumours that the Ethiopian military authorities had opened the railway from Addis Ababa to Dire Dawa, and so one weekend some friends and I decided to get out of the capital and see some of the countryside.

We arrived at the station early in the morning, and pushed our way through the crowds to the ticket office. Two Revolutionary Guards with machine guns seemed unconcerned at our presence, so we made our way along the busy platform to the comparative calm of the carriage. I found an empty window seat and settled in.

The train started on the long twelve-hour haul to Dire Dawa, hundreds of miles east across the plains. City buildings drifted past the window and the train soon reached the green hills of the open countryside, dotted with round thatched farmers' huts.

It was nearly midday when the train began to move slowly uphill into a region of volcanoes. At first, the trees became more and more scarce, and small pebbles were scattered on the ground. The train clanked on up to a desolate plateau, which stretched out as far as the eye could see, like some vast lunar landscape covered with pitted and pock-marked rocks.

The final stretch, from mid-afternoon onwards, was the journey across the lowlands. There were thorny green acacia trees on the plain, and vultures on their branches stood out against the pale light of the late afternoon sun.

It was early evening when the train finally came to a halt in Dire Dawa, an oasis in the wilderness. I hired one of the horse-drawn carriages at the station, and breathed in the sweet smell of fresh rain. I leaned back in the carriage as it swept through the empty, tree-lined avenues of the town towards the only hotel, and savoured the silence.

It was a delight not to have Emma's voice ringing in my ears. She had got onto the train at the beginning of the trip and had not stopped talking the whole time, which had ruined what would have been a wonderful journey.

Writing skills: descriptive language

3 Read the following passage. What is wrong with it?

We went down the rough track towards the jungle until we reached the river that went across the road. We parked the Land Rover in the shade of some rubber trees and got out. We went across the river, which fortunately was not too deep, and then, as we were in no hurry, went through the rice fields on the other side towards the forest. The path that went through the trees was entirely overgrown, so we went along it with considerable difficulty. It was nearly mid-afternoon when we finally got out of the thick undergrowth and got to the bottom of the mountain. Although we were all by now feeling exhausted, we went up the steep slope and went to the rendezvous point just as the sun was going down.

4 Rewrite the passage, trying to include the following verbs. You may also need to make a number of other small changes, to prepositions for example.

arrive clamber cut drive emerge hack your way lead reach wade walk

Vocabulary

Word knowledge: *cut*

5 Complete these phrasal verbs and expressions with *cut* using a suitable word.

a I'm just not cut ______ for this kind of travel – I like my creature comforts.

b We were lucky that the back-up engine cut ______, otherwise we would have crashed.

c The torrential floods cut ______ all access to the village.

d I was really cut ______ by what she said – I wish she'd kept her feelings to herself.

e This hotel is a cut ______ the others we've stayed at – especially with regards to the impeccable service.

f We had to swerve to avoid the driver that cut us ______.

g My plan to go travelling on my own is by no means cut and ______. I'd be very happy to have a travelling companion.

h She's always cutting ______ with negative comments. I wish she'd just listen properly and then have her say.

Exam practice *See Writing guide page 140*

Tip

When checking your work, look for any words (not only verbs) that have been repeated. Where possible, see if you can improve the style by choosing a different word.

6 Read this exam question, and follow stages 1–5 to write your article.

> A travel magazine has asked you to write a description of a nostalgic journey. Write your article giving details of the journey and explaining why it was nostalgic for you. Write your article in 280–320 words.

Stage 1: Read
Think about what type of journey would interest your target readers.
The key word is nostalgic. You will need to talk about memories of a place and why they are important to you.

Stage 2: Think
Think of details that will be included – the exact places and memories that you will talk about. What images do you want to describe?

Stage 3: Plan
Make a detailed plan, using this structure if you wish:
Starting out: preparations, the reason for the journey
The journey: how you travelled, memorable moments along the way
Arrival: the place, your feelings

Stage 4: Write
Choose your language carefully to bring out the sense of nostalgia.

Stage 5: Check
Read through your article. Have you kept the readers' attention?

Reading & Use of English

Part 4

1 **Some people say that the journey is more important than the destination. What is your opinion?**

2 **Now read the text and answer these questions.**

a Why does Oliver prefer to travel by bus?

b If you had been in Oliver's shoes, how would you have decided to travel?

Bus Journeys *Oliver Balch, travel writer*

Darwin opted for a sailboat. Che famously went by motorbike. Me, I'm a bus man. There are few crannies where a rickety local bus won't take you. I've driven with brave (though not always sober) bus drivers across Chile's Atacama Desert and to the edge of the Ecuadorian jungle, over the endless Argentine pampas and to barren Paraguayan outposts.

I'm not alone. Bus is the travel mode of choice for the majority of South Americans, too. Nowhere gives a better flavour of the continent than its often scrubby, chaotic bus stations. And no cultural immersion programme can rival sitting shotgun with a local farmer or market tradesman.

Of my hundreds of bus journeys in South America, a ride through the jungles of northern Bolivia remains the most emblematic. The trip to Cobija, a town on the Brazilian border, was advertised as taking twelve hours. Nothing was said of the balsa rafts to make the half dozen river crossings, nor the almost total lack of tarmac, nor the high probability of getting stuck in the mud.

But when we rolled into town, a full day late, my preference for bus travel remained unshaken. It's true, I could have flown. But if I had, then I'd have definitely missed out on the male bonding that is shovelling mud during a torrential storm and the delights of an old lady's homemade *cherimoya* (a heart-shaped fruit with white flesh and green skin) flan. And not only that, I wouldn't have heard a live (and regularly repeated) version of Bolivia's top 50 all-time-classic folk songs. Even without these, the coachload of accommodation offers I received from my new best friends in Cobija would have made the trip more than worthwhile.

From *The Guardian*

Grammar *See notes page 161*

Counterfactual conditionals

3 **Read this sentence from the text and answer the questions below.**

But if I had, then I'd have definitely missed out on the male bonding that is shovelling mud during a torrential storm and the delights of an old lady's homemade cherimoya flan.

a Which word is 'missing' after *But if I had…*?

b What does the contracted form *I'd* mean in the second part of the sentence?

c What is the connection between the information in the first and second parts of the sentence?

4 **Correct the mistakes in sentences a–e.**

a If you would have travelled by train, it might have been much cheaper than flying.

b I've never been backpacking, but if I would, I'm sure I'd have enjoyed the experience.

c I'm sure if you'd tried a bit harder, you could had learned to speak a little of the local language.

d If you've really been interested in seeing more of the country, you should've arranged to stay an extra few days.

e I'd had stayed to listen to the guide instead of wandering around on my own if the tour had been a bit more interesting.

Mixed unreal conditionals

5 What is the difference in meaning between these two pairs of sentences?

a 1 If money was no object, we would go on a world cruise.
  2 If money was no object, we would have gone on a world cruise.

b 1 If we hadn't gone on that world cruise, we wouldn't have seen so many exciting places.
  2 If we hadn't gone on that world cruise, we would have some money to go on holiday.

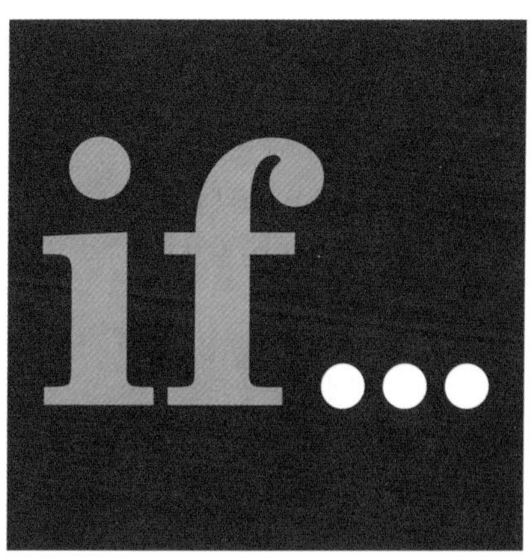

6 Which of these sentences a–f follows on from the sentences in 5 above? You do not need two of them.

a But we just can't afford it now.
b But we couldn't afford it.
c But I don't think we'll ever be able to afford it.
d But we can afford it.
e So I'm glad we did.
f So I'm glad we didn't.

7 Complete a–d with the correct form of the words in brackets.

a If we .... (not/spend) all our money on that adventure holiday last year, we .... (be) going skiing next month.
b If I .... (not/lost) my passport when I was backpacking last month, I .... (not/have) all those problems trying to get another one.
c If I .... (not/get) seasick every time I get on a boat, I .... (cross) the Channel by ferry when I went to France last summer.
d If I .... (not/met) Paul on holiday, we .... (not/be) married now.

Alternative conditional structures

8 Sometimes *if* can be used with, or replaced by, other structures. Read the sentences a–k and answer the questions 1–11 which follow.

a Should you require any further information, do not hesitate to contact me.
b If you should see Tim, give him my regards.
c If I were to go missing, what would you do?
d Had I known what hard work it was going to be, I wouldn't have offered to pack.
e If it had not been for the traffic, I wouldn't have been so late.
f But for Sue's valuable help, we would never have caught the plane.
g Were it not for the reasonable price of the meal, I would definitely have complained.
h Provided/Providing that you plan your trip in advance, backpacking can be fantastic.
i Unless you speak the local language, surviving in another country can be difficult.
j Supposing the flight is cancelled, how are you going to get to your destination?
k They can't decide whether to set off on the expedition now or wait.

1 Which sentences suggest that the situation is possible but not likely?
2 Which sentences refer to past situations?
3 Which phrases mean *without*?
4 Which sentences invert the verb and the subject instead of using *if*? What is the effect?
5 In which of the other sentences can an inversion be used?
6 Which phrase is used to make a condition? How else can you say this?
7 Which phrase has a similar meaning to *If not …*?
8 Which phrase means *if this is the case*?
9 Which phrase is used to express a choice between two possibilities? Is it possible to replace the phrase with *if*?
10 Which of the expressions or alternatives are formal and might be written, and which are informal and would probably be spoken?
11 What other words or phrases could you use to rephrase *supposing*?

Word knowledge: *if*

9 Complete a–g using the phrases below. There is one you do not need to use.

what if   even if   if and when   as if   only if   if only   if so   if not

a .... we have enough money to go on a package holiday, I don't want to do that. I'd rather do my own thing.

b .... I hadn't decided to go on holiday that particular week. But how was I to know that the airports were going to be closed?

c This safety equipment is to be used .... a critical situation arises.

d .... I tried to get a ticket for you to come to Paris, too? Would you like that?

e You may decide to change your date of travel. ...., these tickets can be exchanged.

f Travel rules and regulations in the small print must be adhered to. ...., you may find yourself in a difficult situation.

g .... we ever get to go on holiday I hope it's somewhere hot.

10 Write sentences of your own starting with the words in the list below.

If I hadn't …	*Had it not been for …*	*Whether … or …*
Should you …	*If I were to …*	*Supposing …*
Were it not for …	*Unless …*	*But for …*

Exam practice

Tip

Transforming the sentence may require idiomatic expressions, changes to the verb, different lexical items, or the insertion of extra words like prepositions.

11 Reading & Use of English, Part 4: **For questions 1–6, complete the second sentence so that it has a similar meaning to the first sentence, using the word given. Do not change the word given. You must use between three and eight words, including the word given. Here is an example (0).**

0 *Oliver did not suffer from his experience in the Bolivian jungle.*
worse
Oliver was ***none the worse for*** *his experience.*

1 The local people were so generous that we felt quite at home there.
had
We would not have felt so at home there .... of the local people.

2 Besides mapping the mountain ranges, there were many other reasons for the trip.
to
There .... simply mapping the mountain ranges.

3 After such a traumatic experience, somebody would have insisted that the airline passengers spent a short spell in hospital.
subjected
After such a traumatic experience, the airline passengers .... a short spell in hospital.

4 The delayed passengers were looking forward to arriving at their destination.
wait
The delayed passengers .... at their destination.

5 Brad was determined to drive across the desert.
out
Brad had no intention .... across the desert.

6 The trip was never an ordeal for the travel writer.
looked
The travel writer never .... an ordeal.

Speaking Part 2

Exchanging ideas and reaching a conclusion

1 In pairs, look at pictures A and B below. Talk together for one minute about what effects the invention of these types of transport have had on our lives.

A

B

C

D

Brochure: Travelling holidays

2 Compare your ideas with another pair of students. How similar or different were they?

Evaluating and suggesting alternatives

3 2·22 Listen to some students doing a Part 2 task. Tick the discourse markers they use.

I see where you're coming from but …	*I mean …*
You do have a point there but …	*On top of that …*
Well, let's see …	*At least …*
…, say …	*Whereas …*
However …	*At the same time …*
Anyhow …	*All the same …*
For one thing …	*I guess …*
Then there are …	*To be honest …*
As a matter of fact …	*There is some truth in that, of course, but …*
In any case …	

4 Look again at the discourse markers in 3. Which ones are used to do the following?

a dismiss or move on from what has previously been said
b introduce another point of view
c give yourself time to think
d agree with what someone has said before adding your own opinion
e give an example
f say what you really think
g add to examples you have already mentioned
h qualify or modify what you have said
i introduce a list of points

Tip

Using discourse markers is a feature of natural language. They will help you to structure your responses and express your reactions to your partner's contributions.

Exam practice

5 2·23 Listen to the exam question. Then, with a partner, answer the question. Try to use some of the discourse markers in 3.

1 Where do you think the photos on page 131 were taken? What do you think it would be like to live and work in a place like this?

2 Read the main text, ignoring the missing paragraphs and the words in *italics*. Find out where the writer went and what he was doing there.

Great explorations

I When I left that nautical shop in Ushuaia, Argentina with just a few postcards, I had no idea how much I would regret it later. *I couldn't imagine the real need for a human being to have a nautical chart of Cape Horn*, the southernmost point on the whole planet. Mainly since this would only become a reality after three intense days of navigating the waters that changed the history of the world and viewing the same landscapes that Charles Darwin and Ferdinand Magellan saw.

[1]

II *There was nothing ordinary about that chart. The pen scratches showed the exact route that the vessel had taken in the first stretch of the course*, which went from the capital of the archipelago to Cape Horn in Drake Passage where fearsome waters must be overcome to reach the Antarctic. There were over ten nationalities occupying the sixty-four cabins on the boat, which, with its siblings, exclusively covers the extreme south of Patagonia. They're known as expedition cruises and feature lectures on fauna and flora and documentaries on Shackleton's expedition to Antarctica.

[2]

III 'Ninety dollars,' said the Frenchman. *He was on his honeymoon and his reason for wanting to buy the map was a strong one*. His bride, who had always dreamed of spending her post-nuptial days in Madagascar, wasn't able to hold him back since she was napping in the cabin.

[3]

IV The first expedition to reach Cape Horn in 1616 was composed of two ships and eighty-seven men. *It left from Holland in 1615 with the mission of finding a passage from the Atlantic to the Pacific that could serve as an alternative to the Strait of Magellan*, discovered in 1520 and monopolized by the East India Company.

[4]

V The island where we disembarked on that morning didn't seem like the kind of place where no less than 500 shipwrecks took place. It was cold and windy but the sun provided a more hospitable atmosphere. On one of its extremities there was a monument; on the other, *a lighthouse which is home to traffic controller Patricio Ubal, his wife and their children*.

[5]

VI A seasick Charles Darwin did not disembark at Cape Horn. It was 1832 and the young, inexperienced British naturalist had joined the second expedition of Captain Robert Fitzroy on his frigate, the *Beagle*, in exchange for financial help from his father. *On board were also three natives of Tierra del Fuego whom Fitzroy had taken to England on his last voyage. The most famous of these was Yamana Jeremy Button*.

[6]

VII *The glaciers there remain in the same place, however, exactly as Darwin saw them*. The deep blue of the millennial ice is as impressive as the ferocious noise coming from the huge chunks that break off that living mass. It is an unforgettable spectacle.

[7]

VIII *The auction had come to an end, but our voyage had not*. The next morning, hours before the boat docked in Punta Arenas, we visited the Magellanic penguins on Isla Magdalena. This was the moment São Paulo native Lidia Senatore had been waiting for. Coincidentally, the nautical chart auctioned off had been purchased by her for $150. Luckily for François, Valentine never heard about that.

Exam practice

Tip

Read the main text first, paying special attention to clues about what information might be missing and references to people and places. Underline any references before and/or after the gap which might lead you to find the answer before reading the missing paragraphs.

3 Now read the missing paragraphs. Choose from the paragraphs A–H the one which fits each gap (1–7). There is one extra paragraph which you do not need to use. Use the questions in the missing paragraphs and the words in *italics* in the main text to help you.

Missing paragraphs

A Ushuaia is an unusual place. Half an hour from the city centre, the Cerro Castor ski station is the southernmost in the world and runs until the end of October, when all the others in South America have already closed and the European stations haven't even opened. (*What might this paragraph refer to?*)

B 'Going once, going twice…' In a fit of obsession, Francois raises his hand, 'sold to the gentleman for $250.' Afterwards Valentine snorts: 'How can you pay $250 for a piece of paper?' (*Where and when might you hear the opening words of this missing paragraph?*)

C All the people gathered that night in one of the lounges of the Chilean boat *Mare Australis* had been through this experience and now, on the last night of our journey, were staring at the auctioneer with a genuine greed for that tube with the paper inside. I couldn't help myself. I started off the bidding. (*What might 'that tube' refer to?*)

D These are fascinating people. The coldness with which his mother received her son two years after his disappearance provoked reports of amazement from Darwin, who witnessed this at Isla Navarino, where we disembarked that afternoon. But, instead of the people who used to live there, we only came across the tracks of beavers. (*Who might the son be?*)

E 'How much is the chart of such an historic voyage worth?' chanted the auctioneer in order to raise the bidding, which had already passed $200. I'd stopped at 150 but the Frenchman and the table of Americans showed no signs of giving up. (*Which voyage is being referred to here?*)

F 'Cape Horn was a dream for me. You can't go any further. It's difficult and dangerous to get there and I wanted to share this with her,' lawyer François Marty told me later. He only told his new wife Valentine that they were going to South America. 'Pack a bag for every season, everything from a bikini to ski clothes,' he advised her. (*Why might the lawyer be explaining this to the writer?*)

G This is just a temporary position – it lasts less than a year – but a solitary one. It means having to pass the entire time isolated from the world, without seeing civilization and not even being visited by it during the winter months. (*What might the temporary position be?*)

H More common for visitors are the itineraries which peruse the Patagonian canals further north. Other ships cover an even wider course but they don't pass by Cape Horn. And it was this mythical little island that had attracted those who were in that room. (*More common than what?*)

Text analysis

4 Work through a–f, referring to the text (i–viii) and missing paragraphs (A–H).

a What does the writer imply about the bride's attitude towards spending her honeymoon on a boat in South America? (iii)

b What is the writer suggesting about Darwin's reason for joining the expedition to South America? (vi)

c How does the writer imply Valentine might have reacted if she had known what the nautical chart had originally cost? (viii)

d What impression does the writer create by using: *a fit of obsession* and *Valentine snorts*? (B)

e Why does the writer describe everyone's greed as *genuine*? (C)

f What effect does the use of the word *chanted* have? (E)

Listening | Part 4

1 **What are your main considerations when planning a travel experience? Rate the following beginning with 1 (the least important) to 5 (the most important). Give reasons for your opinion.**

cost *type of travel experience* *destination*
amount of time available *people you go with*

Exam practice

2 2·24 **You will hear five people talking about travel experiences they have had. You will hear the recording twice. While you listen, you must complete both tasks.**

TASK ONE: For questions 1–5, choose from the list (A–H) each speaker's reason for choosing the travel experience.

A fulfilling a lifelong ambition
B acting on a recommendation
C a desire to do something different
D receiving an unexpected sum of money
E a wish to experience something first-hand
F a need to get away from it all
G a decision made on the spur of the moment
H a feeling that the challenge was achievable

Speaker 1		1
Speaker 2		2
Speaker 3		3
Speaker 4		4
Speaker 5		5

TASK TWO: For questions 6–10, choose from the list (A–H) how each speaker feels about their travel experience.

A impressed by how unusual and different everything was
B prepared to tackle a similar challenge again
C disappointed by the lack of excitement
D amazed that it was so difficult
E eager to repeat the experience
F surprised how wonderful it was
G sorry that the pace was so hurried
H irritated by an unforeseen problem

Speaker 1		6
Speaker 2		7
Speaker 3		8
Speaker 4		9
Speaker 5		10

Tip

During the 45 second pause, skim read the options in both tasks, then read them again. As you listen for the first time, put the number of the speaker next to the option you think is correct. Then, on the second listening, check that the option is correct.

Reacting to the text

3 **With a partner, discuss questions a–j. The words in *italics* are all used in the listening extracts. Listen again if necessary to help you answer the questions.**

a How might Speaker 1 have felt when her family *came into some money*?
b Why do you think Speaker 1 found seeing animals in the wild *awesome*?
c Why do you imagine Speaker 2 felt that climbing Kilimanjaro would be a *doddle*?
d What do you think Speaker 2 meant when he said he was *feeling pretty chuffed* with himself?
e What do you think Speaker 3 meant when she said '*I'm not the best of sailors.*'?
f What kind of *scary moments* did Speaker 3 probably experience on board the tall ship?
g How do you think Speaker 4 might have reacted to the scenery he saw in the Scottish Highlands?
h What do you think Speaker 4 meant when he said '*You can say goodbye to a good night's sleep*'?
i Why do you think Speaker 5 had never considered Cuba as a *tourist destination*?
j Why do you think Speaker 5 feels that Cuba *isn't just a carbon copy of umpteen other places*?

Exam strategies

Reading & Use of English

General skills

In any kind of reading, there are two processes (often referred to as 'top down and bottom up') going on – the real world knowledge of, or interest in, the subject you are going to read about, and your ability to decode the grammar and vocabulary into meaningful sections. This is why many course books include some kind of lead-in questions before reading passages to motivate students to find out information. Two of the skills needed in this lead-in process and in tackling various reading task types are skimming and scanning, but there are others of equal importance. Here are some things you can do to improve your reading skills.

- Decide what kind of reader you are: e.g. fast or slow? Do you visualize what you read about? Have you got a photographic memory? Do you need to go back over the same reading material to internalize/remember what you have read?
- Time your reading speed (the average number of words native speakers read per minute is approximately 250). Try to increase your reading speed gradually while still retaining what you have read. This is a useful skill both for the exam and in real life.
- Practise skim-reading for gist/global meaning to find out what a text or paragraph is about without worrying too much about individual words you do not know or understand.
- Practise scanning to find specific information which you will need in order to answer certain questions. When you find the information you need, underline it and put the number of the question beside it. This will save you time in the exam.
- Identify examples where the writer expresses an opinion or adopts a particular attitude.
- Try to read between the lines and understand in more depth what views the writer is trying to put across.
- Be aware of cohesion/text structure and text organization features, e.g. exemplification/reference. This will help you in the Reading and Use of English tasks like the gapped text.
- Learn to manage your time, e.g. decide how long you should spend on any one part of a paper so that you can do all the tasks. Practise doing a whole Reading and Use of English paper in the time available in the exam (1 hour 30 minutes).
- When you learn vocabulary, try to remember it in context, together with words it collocates with, or in word families.

Techniques for the Reading & Use of English paper

Part 1: Multiple-choice cloze (Units 1, 5 and 10)

- After skim-reading the text, read each sentence (not each line) carefully and look at the options to fill the gap.
- Think carefully about the meaning of each word.
- Do not choose the first word you think is correct. Try all the options before you make your choice.
- Ask yourself the same question for every option: Is this the right meaning of the word for the context?
- Check that the word fits with the words before and after it, i.e. it is both grammatically correct and it has the right meaning.

Part 2: Open cloze (Units 2, 6 and 11)

- After skim-reading the text, read the whole text again ignoring the gaps.
- Now read the text again sentence by sentence, not line by line, and look closely at the words and structures before and after each gap.
- Try to say each gapped sentence in your head. This might give you an idea of which word or part of speech could be missing.
- Make sure the word you choose fits grammatically and makes sense in its context.
- When you have finished, read the whole text again to see that it reads well and makes sense.

Part 3: Word formation (Units 3, 7 and 9)

- After skim-reading the text, read the text again, ignoring the words given, and decide what part of speech the missing word in each gap should be, e.g. an adjective, adverb, noun, etc.
- If the missing part of speech is a verb, think carefully about which tense you need.
- Decide which affix is needed to transform the word given.
- Try to remember which prefix is needed for which letter when making a word negative, e.g. *un-* is the most common negative prefix and can be used before words starting with any letter. *im-* is used before the letters *m* and *p*. *il-* is used before the letter *l*. *ir-* is used before the letter *r*.
- Remember that sometimes other letters need to be added, e.g. *suppose* → *suppose**d**ly*.
- Decide whether the word can change its form or be made negative by adding a suffix, e.g.
  relent → *relentless*
  care → *careful*, *careless*.
- Check that you have made all the changes necessary to the word, e.g. *vary* → *invariably*.
- Check that the word makes sense in its specific and overall context.
- Check the spelling of each word again.
- Make sure you transfer your answers onto the answer sheet correctly.

Part 4: Key word transformations (Units 4, 8 and 12)

- Read the sentence before and after the given word in each item carefully and think about how the word might fit into the gap in terms of meaning and form.
- Brainstorm any idioms, phrases or collocations the word could be used with to complete the sentence.
- Remember that the rewritten sentence should be as similar in meaning as possible to the original sentence.
- Remember not to change the key word in any way.
- Think about the other changes you may need to make to the sentence to be able to keep the same meaning.
- If you cannot do one of the questions, go on to the others and then come back to it.

Part 5: Four-option multiple choice (Units 1, 5, 9 and 11)

- After skim-reading the text, read the text again carefully.
- Read the first part of each question and turn all the stems into questions.
- Try to identify which part of the text the question is targeting and try to answer the questions without looking at the options.
- Now look at the options and read each one carefully.
- When you are looking for answers remember that MCQs follow the order of the information in the text, although there is sometimes a 'global' question at the end.
- Even if you think you know the answer, always check that the other options are not correct.
- Try writing your own MCQs for a text in this book which has a different task type. This will help you to 'get inside the head' of the examiner and understand how these questions work, e.g. in 4-option MCQs, one might be almost correct, one might echo the text but say something different, one could interpret the text in an inaccurate way and would therefore be wrong, and one is the correct answer.

Part 6: Gapped text (Units 2, 4, 7, 10 and 12)

- Being aware of the cohesion of a text will enable you to tackle this task type. The difficulty with the gapped text is that it is a text which has been deconstructed. Some students find it difficult to reconstruct the text without actually being able to see it in its entirety, so you need to train yourself to do this properly.
- Try photocopying texts and cutting them into paragraphs and see if you can piece them together coherently. Analyse how you were able to do this.
- Try and predict what might come before or after an isolated piece of information. This will increase your interest in a text, particularly a literary one.
- Make sure you understand the meanings of connectors and link words, e.g. *so that* and *so … that*, and what they are expressing.
- Type out a paragraph and remove all the connectors and reference devices. Put them in a list at the top in the order in which they appear. See if you can put them in an appropriate place in the text.
- After skim-reading the text and missing paragraphs, always read the base text and missing paragraphs again carefully before doing the task.
- Make sure you read the paragraph before and after each gap carefully as the missing paragraph might link with either of these.
- For each gap, try to identify which paragraph is missing by quickly trying to imagine each paragraph in each gap and underlining the words which might help you to find where it belongs.
- Write the number of the gap next to the paragraph you have chosen so that you do not waste time trying to remember what you decided.
- If you are absolutely sure that a paragraph fits a particular gap, make your choice and discount that paragraph from the other gaps.
- When you have finished, try the extra paragraph in each gap to make sure it doesn't fit any of them.

Part 7: Multiple matching (Units 3, 6, 8 and 12)

- After skim-reading the text, read each section again carefully.
- Read each question and try to identify which section it relates to.
- Use a pencil to locate the different areas of information you are looking for. You could underline, e.g. people's names, and circle the information which applies to that person. This will help to check answers again when you have finished the task.
- Check each piece of information against each question.
- If you cannot answer a particular question, leave it and go on to others, then look at it again at the end. You may have missed something.
- Remember that the text, speakers, etc. may use different words from those in the options. If you spot the same words, this does not mean that the question refers to that particular extract.

Writing

General skills

- Read through the task and underline the most important information, e.g. the context, target reader, points to include, length. This will give you the plan of your task, and usually all the information you need to write it.
- The time pressure of an exam makes candidates want to begin writing as soon as possible to make sure that they finish the paper. Although it may initially seem like a waste of valuable time, taking a few minutes to plan your writing will ensure that it is more relevant and better organized.
- Think about who you are going to be writing for or to.
- Decide on a suitable writing style.
- Decide what order to put your information in and how you will lay it out.
- Decide how to link your sentences and paragraphs to the rest of the writing.
- Use a variety of structures and vocabulary: don't keep repeating the same thing.
- Try to write neatly and legibly.
- The word count in the questions is meant as a guide. You will not be penalized for exceeding the upper limit. However, if you write too much, there is the danger that much of it will be irrelevant. You will lose marks for writing a lot of irrelevant information. Keep it focused!
- Do not waste time counting individual words. Instead, work out approximately how many words you write on a page and use this as a guide.
- Practise writing to a time limit to better prepare yourself for exam conditions.
- Leave enough time at the end to check for errors and to see if what you have written makes sense.
- Read widely. Not only will this help you learn more vocabulary and increase your grammatical accuracy but also allow you to appreciate different styles of writing which you can apply to your own writing.

Techniques for the Writing paper

Part 1: Essay (Units 2, 4, 7, 10)

- Spend time reading the two texts carefully and identify the main points in each of the texts.
- Identify whether the two texts present contrasting or complementary views.
- Plan how you are going to answer the question and organize the information.
- Make sure you integrate and paraphrase each of the main points in the texts. If you fail to include any of the main points, you might lose marks.
- Use the key points in the two input texts as the basis for your answer.
- Integrate your own views and opinions with the key points.
- Keep it focused. Avoid including any irrelevant information.
- Make it interesting and engage the reader.
- Write in an appropriate register.
- Try to use a variety of cohesive devices.
- Try to use a range of vocabulary to demonstrate what you are capable of.
- You can use British or American spelling, but it must be consistent.
- Leave sufficient time to check through your essay to avoid any unnecessary errors.
- Practise by doing timed writing to get a feel for exam conditions.
- For more detailed guidance and model answers, please refer to the Writing guide on pages 138 to 148.

Part 2 (Units 1, 3, 5, 6, 8, 9, 11, 12)

- Look carefully at the kind of text that the question asks for: it will be a review, a letter, an article, a report or, in the set text question, an essay.
- Work out exactly who the reader is and choose a suitable style to write in.
- Look at all parts of the question because there will be important information in each part.
- Check that you have covered all the aspects that the question mentions. If you fail to address all strands of the question you might lose marks.
- Do not choose the set text question if you have not prepared for it.
- For more detailed guidance and model answers, please refer to the Writing guide on pages 138 to 148.

Listening

General skills

Listening is a skill which some people are not particularly good at. It requires concentration and an ability to focus on what someone else is saying, rather than on what contribution you would like to make to the conversation yourself, so you need to put yourself in the position of a passive listener. A listening test can also induce panic and is sometimes perceived as being difficult, although results don't always bear this out, so careful and thorough preparation is therefore necessary before the exam.

- Decide what kind of listener you are. Are you a good listener? Can you remember what people say or does your attention tend to wander? Do you easily lose track of what is being said? Being honest with yourself will help you to improve your listening skills.
- Always make maximum use of the time given to read through the questions for the task carefully before listening to the text. This helps to focus on what you are about to hear.
- The skills you acquire for the reading paper will help you to skim-read the questions before you listen and identify the information you are looking for.
- Practise reading, listening, and making a few notes at the same time.
- Try to tune in to the speakers' accents or style of talking quickly at the beginning of the listening task.
- If you miss an item, don't panic. Just guess or leave the answer and go on to the next one, otherwise you may miss that one, too. You can have a go at the missed item when you hear the recording the second time.
- Remember that there will usually be some distraction in a listening task, so do not choose an answer until you have heard everything the speaker says.
- Although it is sometimes possible to predict the kind of answer to expect, it is imperative not to decide what the answer will be before you listen.
- Remember that in the sentence completion task, the words you need will be the same as those you will hear and the words must be spelt correctly, so always check your spelling.
- It often helps to underline the most important (key words) in each MCQ or multiple-matching option. The speaker may say the same thing but use slightly different words.
- Practise listening to radio programmes or watching TV programmes in English if you can.
- Familiarize yourself with different accents so that you are not always listening to only one type of spoken English.

Techniques for the Listening paper

Part 1: Three-option multiple choice (three extracts)
(Units 1, 6 and 11)

- Read through the questions quickly, but carefully, before listening to the text. This helps you to focus on what information to listen for.
- Try to identify what the short listening extract is about, e.g. the speaker's attitude towards something, opinion about something, etc.
- Put a dot beside the answer you think is correct when you listen for the first time. Then make your final choice on the second listening.
- Concentrate on one extract at a time. If you cannot answer a question, leave it or guess and move on to the next one.
- Check or decide on your final answers in the second listening.

Part 2: Sentence completion (Units 2, 7 and 10)

- Read the sentences carefully and try to imagine what kind of information might be missing, e.g. names, facts and figures, but don't try to guess what the word might be. The answer will probably not be an obvious one.
- Don't write the first thing you hear and assume it is the answer. Write it, but then listen to make sure the word is not a distractor.
- The information in the recording might be in a slightly different order from that in the question.
- Remember that answers are usually only one or two words so keep this in mind when deciding on your answer.
- Correct spelling is essential in this task. Because of this, words which present spelling problems are usually avoided.
- If you are unsure of the spelling of a word, don't waste time agonizing over how to spell it. Try and spell it according to its sound and move on to the next item.
- Check that items fit grammatically and make sense.

Part 3: Four-option multiple choice (Units 3, 5 and 8)

- Remember that this is one complete task which requires a longer period of continuous concentration than each of the three extracts in Part 1. There are also four options instead of three so more reading is needed.
- Read through the questions quickly but carefully before listening to the text. This helps you to focus on what information to listen for.
- Put a dot beside the answer you think is correct when you listen for the first time.
- If you cannot answer a question, leave it or guess and move on to the next one.
- Check or decide on your final answers in the second listening.

Part 4: Multiple matching (Units 4, 9 and 12)

- Read both tasks carefully and underline what you think the key words are.
- You need to look at all the answers for both tasks while you listen to each speaker. So, train your eye to glance quickly at all the possibilities as you listen, even if you think you know the answer. Skimming skills will be useful here.
- Don't be too hasty. A statement may look true because it contains phrases from the listening, but it may not have the same meaning.
- As you listen, try to match the meaning, although not necessarily the exact words, with what the speakers say.

Speaking

General skills

Speaking in front of an audience is a skill that many people are not very good at, even in their own language. In an exam situation, candidates are effectively speaking in front of an unknown audience and this can make them feel very nervous. But remember that if you say very little, you won't be able to show off your speaking skills, so the important thing is to keep talking.

- It's important to maintain eye contact with the examiner (except in Part 2 where you have to interact with your partner).
- Speak clearly enough for both the examiners to hear you.
- If there is any background noise, it can be difficult for both examiners to hear what candidates are saying. So, take a deep breath at the beginning of the test and project your voice.
- If you are unsure about the content of visuals, speculate about them. Visuals can often be interpreted in several ways and you are entitled to your opinions about them.
- Arm yourself with some useful fillers, phrases and link words which you can use to give yourself time to think, or to agree or disagree with your partner and structure your responses.
- Don't be afraid to express and justify your own views and opinions about issues connected with the topics.
- Listen carefully to what you have to do, pick up the cues and follow the prompts you are given. If what you say is irrelevant, you will not do so well.
- Examiners will assess you on the following: grammar and vocabulary (range, accuracy and appropriacy); discourse management (organizing a larger unit of discourse, expressing and justifying opinions and developing topics); pronunciation (prosodic features and intelligibility); interactive communication (using general interactional and social language).
- Don't be too nervous, or fidget! The examiner wants you to do well and is not trying to catch you out by asking difficult questions. A little nervousness is fine, as it often leads to a more motivated performance.
- Show the examiner what you can do. You have spent a long time preparing for this examination. Don't waste the opportunity to display what you have learned!

Techniques for the Speaking paper

Part 1: Conversation (Unit 1)

- This part of the test is to relax you and help you to tune in to the voice of the examiner and perhaps your partner. The questions will be about you, your hopes, likes, dislikes, opinions, etc. so don't panic. Try to enjoy this part.
- Don't just answer the question with a one-word answer. Try to expand on your response and give the examiner a little more information.
- Don't take too long to answer the question. Start talking as soon as possible to maximize your test time.
- The examiner will stop you when the time for this section is up by saying 'Thank you'.

Part 2: Collaborative activity (Units 2, 6, 8, 11, 12)

- In this part of the test, you are expected to interact with your partner. It is important, therefore, that you give your partner the opportunity to speak as well as making a contribution to the conversation yourself. If you have a reticent partner, then invite them to join in. If you have a dominant partner, interrupt politely to say what you think, too.
- Listen carefully to what you have to do and try to remember what it is. The title above the visuals will help you. Although you can ask the examiner to repeat the task, this wastes valuable test time so it is better not to do this if it's not necessary.
- Don't be too dogmatic in your views. Trying to see both sides of an issue or argument may give you more scope to show what you can do with the language you know.
- Don't worry about timing. Keep talking. The examiner will stop you when the time is up.

Part 3: The long turn (Units 3, 4, 5, 7, 9, 10)

- Start talking as quickly as possible and think as you go along. Silence is time wasted!
- Remember you are not being examined on your ideas, only your ability to express them, so don't be afraid to speak your mind.
- You don't need to use the ideas below the question, but they might help you to structure your response.
- Try to use discourse markers as pointers to what you are going to say, and a range of grammar and vocabulary.
- If you know you've made a mistake, try and correct it.
- If you can't think of a word, you can always paraphrase it.
- Listen to what your partner says in the long turn as you will be asked a follow-up question related to the topic.
- You will also be asked to join in the discussion after your partner has answered a follow-up question, so listen to what your partner says initially.

Developing the topic

- Listen carefully to the questions as you will not see them written down.
- Try to answer the question without going off the point. This will make your contributions more relevant.
- Don't make your answers too anecdotal or personal. These questions are asking for your opinions and ideas, agreement and disagreement, etc. on themes related to, but wider in scope than, the topics in the long turn.
- Sometimes the examiner may address a question to both candidates. Make sure you allow your partner the chance to speak after you have made your contribution.
- There are no right or wrong answers to the questions so you can say what you think.
- If you disagree with your partner, do so politely, acknowledging their contributions but adding your own.
- Don't worry about timing. The examiner will stop you when the time is up.

Writing guide

Part 1, Essay

Understanding the task

1 Read the exam question and answer questions a–c below.

Read the two texts below.
Write an essay summarizing and evaluating the key points from both texts. Use your own words throughout as far as possible, and include your own ideas in the answer.
Write your answer in 240–280 words.

Chasing the yankee dollar
The concept that money brings happiness is flawed and naïve for two fundamental reasons. Firstly, being rich is only relative to the spending power of others within our circle, so inevitably we compare ourselves to this cohort. In other words, the desire is not necessarily to be wealthy but wealthier than others. In addition to this, we set ourselves goals, such as the purchase of a car or the acquisition of a house; on attainment of such achievements we feel a sense of satisfaction. Yet this is short-lived, and the endless cycle requires new goals and targets to make us happy; inevitably, these methods will never bring happiness.

It isn't just the money
It is widely accepted that the happiest countries are also among the richest, but the reason for this is not immediately obvious. A glance around society proves that money in isolation does not bring happiness. It is clear that people don't derive genuine fulfilment from the shallow hoarding of consumer products, or even the purchase of high-end goods. However, whilst wealth on its own might not engender a feeling of happiness or satisfaction, what it does do is to facilitate access to products and services that promote a sense of well-being, such as health and education.

a Do the texts contain complementary or contrasting perspectives?
b Paraphrase the two main points in each of the two texts.
c What are your initial thoughts and reactions to the ideas?

2 Read the model answer and pay particular attention to the comments 1–12.

The pursuit of happiness and wealth are two dreams and concepts that occupy much of humanity, but to what extent are the two interconnected? Can it really be argued that the acquisition of money and material goods is a prime signifier of fulfilment? Both texts (1) discuss the nature of these concepts, but from a different perspective (2).

The first passage (3) argues that people chase riches to feel superior to others and to attain a given target (4). I personally feel (5) this will resonate with many people because we are conditioned by society to believe that this is what gives our lives meaning. Having possession (6) of more and more items generates a temporary feeling of satisfaction, and acquiring these in the pursuit of status leaves the ever-present fear that other people will surpass our efforts.

In contrast, the second text (7) proposes that the interconnected nature of wealth and other services such as education and health means that inevitably money does result in happiness (8). Whilst (9) we might not exactly feel euphoric in the midst of some medical procedure or when standing in line outside the classroom door, I would agree that (10) having sufficient prosperity to take advantage of these services is a vital part of our sense of well-being. Were these services stripped away (11) or put beyond the reach of affordability, the negative impact on our mental as well as physical health would be considerable.

In conclusion, it could be argued that flash cars and mansions allow limited progress along the path to happiness. However, if those fundamental services, which are facilitated by money and taken for granted by us all, were ripped from our grasp, I have no doubt that levels of contentment would fall (12).

Comments on the model answer

1 A good reference to both texts in the introductory paragraph.
2 This signals a good early reference to the contrastive nature of the texts.
3 Focuses attention on the ideas in text 1.
4 Good paraphrase of text.
5 Clear shift to personal stance indicating evaluation.
6 Good use of a participle clause and helps maintain the link with the previous sentence.
7 Clearly marks the transition to the second text to give a balanced alignment.
8 Good paraphrase of text.
9 Good use of concessionary clause.
10 A clear indicator of personal opinion.
11 Good use of inversion which suits the more formal style.
12 Re-states the writer's main argument.

Improve the essay

3 Look at the essay below answering the same question as the model answer. Read the essay and try to improve areas you think are weak.

Happiness is a feeling many people desire, and we consequently strive to achieve this state. For some, it is a flawed and naïve concept that money brings happiness but for others, money enables people to acquire the products and services that they can derive satisfaction from.

From one perspective, for some people it is only important to feel rich relative to others within their circle. When we feel wealthy in comparison to this cohort we perceive that we are rich. Additionally, we set ourselves goals and, when we meet these goals, we feel a sense of satisfaction. Unfortunately, this feeling is short-lived and the endless cycle means that new goals and aims are needed to make us happy.

Another perspective is that money in itself does not bring happiness but it enables people to purchase the products and services that they derive satisfaction from. Not from typical material goods but through other more basic and important needs. The richest countries unsurprisingly are also the happiest countries. Whilst money on its own might not bring happiness, it does let people access health and education that provide much satisfaction. It's not the money on its own that makes you happy but the things it's linked to like health and education.

In conclusion, happiness is a goal many wish to pursue and so they look for different ways to achieve it. It does however allow access to basic services from which much satisfaction is derived.

Useful language
Cohesive language

Expressing similar ideas
Furthermore, …
In addition, …
Moreover, …
Likewise, …
Similarly, …

Expressing opposing ideas
However, …
On the other hand, …
Nevertheless, …
Nonetheless, …

Expressing results
accordingly …
as a consequence …
hence …
thus …
for these reasons …
consequently …

Contrasting two statements
Instead, …
On the contrary, …
Rather (than) …

Restating or explaining
in other words …
in particular …
that is (to say) …
specifically …

Concluding
All in all, …
In brief, …
In conclusion, …
To summarize, …

Exam practice

4 Look at this further example of a Part 1 essay task and practise writing an answer.

Read the two texts below.
Write an essay summarizing and evaluating the key points from both texts. Use your own words throughout as far as possible, and include your own ideas in the answer. Write your answer in 240–280 words.

Out of control
The boom-bust cycle of world economies is hardly a modern phenomenon, spanning some 400 years in various guises. The pursuit of wealth through speculation on markets exemplifies the inextricable link, to the human eye, between money and happiness. However, were it simply a matter of acquiring enough valuable commodities to maintain a certain standard of living then perhaps the constant maelstrom of economic growth followed by the despair of recession could be avoided. Unfortunately, once one man becomes rich, another seeks to attain the same or a higher position until the value of such goods and services reaches yet again an unsustainable level and the inevitable decline ensues.

Basic needs
Striving for greater riches is something which transcends every aspect and level of society. Stereotyped as the greed of the rich elite, this perspective naively hides the fact that the vast majority of the world exists below the poverty line. At least 80% of humanity lives on less than $10 dollars per day and is fighting a constant battle for survival. It is therefore not surprising that to a certain extent money is equated with happiness, since the income derived from (often strenuous) labour enables individuals to eke out a meagre existence and the simple provision of food and shelter is not a simple given fact but a pleasure and comfort for all.

Part 2, Article

Understanding the task

1 Read the exam question and answer questions a–d.

> A newspaper has asked readers to write an article on the current debate surrounding the impact of mobile devices on our lives. Write your article (280–320 words) for the comment and debate section of the newspaper giving your views on the positive and negative impacts on our lives?

a Which word in the exam question indicates that your article should be discursive?

b What aspect of the question means that the article should not consist of a history or description of mobile electronic devices?

c What expectations might readers have of articles in the comment and debate section of the newspaper?

d What style would be appropriate for this article?

2 Read the model answer and pay particular attention to the comments 1–12.

> When I took (1) a seat on a long-distance train journey recently, I was irritated to discover that I'd left my wallet at home. What really made me panic, though, was (2) the realization that I'd also left behind my mobile phone. Two hours without communication or music: how ever was I going to survive? (3)
>
> And yet, as little as two or three decades ago, modern mobile devices such as these belonged to the realms of science fiction. Who would have thought it possible to bank, shop, watch movies, and listen to music and much more from something as minuscule as today's portable electronic products? Yet as with any technological development, the outcome for us all can be as damaging as it is beneficial (4). The instantaneous nature with which we receive so many products and services is truly astounding. In the case of music and literature, to name just two, you can carry in the palm of your hand the same amount of books and music that would have once been crammed into an entire room.
>
> Communication via phone (5), text, messaging, email, video calls enables us to try (6) a million and one ways to track someone down. Yet it is this very method of communication that is (7) dramatically transforming our society into something almost unrecognizable. Youngergenerations have always sought to differentiate themselves form what preceded them, and classic examples of this (8) are clothing or music revolutions. Now this platform literally enables entire sectors of society to isolate itself from another, and to some extent can be seen to be causing factions within society (9).
>
> Seldom would anyone with a love of culture argue (10) that having the world of literature and music at your fingertips is in anyway a treacherous path down which society is heading (11). Yet, whilst I embrace aspects of this technological revolution, I do feel it is having a detrimental impact on something that sets man apart from other species – the ability to converse (12).

Comments on the model answer

1 The inclusion of personal experience engages the reader in an appropriate way for an article

2 The use of a cleft sentence draws readers' attention to a specific point

3 The sardonic tone underlines the writer's stance

4 Clearly highlighting stance

5 Use of nominalization to make phrasing more concise and easier to read.

6 Good use of pronouns to personalize the example and involve the reader, while at the same time broadening the frame of reference to include society at large.

7 Effective use of an emphatic device that helps convey the writer's stance

8 Clearly highlights exemplification

9 Good use of hedging.

10 Good use of inversion after a negative adverbial to create a more dramatic effect.

11 Interesting, emphatic choice of vocabulary.

12 Thought-provoking concluding sentence.

Improve the article

3 Look at the article below answering the same question as the model answer. Read the article and try to improve areas you think are weak.

> Modern mobile devices perform a large number of functions. Many people in the past would not have imagined that so many functions could be performed on one device. This technological development has had many positive and negative impacts on our lives. Questions that once led to much debate can now be answered in seconds. The web is a great source of knowledge that allows questions to be answered instantly. For forgetful people as well mobile devices have many benefits. You can watch televisionon demand twenty four seven. It is even possible to send a text message to a television telling it to record a TV programme.

writing guide

At the same time, technology is changing the way people chat. Normally, conversation makes it almost impossible to talk to more than one or two people at any one time. Social media allows for literally hundreds of people to take part in one conversation at the same time. It also allows people from all around a country or even the world to interact. It is even possible to join in a conversation two hours after it started and see what everyone has been saying. Therefore it could be argued that the internet has actually added something to conversations rather than taken it away.

It is perhaps a difference between the ages that makes some people view technology as being a negative influence. Few young people would complain about being able to chat in this way, but I doubt many grandparents would enjoy using such a method of talking.

Useful language
Giving examples

For example/instance, …
By way of illustration, …
A good/classic/well-known example/illustration (of this) is …
An example of this is the way in which …
… illustrates this point/shows this point clearly.
This can be illustrated by …
In the case of …
Take … (as an example)
such as …

Note: Examples in articles can take the form of an anecdote or description of personal experience, and are often included without an introductory expression.

Exam practice

4 Look at this further example of a Part 2 article task and practise writing an answer.

A newspaper has asked readers to write an article on the current debate surrounding the impact of television on our lives. Write your article (280–320 words) for the comment and debate section of the newspaper giving your views on changing trends and their impact on our lives.

Part 2, Letter

Understanding the task

1 Read the exam question and answer questions a–d.

> You have recently read a newspaper article which stated that 'most people in society are far too reliant on convenience food and this is having a detrimental impact on people's diets'. You decide to write a letter (280–320 words) responding to the points raised and expressing your own views.

a Based on the quote, what do you think was the underlying tone of the extract?
b Is it appropriate to give examples?
c What points might have been raised?
d What register will be appropriate for this task?

2 Read the model answer and pay particular attention to the comments 1–11.

Dear Editor,

I am writing in response to (1) the article on changing diets in society and would like to share my views. Whilst (2) some interesting issues are raised that will no doubt encourage enthusiastic debate, some of the points expressed are fundamentally flawed and somewhat exaggerated (3).

Having said that, I would be inclined to agree that a proportion of our society does, unfortunately, represent the caricature depicted in the article. Yes, there is an element of society that is dependent on pre-packaged microwave food (4) to provide necessary sustenance in a quick and simple form; however (5), to assume that this means people do not prepare fresh food at all, or that fast food alone is to blame for an increase in illnesses, is quite frankly ludicrous.

Many packaged foods in fact provide people with a more than adequate nutritional balance and actually save people money, whilst at the same time cutting down on waste. It is a well-known fact, which the article fails to acknowledge (6), that frozen vegetables provide higher levels of vitamins than many fresh products due to the deterioration in levels of nutrients as the fresh product ages (7).

As far as people not being willing to prepare food is concerned, I'm afraid I again have to take issue here (8). Yes I too am 'guilty', for want of a better word, of opening packets of ready-made food but at the same time I frequently concoct (9) my own dishes. The world is not black and white, and thus should not be viewed so one-dimensionally.

To sum up (10), I, in common with many others, do not fall into the category of polar opposites suggested by the article. Whilst (11) we may at times enjoy convenience, many of us equally derive great pleasure from our creativity in the kitchen. I look forward to following subsequent articles on related issues.

Yours faithfully

Comments on the model answer

1 Good use of letter writing conventions.
2 Concessionary clause helps set out writer's viewpoint.
3 Good use of more emphatic lexis.
4 Paraphrased the wording in the question.
5 The writer skillfully disagrees with the magazine: *Having said that … Yes, there is an element of society … however … .*
6 The writer has tried to add a variety of structures.
7 The paragraph as a whole contains examples that successfully support the writer's main argument.
8 Appropriate use of register to politely disagree with someone.
9 More vivid alternative to 'prepare'.
10 The use of a concluding phrase shows good organization.
11 Good use of a concessionary expression to acknowledge a contrasting view.

Improve the letter

3 Look at the letter below answering the same question as the model answer. Read the letter and try to improve areas you think are weak.

Hi,

I saw your article the other day and thought I'd like to have my say. There are a number of things I really don't agree with. The first issue that I disagree with is that people rely on convenience foods. Convenience foods do make up a part of many people's diets but they are not the only thing people eat. People eat all sorts of products and convenience foods do play a part in most people's diets but I don't really see that as a modern phenomenon or a concern. The phrase 'TV dinner' was coined more than fifty years ago, so it is hardly a new thing that people are eating convenience foods. It is not as if this has changed overnight and people are all of a sudden eating convenience foods; this has been going on for a long time. However, I don't think people really rely on convenience foods, they are simply that – convenient. Modern life requires people to multi-task. So people buy convenience foods to help them do other things in their lives. When people have the time they cook. Personally I cook every weekend. I also cook quite often during the week. Many other people do the same. In fact I would say cooking is a hobby for me. It is also a hobby for many other people. So I don't agree that many people do not prepare food. The opposite is true, in fact: many people cook for a hobby.

Thanks

Useful language
Structuring a letter

Opening phrases
I'm writing to express my (concern, etc.*) at/about …*
I'm writing in response to … .
I am writing in reply to … .
I'm writing with regard/reference to …

Expressing personal opinion
I would definitely agree that …
It would appear to me that …
Having said that,
As far as … is concerned …
I would (however) take issue with …

Closing phrases
I look forward to (hearing, receiving, etc.*) …*
I would therefore be grateful if you could …

Exam practice

4 **Look at this further example of a Part 2 letter writing task and practise writing an answer.**

You have read a newspaper article which stated that 'thousands of dollars are chucked down the drain annually on so called alternative medicine'. Readers were asked to send in their opinions. You decide to write a letter (280–320 words) responding to the article and expressing your own views.

Part 2, Review

Understanding the task

1 Read the exam question and answer questions a–d.

> A newspaper has asked readers to write a review of a hotel they have recently stayed in. Write your review (280–320) for the travel section of the newspaper saying who you would recommend the hotel for and why?

a Who might the readers of the article be?
b What three main elements should your review consist of?
c What part of the question suggests that you need to be evaluative in your writing?
d What style of writing would you expect to use?

Text analysis

2 Read the model answer, paying particular attention to the comments 1–12.

In the dim and distant past (1), Sicily was well off the beaten track (2) of the international tourist market, but a robust tourism strategy (3) has thrown open the doors on some once little-seen gems (4). Unfortunately, floods of tourists on cheap flights have swamped some resorts beyond recognition, but with just that little bit more effort there are some delightful hideaways (5) to be found.

Castel Di Tusa nestled (6) within a charming bay on the Tyrrhenian coast is one such place. In theory, there should be little to draw the tourists here were it not for the 'Art Hotel', Artelier Sul Mare. The compelling pull of the beaches, shops and restaurants in the much larger Cefalu is that bit more (7) convenient for the hordes (8) pouring out of the airport, but those that persevere and seek out this peaceful oasis are in for a treat.

Each room has a contemporary style and an artist's take on a concept. It is as if you are staying in an art gallery. Whether you stay in the same room every night or experience the huge array of talent on display by hopping from room to room is your prerogative, but which ever you choose, drifting (9) to sleep in this peaceful utopia (10) is an experience to remember. Whilst (11) you might not have a swimming pool, gym and flat screen TV you can experience dinner in the stunning surrounds of the terrace on the edge of the shore.

If (12) you expect all the trappings of five star luxury this would not be the place for you, and unless (13) you have particularly cultured teenagers it would not be the most energizing of breaks for them, however for those that enjoy the charm of peaceful idyllic surroundings in the comfort of some truly stunning rooms then this is the place to go (14).

writing guide

Comments on the model answer

1 & 2 Good fixed expressions engage the reader, offering an alternative to 'once' and 'away from'.

3 Neat use of a nominal structure as opposed to the more wordy 'strategy aimed at attracting tourism'.

4, 5 & 6 Evocative lexis frames the setting and suggests an approving stance.

7 This extension of the standard comparative form indicates a critical attitude, reinforcing the negative term 'the hordes'.

8 The use of 'hordes' has negative connotations, and contrasts the notion of mass-tourism with the fine atmosphere of the hotel in the review.

9 & 10 Use of ethereal noun and verb helps create an evocative mood that reflects the writer's positive view of the destination.

11 Good concessionary structure that compares the alternatives.

12 & 13 Use of the conditional 'if' and 'unless' clauses maintains the reader's interest and strengthens the concluding statement.

14 A good way of organizing the ideas to have maximum impact on the reader

Improve the review

3 Look at the review below answering the same question as the model answer. Read the report and try to improve the areas you think are weak.

When economic times are difficult, many people look for a cheap holiday. One economical option can be to opt for a holiday that includes everything. You will not have to spend anything more than you planned. Making this as cheap as your choice of destination. One great option for cheap all-inclusive hotels is Tunisia.

The Club Hotel Riu Marco Polo is next to the beach and has a large swimming pool with sea views. For those who like sports activities, there is lots to do in the sea and on the beach with volleyball, canoeing, sailing and wind-surfing. There is a kids club and lots of sports for people to do such as tennis and football. There is also a kids' pool and lots of playgrounds. In the evening there are lots of bars and restaurants suitable for all members of the family with, amongst others, both an Italian and Asian restaurant to try. All the food and drink is included and served throughout the day.

The rooms are comfortable and come with lots of

facilities. Each room has got a phone, satellite TV to watch your favorite programs, mini-fridge for snacks and drinks and air-conditioning to keep you cool. Family rooms also have a separate lounge to relax in. Like most hotels now, some rooms have sea views if you are willing to pay extra.

Many people like having lots of things to do and lots of food and drink to choose from. The hotel has so much to offer that once you are there you never need to leave.

Useful language
Comparison and contrast

Comparison markers

Similarly, …
In a similar way, …
In the same way as …
In common with …
Like …
Equally, …

Contrast markers:

However, …
Whereas, …
Whilst …
While …
On the one hand, …
On the other hand, …

Instead of …

Unlike …
By (way of) contrast, …

Exam practice

4 **Look at this further example of a Part 2 review task and practise writing an answer.**

A newspaper has asked readers to write a review of a restaurant they have recently eaten in. Write your review (280–320) for the travel section of the newspaper saying why you would or would not recommend the restaurant.

Part 2, Report

Understanding the task

1 Read the exam question and answer questions a–e.

As part of a globalization project at college, you have been asked to write a report (280–320 words) on the impact of the English language on your society. In your report you should describe the positive and negative effects English is having on your society and make recommendations to minimize any negative impact that English has had on society.

a Which key words tell you what information to include?
b Are you required to give suggestions?
c Do you expect to have to give your own opinions? How will this affect style?
d What will the target reader expect to achieve by reading the report?
e How do you expect to organize the information in your report?

2 Read the model answer and pay particular attention to the comments 1–17.

Introduction (1)
The purpose of this report (2) is to analyze the impact of the English language on our society. The report will comment on specific observations and focus on both the positive and negative effects that English has had (3).

Main areas of impact
Across the globe the English language has infiltrated virtually all facets of life and echelons (4) of society. However, it is in education and the world of work that (5) we are witnessing the most pervasive impact. To be able to function competently in both of these settings (6), there is an increasing requirement for proficiency in English. This (7) trend inevitably brings with it both positive and negative consequences.

The negative impact
Traditionally, English was seen as a subject in much the same way as Maths or Biology. However, with the recent introduction of bilingual education in many of our schools, its role has evolved and the issues around this have been magnified. Success in a school subject often hinges on (8) a student's ability in English. More affluent members of our society are able to pay for remedial help, a solution that is not available to all. Similarly, many people are finding it increasingly difficult to secure employment as more and more companies set English proficiency as a baseline (9) in their application procedure.

The positive impact
In an ever-shrinking world of increased cross-border trade (10), English is of paramount importance (11) if our society is to remain (12) competitive. A workforce more proficient in English has allowed us to remain so (13) through forging new agreements (14) with foreign companies and expanding our trade links into new markets. At a more local level, more widespread knowledge of English has also given our tourism industry a much needed boost as locals are in a much stronger position to communicate effectively with foreign visitors, creating (15) a much more welcoming environment for them when visiting.

Conclusions
The benefits of adopting English cannot be underestimated. However, some of these benefits have come at the expense of some members of our society. Those without a good level of English are increasingly being marginalized and disenfranchised (16). More support for the less affluent segments of our society would ensure that the benefits of speaking English trickle down to all (17).

Comments on the model answer

1 Sub-headings signpost the information clearly.
2 Signals the intent of the report clearly.
3 Change of clause structure helps to avoid repeating 'society' again.
4 Interesting, ambitious use of vocabulary.
5 Good use of a cleft sentence.
6 Good use of fronting to maintain focus.
7 Avoids repetition.
8 Good alternative to 'depend on'.
9 Interesting choice of vocabulary.
10 Good use of fronting and interesting vocabulary.
11 Strong collocation.
12 Good use of more complex grammar.
13 Avoids repetition.
14 Interesting use of vocabulary.
15 Good use of adverbial clause.
16 Interesting choice of vocabulary.
17 Good use of hedging and more complex vocabulary.

Improve the report

3 Look at the report below answering the same question as the model answer. Read the report and try to improve areas you think are weak.

What impact has the English Language had on Bahraini society? This report will look at the impact English has had there. It is fascinating to observe the number of areas in which English has impacted on modern life, but the effect is not the same across all of society. More than fifty percent of Bahrain's population are non-Bahraini citizens. So inevitably a number of languages are spoken in different parts of society. Areas that have been particularly affected are those of education and employment. This is in part due to the fact that these two areas are interconnected. Private education has become more diverse both in its content and the language used to instruct students. This means that graduates of these schools can study and work anywhere in the world. English is largely the language used for the purposes of instruction in private sector schools. State education is often in the medium of Arabic and levels of English are not high meaning these high school graduates will have limited employment opportunities. The graduates of the private education system often live, work and study abroad and consequently are able to bring back to our society a wider range of skills and knowledge to the benefit of the whole wider society. The level of English obtained from state education English is not likely to be as high, resulting in a number of negative impacts on these students' career prospects and ultimately creating a greater divide in social classes. English is having a positive effect on the wealthy sectors of society and a negative effect on the poorer sectors of society. English has become a tool of power and control and through no intention of the language's native speakers.

Useful language

Expressions for referring back and signalling intent

Referring back

As mentioned previously, …
As stated earlier, …
See above for …
As has already been discussed, …
With reference to …

Signalling intent

The purpose of this report is to …
This report sets out to …
The report will comment on …
Below is an explanation of …
The focus of this report is …

Exam practice

4 Look at this further example of a Part 2 report task and practise writing an answer.

You have recently been on an exchange programme to another country as part of your university studies. Your tutor has asked you to write a **report** (280–320 words) of the main similarities and differences between your culture and the country you have just visited. In your report you should also make recommendations for future students who may travel there.

Part 2, Set texts

There will be two questions in the exam on the set texts. These are always questions 5a and 5b in Part 2 of the Writing paper. Set text questions are optional. Each question will be based on one of the set texts. As the set texts can change from year to year, check with Cambridge ESOL for the most current texts. The information can be found on their website.

Preparing for the set text task

Do not attempt to answer any of the set text questions unless you have read the book and studied it very carefully. If there is a film version, it is acceptable to watch this. However, it is advisable to watch the film *and* read the book. Whilst reading the book (or watching the film version), it is a good idea to keep a note of important aspects that you can use to answer the exam questions. In the exam, candidates with the best marks show a thorough knowledge of the texts. Here is a list of things to consider:

- **Overview** It is important to have a clear understanding of the plot, the key events, and how these events are interconnected.
- **Themes** Make a note of the key themes represented in the book. How true are these events today? What is your opinion of these themes?
- **Narrative** Who narrates the story? What effect does this have on the reader? What is the narrator, or author's, tone or attitude?
- **Characters** Make a note of main characters' physical appearance and personality traits. What is their behaviour like? Why do they behave like this? What are their attitudes? What is their motivation? How are they motivated? Do these aspects change as the story progresses?
- **Setting** Make notes on the place, the society and the world in which the story is set. What is the relationship between the characters and the world they live in? Does the setting reflect the characters, attitudes, beliefs and traits?
- **Quotes** Keep a record of important quotes that you can use to illustrate your answer.

Answering the set text questions

Here is a list of things to consider when answering a set text question:

- Read the question carefully, underlining any key words.
- Identify what the question is asking for. The question will have two or three elements.
- It could be a report, a letter, a review, an essay or an article. Write in an appropriate style (see relevant pages in the Writing guide for these different task types).
- Identify the target reader and write in an appropriate register.
- Plan your response.
- Try to address *all* elements of the question equally.
- Do not write a summary of the plot. The question will ask for more than this.
- Include, where appropriate, quotes to support your opinions.

Useful language

Themes

… draws attention to …
… a commentary on …
… the theme runs through …
… marks the …
… revolves around …
… interwoven themes of … and …

Narrative

… see through the eyes of …
… is told from the point of view of …
… draws the reader into the story.
… captures the readers' attention.
… adopts a position which …
… creates a sense of …
… written in the first-person …
… jumps from … to …

Characters

… is portrayed as …
… comes across as …
… the protagonist undergoes …
… is presented as …
… a prime example of …

Setting

… is set against a backdrop of …
… is set in …
… alternates between … and …
… plunged into …

Grammar notes

Unit 1 Past verb forms

Past simple

We use verbs in the past simple to create distance from present time when we describe earlier situations (1). We use the present simple for things that are generally true or happen regularly (2).

1 Scott **played** rugby for his school.
Did you **live** in Paris?
I **didn't have** much fun as a child.

2 We **play** bingo on Monday nights.
Do women **live** longer than men?
I **don't go** out much.

- **We can use a present form when talking about a past situation if a description is still true:**
I stayed out of the sun most of the time there because I **have** fair skin and I **burn** easily.

We can also use verbs in the past to create distance from present reality when we describe hypothetical situations (3). We also use this distancing effect of verbs in the past as a less direct and more polite way of making requests or offers and expressing personal opinions (4).

3 If I **wasn't** tired, I'd go with you.
Supposing you **found** a bag of money, would you keep it?

4 **Did** you **want** to go out tonight?
I **thought** we might get a bite to eat later.

We use a verb in the past for a future event after the expression *it's time (that) …*.

5 It's getting late and it's time (that) we **went** home. (~~it's time we go home~~)

Past continuous

We use the past continuous to describe actions in progress at a specific time in the past.

6 What **were** you **doing** at 8.30 last night? ~ I **wasn't doing** much. I **was** just **reading**.

In sentences with *when*- and *while*-clauses, we can use the past continuous to describe an activity in one clause that is in progress before an action in another clause (7). The activity that starts later may interrupt the first activity (8).

7 *While* he **was driving**, I fell asleep.
We saw Henry *when* we **were walking** in the park.

8 *When* you phoned, I **was listening** to the news.
David **was jogging** *when* he slipped and fell.

We can use the verb *hope* in the past continuous to talk about an earlier plan (9) or as a way of making a request more polite (10).

9 We **were hoping** to spend a couple of weeks in Spain, but it was going to be too expensive.

10 I **was hoping** you could help me understand how the new copy machine works.

We can use the past continuous for general background information (11) and with verbs of 'saying' as a background before reporting some news (12).

11 We **were having** lunch with friends when I heard about the new contract.

12 One of them **was telling** me negotiations were over. He **was saying** that it was a done deal.

We can use the adverb *always* with the past continuous to emphasize that something happened repeatedly and, in many cases, that it was annoying.

13 They never bothered to look at a map and, as a result, they **were** *always* **getting** lost.

Past perfect

We use the past perfect when we are describing an action with the past simple and we want to refer to an action further in the past (14). We can also use the past perfect to describe earlier hopes or desires that were not fulfilled (15).

14 We tried to catch him during his office hours, but he **had** already **left** for the day.

15 We **had hoped** to have the party outside in the garden, but it rained all day.

We use the past perfect in clauses with *after* or *when* to emphasize that an action was earlier.

16 Our team surprised everyone by winning *after* nobody **had given** them a chance.

- **Note that two verbs in the past simple can suggest a cause and effect:**
When I **called**, he **came**.

Used to and *would*

We can describe past habits and states with *used to* (17), often when establishing a time frame for a narrative episode (18).

17 I **used to** play hockey. **Did** you **use to** have a dog? There **didn't use to** be so much traffic.

18 My parents say that when I was a child, I **used to** carry this old ragged teddy bear around.

- **Don't confuse *I used to play* (= past habit) with *I was used to playing* (= 'familiar with')**

We also use *would* in narrative episodes when we describe regular past actions (not states), usually after a past time frame has been established.

19 **I'd** take that teddy bear everywhere with me and I **wouldn't** let anyone else touch it.

- **In speaking, we usually use the reduced form *'d* instead of *would* after pronouns.**

We often use *would* for hypothetical situations, especially in unreal conditionals (20), and when we cautiously express an opinion or make a request (21).

20 **Would** you stay with me no matter what happened?
It **would** be quicker if we took a taxi.

21 I **would** describe James as an average student.
Would you check that I've done this right?

We can use *would* for a future event that is described from a point of view in the past. This structure is sometimes called 'the future in the past'.

22 After that first brief meeting with Ben, Cristina just knew she **would** have to see him again.

We can use *would* (= 'be willing to') to describe willingness (23) and the negative form *wouldn't* (= 'not be willing to') when someone refuses to do something (24).

23 Most people **would** pay more for better health care.
I **would** stay longer, but I miss my pets.

24 She had a lot of influence, but she **wouldn't** help us. She **wouldn't** even listen to our plan.

We use *would* with verbs such as *love* or *prefer* (25), and in the expression *would/'d rather* (26), when we are expressing a preference. In a clause following *would rather*, we use a past tense.

25 They **would** *prefer* it if I didn't talk about the project yet. I'd love to stay here with you.

26 *I'd rather* you **didn't leave** yet because I might need your help later.

We sometimes use *would*, with stress, when we are criticizing a particular action in the past.

27 I was hoping to keep this a secret, but you **would** go and tell everyone about it.

Unit 2 Future time

Future: *will* and *shall*

There is no single form used as the future tense. We usually use *will* plus the base form of the verb to give or ask for information about the future (1) and to talk about possible future actions when we make promises, requests or threats (2). We use contracted forms after pronouns (*'ll*) and in negatives (*won't*) unless we are being formal or emphatic.

1 Christmas **will be** on a Friday.
The meeting **won't start** until 9:30.
When **will** you **leave**?

2 We'**ll help** you clean up.
I **won't tell** anyone.
Will you please **go**?

We can use shall with *I* or *we* to express determination, or in questions to make offers or suggestions. It is becoming rare as a way of referring to future time.

3 We will forgive, but we **shall** never forget.
Shall I start the ball rolling?
Let's go, **shall** we?

Future continuous, future perfect and future perfect continuous

We can use *will* + *be* + present participle as the future continuous to talk about future actions in progress at a particular time (4), to express plans or intentions (5) and to make polite enquiries about future plans (6).

4 Next week at this time, you **will be lying** on the beach and we'**ll** all still **be slaving** away here.

5 I'**ll be sending** in my application tomorrow.
After finals, we'**ll** all **be scrambling** to find work.

6 Where **will** we **be staying**? **Will** we **be paying** for the accommodation ourselves?

We can use *will* + *have* + past participle as the future perfect to say that something will be completed by a particular time (7). We use *will* + *have been* + present participle as the future perfect continuous when we look ahead to a future time and imagine an action lasting from a point in the past up to that future time (8).

7 By next summer I'**ll have finished** my degree. It's 5:30.
Will Jay **have left** work already?

8 At the end of this month, I'**ll have been struggling** to make ends meet for a whole year.

Will or *be going to*?

We use *will* for a prediction based on past experience or knowledge (9), especially in the main clause of predictive conditionals (10). We use *would* or *was/were going to* when we describe a past prediction about the future (11).

9 As soon as the victorious British team lands at Heathrow, all their fans **will start** celebrating.

10 If you don't put anything away for a rainy day, you'**ll have** nothing to fall back on later.

11 When I was younger, I thought I **was going to be** a rock star and I **would** never **have** to work.

We use *be going to* for a decision already made (12) and *will* for a decision at that moment (13).

12 She's fed up with public transport so she'**s going to** buy a car.

13 I need someone to take this to the post office. ~ **I'll go**!
That's the phone ringing. ~ **I'll get** it!

We can use *will* or *be going to* in many contexts with no difference in meaning. In questions, we can use *will* for open questions, no plans assumed, and *be going to* when there is an emphasis on intention.

14 What **will** you **do** next?
What **are** you **going to do** next? (= What is your plan?)

Present simple and present continuous for the future

We can use the present simple or the present continuous for future events in a schedule or timetable (15) and to talk about future actions we have planned or arranged (16). We can also use the present simple of *be* + infinitive to talk about official plans or preconditions (17).

15 The new course **starts** in January.
I think Kate **is heading** out of here first thing tomorrow.

16 I **see** the doctor next Friday.
We**'re playing** golf tomorrow. (NOT ~~It's snowing tomorrow.~~)

17 King Harald **is to visit** Oslo in May.
If we **are to catch** the bus, we'd better get a move on.

The future in clauses and phrases

In adverbial clauses, we usually use the present simple for future actions.

18 People **will** get serious about conservation **when** their water bills **start** to soar. (~~will start~~)

In clauses beginning with *after*, *as soon as*, *once* and *when*, we use the present perfect for a future action viewed as complete (19) or the present continuous for a future action viewed as ongoing and incomplete (20). We can use *not … until* in a similar way (21).

19 They **will** only get serious about conservation *when* their water bills **have started** to soar.

20 They **will** only get serious about conservation *when* their water bills **are starting** to soar.

21 People **won't** get serious *until* their water bills **start**/**have started**/**are starting** to soar.

We can use phrases with *about to*, *due to*, or *expected to* + base form of the verb to distinguish between future events as happening very soon (22), happening according to a schedule (23), or happening based on an expectation (24).

22 Hurry up. I'm *about to* **have** a meltdown.
Our flight is *about to* **leave**, you know.

23 We have plenty of time. Our flight isn't *due to* **leave** for another two hours.

24 The weather is really bad. Our flight isn't *expected to* **leave** any time soon.

- **Don't confuse *due to leave* (= 'scheduled to') with *due to the rain* (= 'because of ').**

We can use future phrases with an adjective such as *likely* + infinitive to say how sure we are about a future event (25) or an adjective such as ***ready*** to say if we are prepared or not (26).

25 Our team **is bound** / **certain** / **guaranteed** / **likely** / **sure** / **unlikely** to come out on top.

26 Our team **is ready** / **prepared** / **set** to fight for a place in the final four.

- **Don't use *probably* in this way:**
They will probably win. (~~They are probably to win.~~)

Unit 3 Focus and emphasis

In spoken English we can use intonation and stress to focus on or emphasize one part of a sentence. In written English, special structures are often used. For example, we can add auxiliary *do* for emphasis (1) or contrast (2) in affirmative statements.

1 What a lovely spread. You **did** go to a lot of trouble!

2 The report isn't comprehensive, but it **does** point to a number of shortcomings.

Fronting and inversion

We can also focus attention on one part of a sentence by moving it to front position, known as 'fronting'. We use fronting for emphasis (3) and also to link a sentence more closely to the preceding sentence (4).

3 Complaints about poor communication inside the organization are increasing. **This type of problem** we can't ignore. (= We can't ignore this type of problem.)

4 We looked at one new manager's experience trying to modernize her department. **At every turn** she was confronted by bureaucratic red tape.

After fronting, we often put the verb or auxiliary verb before the subject. This is called inversion. We use inversion after negative words (5), phrases beginning with *not* (6), and after negative adverbs such as *never* or *seldom* in front position (7).

5 I don't like it. *Neither* **do my parents**. *Nor* **does anyone else** that I've asked.

6 *Not until much later* **did we** learn that the earlier experiment had been a failure.
Not only **were many of the patients** worse off, some of them had actually died.

7 *Never* **had I** heard such nonsense.
Seldom **do people** get such an opportunity.

- **Others used like this: *at no time*, *hardly*, *no way*, *not once*, *rarely*, *scarcely***

We use inversion after *only* with prepositional phrases (8) and time expressions (9).

8 I've looked everywhere for it. *Only in Italy* **can you** find this kind of ice cream.

9 *Only after the test* **will we** know if it worked.
Only then **can we** decide what to do.

Focus structures

We often use *there* with *be* to focus attention on the subject as new information (10) or to highlight the current importance of information already known (11).

10 People don't like the new tax and **there have been** protests in the streets already.
(better than: and protests have been in the streets already)

11 I think we should go early. **There is** always the problem of finding parking.

We can also use structures called cleft sentences to focus on one part of a sentence. In a cleft ('divided') sentence, we divide a sentence into two parts in order to focus clearly on one part. Some sentences begin with *it* and are called *it*-clefts (12). Others begin with *what* and are called *wh*-clefts (13).

12 (Martin + ate your pizza.) ➞ **It** was *Martin* who ate your pizza.
(Martin ate + your pizza.) ➞ **It** was *your pizza* that Martin ate.

13 (He really likes pepperoni pizza.) ➞ **What** he really likes is *pepperoni pizza*.

It-clefts

We usually form *it*-clefts with *it* + *be* + an emphasized part + a relative clause beginning with *who* (14), *that* (15) or no relative pronoun (-), as in (16).

14 **It was** *Colin* **who** tried to call you earlier. **It wasn't** *Colleen* **who** phoned.

15 **It is** *ballroom dancing* **that** she likes more than anything else.

16 **It won't be** *the cold* (-) you'll get tired of during the Arctic winter, **it will be** *the long hours of darkness* (-) you won't be able to get used to.

We usually use ***it*-clefts** to focus attention on a noun or pronoun (17), but we can also focus on a prepositional phrase (18) or an adverbial clause (19).

17 **It wasn't** *me*, **it was** *Jenny*, who was out of sync with the rest of the group.

18 **It was** *in 1836* that Dickens really started to find fame as a writer.

19 **It's** *because the seasonal rains didn't materialize* that everything looks parched.

Wh-clefts

We form *wh*-clefts with a *what*-clause + *be* + an emphasized part. The emphasized part can be a noun phrase (20), a gerund (21), or a noun clause (22). We usually use *What* as the object of its clause, but it can also be the subject (23).

20 I can't stop yawning. **What** I need **is** *a cup of coffee*. (= I need a cup of coffee.)

21 **What** I enjoy most **is** *swimming* in the sea on a hot day.

22 **What** I hadn't realized **is** *that people go out binge shopping as a form of therapy*.
What I'll never understand **is** *why people think money is the key to happiness*.

23 Social change is coming. **What** causes it will not be *a violent revolution*. It will happen almost imperceptibly through the medium of social networking.

We can also use *wh*-clefts to focus attention on verb phrases. We use a form of the verb *do* in the *what*-clause plus the basic verb in the emphasized verb phrase (24). We sometimes use an infinitive as the emphasized verb phrase after *to do* in the *what*-clause (25).

24 The woman next door has an unusual job. **What** she **does is** *repair old clocks*.

25 David is always off on some adventure. Now **what** he is planning **to do is** *(to) go to Africa and (to) study bonobos in the wild*.

We sometimes use *all* in place of *what* to emphasize 'the only thing'.

26 I'll stop yawning soon. **All** I really need **is** a cup of coffee.

Unit 4 Perfect aspect

Present simple, present continuous and present perfect

We use the present simple for things that are generally true (1) and with stative verbs (2).

1 It **rains** more in winter.
Birds **don't sing** at night.
Do women **live** longer than men?

2 Anya **loves** chocolate.
They **don't believe** us.
He **owns** his flat. (~~He is owning his flat~~.)

We use the present continuous for actions currently in progress (3) and for temporary states (4).

3 I'**m calling** to let you know I'**m coming**, but it'**s snowing** and the traffic **is moving** slowly.

4 Wendy **is being** wild tonight. She **is having** a graduation party. (~~She has a party tonight~~.)

We use the present perfect to describe an action or situation that started in the past and connects to the present (5), especially with stative verbs (6), and after expressions such as *this is the first time that …* (7).

5 How long **have** you **worked** here? ~ I'**ve worked** here since 1997. (~~I work here since 1997~~.)

6 I **have known** Tony for about five years. (~~I know / I'm knowing Tony for five years~~.)

7 *Is this the first time* you **have been** to an opera?
This is the first time I'**ve** ever **tried** sushi.

- **We usually put the adverb after the auxiliary and before the verb (I have ever tried)**

We can use a perfect form with *having* + past participle or *to have* + past participle to emphasize that an event happened before now.

8 The mountaineers were excited about **having reached** the summit. They are thought **to have** already **started** their descent.

Present perfect or present perfect continuous?

We use the present perfect continuous to focus on an activity or process going on from a point in the past up to the present (9) and to ask or talk about anything happening during that period (10).

9 They **have been repairing** our street and it **has been causing** a lot of traffic problems.

10 What on earth **have** you **been doing**? ~ I'**ve been mucking** around in the garden.

We use the present perfect continuous to describe an action or series of actions as part of a continuous process up to the present (11). We can use the present perfect to specify the number of times we performed an action rather than focus on continuous activity (12). In many cases, these tenses are interchangeable unless we want to emphasize that the activity was continuous.

11 He**'s been calling** for you. It **has been raining** a lot recently.

12 He **has called** 4 times and he **has asked** for you each time. (~~He has been calling 4 times~~.)

We can describe an action as a process going on from earlier up to the present (present perfect continuous – 13) or as the present result of an earlier action (present perfect – 14).

13 We**'ve been making** chicken soup. That's why the kitchen is hot and steamy.

14 We**'ve made** chicken soup. That's what everyone's eating. Would you like some?

Present perfect or past simple or past continuous?

We use the past simple for completed actions in the past (15) and the past continuous for actions in progress at a specific time in the past (16).

15 The light bulb **was** invented by Edison.
I **made** mistakes because I **didn't try** very hard.

16 We **were having** problems with the car last week. It **was coughing** and **spluttering** a lot.

We use the present perfect when we think a situation may not have ended (17) and the past simple when we think the situation ended before now (18).

17 I **have lived** in London for a year.
She **has known** him since school.
Has Jason **been** ill?

18 I **lived** in London for a year.
She **knew** him in school.
Was Jason ill all last week?

We use the present perfect with expressions such as *lately* for a time up to now (19). We use the past simple with expressions such as *yesterday* for a time that ended earlier (20).

19 **Have** you **seen** any good films *lately*?
So far my manager **hasn't given** me a pay rise.

- **Others: *already, ever since, recently, since then, up to now, yet***

20 **Did** you **see** that film *last night*?
I **didn't do** the work *yesterday*. (~~I haven't done it yesterday~~.)

- **Others: *a week ago, back then, in the 1980s, the year before last, once upon a time***

In clauses beginning with *after*, *as soon as*, *once* and *when*, we can use the present perfect for completed actions in the future (21) and the past simple for completed actions in the past (22).

21 *As soon as* he **has made** his copies, I will do mine. We'll leave *after* they **have finished**.

22 *As soon as* he **made** his copies, I did mine. We left *after* they **finished** the repairs.

Past perfect or past simple?

We use the past perfect (*had won*) when we want to refer to events before other events in the past simple (*won*) or a specified past time (*2002*).

23 Jenny Fisher **won** her first gold medal in *2002*. She **had won** two silver medals in previous Olympics, but this was her first gold.

With the past simple (*arrived*) in a *when*-clause, we use the past perfect (*had started*) in the main clause for an earlier action (24) and the past simple (*started*) for a later action (25).

24 When he **arrived** in the morning, we **had started** work.
(= started work before he arrived)

25 When he **arrived** in the morning, we **started** work.
(= started work after he arrived)

In conditionals, we use the past perfect for something that did not happen (26) and the past simple for something that might happen (27).

26 If you **had come**, you could have stayed with us.
If **I'd known**, I would have helped you.

27 If you **came**, you could stay with us.
If I **saw** anyone doing that, I would try to stop it.

Past perfect or past perfect continuous?

We use the past perfect continuous for events in progress before another event in the past (28). We can use the past perfect continuous to focus on the duration of a period before the past (29), or use the past perfect to focus on the completion of that period (30).

28 I **had been thinking** about that before you mentioned it. Others **had been talking** about it.

29 Jack **had been working** as a systems engineer since he graduated and he was getting bored.

30 Jack **had worked** as a systems engineer since he graduated and he was bored.

We can focus on an action as a process going on before a past event (past perfect continuous – 31), or as the past result of an action earlier in the past (past perfect – 32).

31 We **had been making** chicken soup so the kitchen was still hot and steamy when she came in.

32 We **had made** chicken soup so we offered her some when she came in.

Future or future perfect?

We use *will* with verbs to talk about future events and in making predictions (33). We can use *will have* in the future perfect to say that something will be completed by a particular time (34).

33 Christmas **will be** on a Friday. If the sun doesn't shine, we **will have** to change our plans.

34 It's 5:30. **Will** Jay **have left** work already? By next summer **I'll have finished** my degree.

- **Other modals can be used instead of *will* + perfect:** Jacob was late because he had to walk to work. Normally he **would have driven** his car. I think it **must have broken** down.

Unit 5 Modals

Modals

The modals are auxiliary verbs such as *may* or *must* that we use with the base form of the verb when we talk about things in terms of prediction, possibility, necessity, deduction or obligation.

1 We **may be** in for a spell of bad weather. So we really **must get** the roof repaired soon.

- **Others: *can, could, might, ought to, shall, should, will, would***

We use a modal with *have* plus a past participle to form the modal perfect (2) and a modal with *have been* plus a present participle to form the modal perfect continuous (3).

2 I **shouldn't have left** my phone on the table. Someone **must have walked** off with it.

3 The thief **must have been hanging** around nearby. He **might even have been watching** me.

We use a modal with *be* (4) or *have been* (5) + past participle to form modal passives.

4 Some things **cannot be explained** by reason. This shirt **should be washed** by hand.

5 The work area **should have been cordoned off**. Some passers-by **could have been** injured.

Prediction: *will, would*

We use *will* for a predictable situation (6) and *would* for a hypothetical situation (7). We use *would have* plus a past participle for a past event or experience that is imagined (8).

6 He **will look** better without that scruffy beard. (= I think he's going to shave it off.)

7 He **would look** better without that scruffy beard. (= I don't think he's going to shave it off.)

8 It was an awesome party. You **would have loved** it. You **would have had** a blast.

Possibility: *may, might, can, could*

We use *may/might* to say that something is possible now or later (9) and *may have/might have* plus a past participle to say it is possible that something happened before now (10).

9 Taking these pills **may/might cause** drowsiness. You **may/might fall** asleep at the wheel.

10 I **may/might have lost** my key somewhere. It **may/might have dropped** out of my pocket.

- **We can use *might have* plus a past participle to convey annoyance at something not done:**
  I waited at home all morning for the plumber. He **might have phoned** me to say he'd be late.

We use the expression *may/might (just) as well* when we make a possible comparison, usually negative, between two things.

11 The soup was horrible. We **might (just) as well** have been drinking dishwater.

We also use *can/could* to describe a type of behaviour that is (*can*) or was (*could*) common or typical (12). We use *could*, not *can*, when we speculate about things happening now or later (13). We use *could have* plus a past participle when we speculate about the possibility of an earlier event (14). We can use *might/might have* in place of *could/could have* in these speculative uses.

12 Some dogs **can be** very dangerous.
The old house **could be** quite cold, even in summer.

13 My car won't start. **Could** something **be** wrong with the engine? (~~Can something be wrong?~~)

14 That area is dangerous. You **could** easily **have fallen** down. You **could have hurt** yourself.

- **We can use *could have* plus a past participle to convey annoyance at something not done:**
  I sent Susan a card and some money. She **could have written** a short thank you note at least.

Necessity: *must, need to*

We use *must* to say that something is necessary and *mustn't/must not* when we tell people not to do things or to say that something is a bad idea.

15 Plants **must have** light to grow.
Empty boxes **must not be** stacked near the emergency exit.

We can also use (*not*) *need to* for something that is (or isn't) necessary (16). We use *didn't need to* when we mean that it was not necessary to do something (17). We use *needn't have* plus a past participle when we mean that something unnecessary was done (18).

16 All plants **need to have** light. There are some plants that you **don't need to water** every day.

17 I knew there wouldn't be a test, so I **didn't need to study**. I watched TV instead.

18 I studied all night then found out the test was cancelled. I **needn't have studied** at all.

Deduction: *must, can't, couldn't*

In positive deductions we use *must* for what we think is likely now (19) and *must have* plus a past participle for what we think is likely to have happened already (20).

19 You're shivering. You **must be** cold. Something **must be** wrong with the heating.

20 It's chilly in here. Someone **must have left** a window open. It **must have been** the cleaners.

In negative deductions we use *can't* for what we think is not possible now (21). We use *can't have/couldn't have* + past participle for what we think was not possible earlier (22).

21 The bill is over $80. That **can't be** right!
You **can't be** 30 years old! (~~You mustn't be 30!~~)

22 I was surprised by how young the police officer was. He **can't/couldn't have been** a day over eighteen.

Obligation: *should*, *ought to*

We use *should* to express an obligation (23), to say what we think is a good idea (24) and to give advice or a warning (25).

23 The police **should crack down** on speeding. Drivers **should** really **slow down** near schools.

24 Teachers **should get** more pay.
Children **should be taught** to say 'Please' and 'Thank you'.

25 You **shouldn't go** swimming right after eating.
You **shouldn't walk** in the park at night.

We use *should have/shouldn't have* + past participle when we think that something desirable did not happen (26) or that an obligation was not fulfilled (27).

26 I **should have rehearsed** more before playing.
I'm sorry. I **shouldn't have left** such a mess.

27 They **should have told** us that it was dangerous.
They **should have put** up warning signs.

We can use *ought to* and *ought to have* with the same meaning as *should* and *should have*.

28 You **ought not to walk** in the park at night.
They **ought to have put** up warning signs.

Unit 6 Relative clauses

Defining and non-defining relative clauses

Relative clauses (or adjective clauses) are subordinate clauses connected to a noun phrase in another clause. They are usually introduced by the relative pronouns *who* and *whom* for people, *which* for things and *that* for both. Some relative clauses are used without a relative pronoun (-)

1 We have friends **who/that** live in Cornwall and **whom** we often visit in the summer.

2 They have a cottage **which/that** is near the most beautiful bay (-) I've ever seen.

There are two types of relative clause: defining and non-defining. We use a defining clause for essential information that identifies the people or things we are talking about (3). We use a non-defining clause, separated by commas, to add extra information (4).

3 My uncle **who** lives in London is an architect. (NOT = my uncle who lives in *Liverpool*)

4 My uncle, **who** lives in London near Hyde Park, has invited us to stay with him at Christmas.

In defining relative clauses, we use *who*, *which* or *that* to refer to the subject (5) or object (6). We can also use *whom* or no relative pronoun (-) for the object (7).

5 I remember the people **who/that** used to live next door. (= *the people* used to live next door)
They had a little dog **which/that** barked a lot. (= *the dog* barked a lot)

6 I loved the beautiful bouquet **which/that** (-) you sent. (= you sent *the bouquet*)

7 I never met the man **who/whom/that** (-) Jane married. (= Jane married *the man*)

- **We don't repeat a pronoun:**
I never met the man that she married (~~him~~).

In non-defining relative clauses, we use ***who***, ***whom*** or ***which***. Don't use ***that*** or no pronoun (–).

8 David and Ann, long-term tango partners, **who/whom** everyone overlooked in the early stages, were on fire in the final round.

9 Halloween, **which** is celebrated on October 31st, can be quite frightening. (~~that is celebrated~~)

We use ***whom*** or ***which*** after prepositions (10), especially after expressions such as ***some of*** or ***both of*** describing how many or how much (11).

10 Harry McGurk, **after whom** the famous effect is named, worked at the University of Surrey.

11 Captain Scott Carter wrote two maritime histories, **both of which** became bestsellers.

We can use ***which*** (12), or a prepositional phrase containing ***which***, such as ***in which case*** or ***by which time*** (13), to add comments about the whole clause before it.

12 One of the candidates told us he had a PhD**, which** turned out to be untrue.

13 Students may arrive with limited proficiency, **in which case** an extra class is recommended.

We can also use ***where*** (14) instead of ***in which*** after a noun such as ***case***:

14 In many **cases where** a request has been made, it has met with a flat refusal.

- **Other nouns used with *where*: *activity*, *example*, *experience*, *point*, *situation*, *society*, *stage***

Reduced relative clauses

A relative clause formed with a participle and no relative pronoun is called a reduced relative clause. We use present participles for active verbs (15) and past participles for passive verbs (16).

15 I think there are two students **waiting outside**. (= who are/were waiting)

16 The strawberries **dipped in chocolate** are delicious. (= which are/were/have been dipped)

We can use a participle from a simple passive to describe a general situation (17) or a continuous passive to emphasize that a situation is continuing (18).

17 We are concerned about people **held** in prison without a trial. (= who are held)

18 We are concerned about people **being held** in prison without a trial. (= who are being held)

We can move reduced non-defining relative clauses from middle position to front position.

19 **Played indoors with cheaper equipment**, ping pong became more popular than tennis. (= Ping pong, which was played indoors with cheaper equipment, …)

20 **Dripping with sweat**, the marathon winner raised his hands in triumph. (=The marathon runner, who was dripping with sweat, …)

We don't use a participle instead of a verb that describes a single or sudden action (21) or a verb with a subject that is different from the relative pronoun (22).

21 There was a sudden bang **that woke me up**. (~~sudden bang waking me up~~)

22 This isn't the information **that I was told before**. (~~the information told before~~)

We usually use an infinitive, not a participle, after a noun phrase with the adjectives *first*, *second*, etc.

23 Neil Armstrong was the first person **to walk** on the moon. (~~the first person walking~~)

Reduced adverbial clauses

An adverbial clause that is formed with a participle is called a reduced adverbial clause. As in reduced relative clauses, we use present participles for active verbs (24) and past participles for passive verbs (25).

24 **Waiting for the train**, I can usually catch up with the day's news. (= When I am waiting)

25 **Driven to desperation by hunger**, you might consider eating a frog. (= If you are driven)

We can include some conjunctions, such as *when* or *if*, in reduced adverbial clauses (26), but not others, such as *because* (27).

26 *When* **waiting for the train**, I can usually catch up with the day's news.
If **driven to desperation by hunger**, you might consider eating a frog.

27 **Not knowing her real name**, I referred to her as 'Hurricane'. (~~Because not knowing~~)

- **Other conjunctions used in reduced clauses: *after*, *although*, *as if*, *before*, *since*, *while***

We use reduced adverbial clauses when the subjects of the main clause and the adverbial clause are the same (28). We avoid using reduced clauses when the subjects are different (29).

28 **Barking loudly**, the dog scared us. (= Because it was barking loudly, the dog scared us.)

29 **Because it was barking loudly**, we were scared. (~~Barking loudly, we were scared~~)

Unit 7 Continuous aspect and stative verbs

Present simple and present continuous

We use the present simple for things that are generally true (1), for informal reports and instructions (2) and with stative verbs (3).

1 Giraffes **live** in Africa.
Birds **don't sing** at night.
Do you **play** cards on Mondays?

2 It **says** here the strike is over.
I **suggest** you **call** the manager and **report** the problem.

3 Jenny's cough **sounds** terrible. Do you **know** if she **has** a sore throat too?

We use the present continuous for actions in progress (4), especially with verbs that have 'change' as part of their meaning (5) and stative verbs describing temporary states (6).

4 What **are** you **doing**? ~ **I'm eating** breakfast and **reading** the morning news.

5 Your child **is developing** normally.
The planet **is getting** noticeably warmer.

6 Why **are** you **being** so careful not to spend anything? ~ **I'm having** cash-flow problems.

We can use the present perfect continuous to focus on an activity or process going on from a point in the past up to the present.

7 We **have been reading** about asteroids.
It **has been raining** a lot recently.

Stative verbs

Stative verbs are used to describe states, not actions, and therefore are used more commonly in the simple form. We use stative verbs to describe the experience of our senses (8), thinking (9), possession (10) and emotional states (11).

8 Some types of cheese don't **smell** very good, but they **taste** great. (~~they're tasting great~~)

9 A lot of people **believe** in ghosts.
I just don't **understand** algebra.

10 We **have** a dog and two cats.
Does this pen **belong** to you? (~~Is this belonging to you?~~)

11 I don't **hate** Brussels sprouts, but I **prefer** other kinds of vegetables.

- **Other stative verbs: *consist of*, *contain*, *depend on*, *dislike*, *doubt*, *hear*, *imagine*, *include*, *involve*, *mind*, *own*, *realize*, *regard*, *remember*, *suppose*, *want***

We also use linking verbs such as *be*, *appear* and *seem* like stative verbs.

12 Jane is a new student. She doesn't **appear** to have any friends. She **seems** to be very shy.

We can use some verbs, such as *mean* or *measure*, as a stative verb (13) or an action verb (14), with different meanings. We can use a verb such as *feel* in both the present simple and present continuous to describe the current state of the subject (15) or in the continuous to say what action the subject is performing (16).

13 'Aloha' **means** 'love' in Hawaii.
The main living area **measures** about forty square metres.

14 **I've been meaning** to talk to you.
Why **are** you **measuring** the height of the wall?

15 Jenny looks a bit rough, but she says she **feels**/**is feeling** fine.

16 The vet **is feeling** the cat's stomach to check for swelling.

- **The verb *need* is not used in the present continuous, but can be used in the future continuous to make a polite enquiry:**
Will you be needing a ticket or have you already bought one?

Unit 8 Infinitives and gerunds

Infinitives

We use infinitives (***to*** + verb) and negative infinitives (*not to* + verb) after verbs (1), adjectives (2) or nouns (3).

1 We agreed **to meet** on Fridays.
He promised **not to tell** a soul about their secret liaison.

2 We'd be happy **to give** you a hand.
I was sorry **to hear** that you weren't feeling well.

3 She made a decision **to confront** the criminal. It wasn't her intention **to attack** or injure him.

We can use a passive form of the infinitive (*to be* + past participle – 4) and a perfect infinitive (*to have* + past participle) for an earlier action (5).

4 The workers want **to be paid** today.
I pleaded with her **not to be taken in** by his smooth talk.

5 I hope **to have read** the guidebook before we go to Berlin.
You seem **to have been** very busy.

We can use an infinitive (*to get*) to express purpose and *only* with an infinitive (*only to find out*) when we want to express a result.

6 We made a big effort **to get** to the meeting **only to find out** that it had been postponed.

Bare infinitives

We use bare infinitives (base form of the verb) after modals (7) and after verbs such as *make* or *let* with objects (8).

7 I *can't* **stay** long. What *will* we **do** if they tell us we *must* **pay** more? (~~we must to pay~~)

8 Please *make* her **stop** that noise. They won't *let* us **leave** unless we pay more. (~~let us to leave~~)

Gerunds

We use gerunds (verb + *-ing*) like nouns: as subjects (9), as objects after verbs (10) and after prepositions (11). We can use determiners such as *the* or *his* before gerunds (12).

9 **Studying** makes me sleepy.
My doctor says that **swimming** is the best exercise.

10 We don't mind **waiting**.
Paul enjoys **not having** a job.
I suggested **taking** a coffee break.

11 She watches TV *instead of* **working**.
Ryan got angry and left *without* **saying** another word.

12 Do **the dusting** first, then **the vacuuming**.
The baby's okay, but **his crying** upsets me.

- **We can use a perfect gerund (*having* + past participle) to focus on a complete action in the past:**
Karl felt guilty about not **having saved** enough money to buy Lucy an expensive present.

We can use gerunds in phrases with objects and complements (13). We use present participles, not gerunds, in participle clauses that are similar to reduced versions of relative clauses and adverbial clauses (14). (See Grammar notes, Unit 6, examples 15–29.)

13 **Helping people** is more fulfilling for me than **making a lot of money** and **feeling miserable**.

14 Two American tourists (who were) **visiting** London on their honeymoon were attacked by a group of young people while (they were) **walking** near Hyde Park late last night.

Verbs used with infinitives and gerunds

We use infinitives, not gerunds, after verbs such as *hope* and *offer* (15). After verbs such as *tell* and *warn*, we must include a noun phrase to identify the subject of the infinitive (16).

15 I'm *hoping* **to get** a day off soon. We *offered* **to pay** for the damage (~~We offered paying~~)

- **Other verbs used with an infinitive: *agree, aim, claim, decide, fail, plan, refuse, vote, want***

16 They *told us* **to wait** for them. We *warned everyone* **not to leave** their doors unlocked.

- **Other verbs used with a noun phrase + an infinitive: *force, order, persuade, remind, tempt***

After *advise, allow, encourage* and *permit*, we use a noun phrase before an infinitive (17). We can also use these verbs with a gerund to describe an activity in general terms (18).

17 They *advised us* **to cook** the eggs thoroughly.
The hotel doesn't *permit non-residents* **to swim** in the pool.

18 They *advise* **cooking** eggs thoroughly.
The hotel doesn't *permit* **swimming** in the pool after ten o'clock.

After *regret, remember, stop* and *go on*, we use an infinitive for something that happens later (19) and a gerund for something that happened or was happening before (20).

19 *Remember* **to take** an umbrella.
After Steve Jobs left Apple, he *went on* **to develop** Pixar.

20 Don't you *remember* **taking** it earlier?
After he left the company, it *went on* **losing** money.

- **We can use *stop* + object + gerund:**
The main goal was to *stop people* **drinking** and **driving**.

Some verbs have different meanings when used with an infinitive or a gerund. We use *mean* with an infinitive (= 'intend') or with a gerund (= 'result in') (21). We usually use *dread* with a gerund (= 'be anxious about'), but the verb is also used with an infinitive in expressions such as *I dread to think* (= 'I don't want to think') (22).

21 I *meant* **to ask** you about your new job. Will it *mean* **spending** more time on the road?

22 I *dread* **getting** sick again.
I *dread* **to think** of how I'm going to pay my bills.

We can use some verbs, such as *like*, *start* or *try*, followed by either an infinitive or a gerund with little difference in meaning.

23 I *tried* **to learn/learning** German, but it was hard.
Have you ever *tried* **to ski/skiing**?

- **Note that after *try your best*, we only use an infinitive:** We **tried our best to be** on time.

24 Bob *likes* **to listen/listening to** jazz.
Their child *started* **to talk/talking** at 9 months.

- **Other verbs used like this: *begin*, *continue*, *hate*, *intend*, *love*, *prefer***

Gerunds and other nouns

We can create nouns called gerunds from the *-ing forms* of both action and stative verbs (25). We tend to avoid using gerunds when an alternative noun is available (26). In some cases, as with *smoke* and *smoking*, the two nouns have different meanings (27). (See also Grammar notes, Unit 8, examples 9–12 on page 159.)

25 A recent **finding** from research on neutrinos has complicated our **understanding** of the physical universe and challenged traditional **thinking**. (~~our understand~~)

26 The **threat** of conventional nuclear war has diminished with the **negotiation** of new treaties and the **reduction** of weapons stockpiles. (~~the threatening~~; ~~the negotiating~~; ~~the reducing~~)

27 It's my **smoking** that annoys her the most. She can't understand why I haven't given up yet. (= She's annoyed by the fact that I am smoking, not by the smoke.)

Unit 9 The passive

Uses of the passive

We use the passive (verb) to focus on what happens to the subject as the person or thing that experiences the action. The subject of the passive is usually the main topic of the sentence (1), often a pronoun referring back to something in a previous sentence (2).

1 One of the mysteries of science is an electrically neutral particle called a neutrino. *The existence of neutrinos* **was predicted** twenty years before *the first one* **was** actually **discovered** in a laboratory.

2 *They* **are produced** by a nuclear reaction in the sun. *They* **are believed** to pass through solid objects, such as our bodies, without having any effect.

We often use 'reporting' (3) and 'thinking' (4) verbs in the passive, plus an infinitive, when we want to avoid presenting information as established fact.

3 The two former rivals **are rumoured to be** in secret negotiations. (~~rumoured in negotiations~~)

4 Businesses don't want to conduct interviews. They **are thought to be** too time-consuming.

- **Other verbs used in this way: *allege*, *believe*, *claim*, *consider*, *feel*, *imagine*, *report*, *say***

The passive with *by*-phrases

The agent is the person or thing that does or causes the action. In active sentences, the agent is the subject (5). In passive sentences, we don't usually mention the agent. We include the agent in a *by*-phrase after the verb when the meaning is not complete without it, or when all the key information cannot be conveyed without it (6).

5 *Shakespeare* wrote Hamlet. *Many famous actors* have played the title role.

6 Hamlet **was written** *by Shakespeare*. The title role **has been played** *by many famous actors*.

We don't usually include pronouns (7) or predictable general agents (8) in a *by*-phrase.

7 We completed the final report on time. → The final report **was completed** on time (by us).

8 Workers must always wear safety helmets on the work site. → Safety helmets **must** always **be worn** on the work site (by workers).

The passive with *get*

We can use *get* + past participle (9) instead of *be* + past participle (10) as a passive, usually in informal contexts, as another way to talk about the subject experiencing the action.

9 I'll **get paid** on Friday.
My books **got damaged** when the basement **got flooded** last year.

10 I'll **be paid** on Friday.
My books **were damaged** when the basement **was flooded** last year.

We can also use *get* + object + past participle to say that the subject causes the action (13). We use a reflexive pronoun when the object is the same as the subject (14).

11 I have to **get** *a special photo* **taken** before I can **get** *my passport* **renewed**.

12 Some of the demonstrators came to the protest determined to **get** *themselves* **arrested**.

The passive with *have*

We can use *have* + object + past participle as a passive in two ways. We can say that the subject experiences the action (13) or the subject causes (or arranges for) the action to be performed (14).

13 My neighbour has such bad luck. Yesterday she **had** *her purse* **stolen** in the supermarket.

14 If you fill out a form at the post office, you can **have** *your mail* **forwarded** to your new flat.

We can also use *have* + object + the base form of the verb (15) or + a present participle (16) to say that the subject causes (or arranges for) the action.

15 The clinic **has** *all new patients* **complete** a questionnaire about their medical history.

16 His story was so sad it almost **had** *us* **crying**. We'll soon **have** *you* up and **running** again.

Unit 10 Contrast, reason and manner clauses

Contrast clauses

We use *although* ('despite the fact that') at the beginning of a clause that contains information that contrasts in an unexpected or surprising way with information in another clause.

1 **Although it is known for sunshine and beaches**, Hawaii also boasts mountain peaks that are covered in snow during the tropical winter.

We often use *though* instead of *although* in informal situations (2). We can use *though* (not *although*) after adjectives or adverbs moved to the beginning of the clause (3).

2 **Though Kate's clever**, she isn't doing very well at school. He has to work **though he's ill**.

3 **Though** the test was **difficult**, we all passed. → **Difficult though** the test was, we all passed.

When we want to emphasize a contrast, we can use *even though* when we are talking about past or present situations (4) and *even if* for future, possible or unlikely situations (5). We don't use *even* with *although* or as a conjunction by itself.

4 Bill kept playing golf **even though it was raining**. (~~even although it was raining~~)

5 Bill would play golf **even if it was snowing**. (~~even it was snowing~~)

- **Subjunctive *were* is sometimes used after *even if*:** He'd play golf **even if** it **were** snowing.

In place of *although/though*, we can use *if* with an adjective (phrase) when we express an opinion containing a contrast (6). We sometimes use *if* with the same meaning as *even if* (7).

6 The food throughout our trip was amazing, **if a bit too spicy at times for my taste**.

7 I still don't think I could eat worms or any other creepy crawlies **if/even if I was starving**.

We can use other conjunctions such as *whereas* (8) and *while* (9) to express a contrast between two clauses. The phrase *much as* is also used in contrast clauses with verbs such as *like*, *hate* or *want* (10).

8 Boys were encouraged to be adventurous **whereas girls were always told to stay clean**.

9 **While no one doubts his ability**, his arrogant attitude has been difficult to accept.

10 **Much as I like music**, I can't listen to opera for long. **Much as I want to**, I can't help you.

We can use *despite the fact that* instead of *although* to introduce a contrast clause (11). We can also use prepositions *despite* and *in spite of* + gerunds instead of a clause with *although* (12).

11 **Despite the fact that he had lots of friends**, he still felt lonely sometimes.

12 **Despite studying hard**, I failed the test. She wasn't satisfied **in spite of being paid extra**.

Reason clauses

We use *because* to introduce a clause with a reason or explanation for another event.

13 **Because there was an accident**, we arrived late. I didn't eat **because I wasn't hungry**.

We can also use *as* or ***since*** instead of *because* in reason clauses (14). We can use *as* or *while* to talk about time and reason together (= 'while and because' – 15).

14 **As it was late**, we decided to stop working. **Since he'd studied Latin**, I asked him to translate it.

15 **As/While we're on the subject of money**, I'd like to ask about next year's budget.

We can use *now (that)* like *as* or *since* to introduce a clause explaining a present situation.

16 **Now (that) we're married**, we never go out. I enjoy opera **now (that) I know more about it**.

We can use other conjunctions such as *for* (17) and *in that* (18) instead of *because* to add a reason or explanation for a preceding statement.

17 It would be wise to save some of the money, **for there may be unexpected expenses later**.

18 We definitely have a problem **in that there are more students than we have room for**.

Manner clauses

We can use manner clauses beginning with *as* (= 'in the way that' – 19) or *just as* (= 'in exactly the way that' – 20) when we are describing how something was or how it was done.

19 The film depicts life **as it was in 1900**. Complete each exercise **as I showed you**.

20 I wrote the note **just as you told me to**. It all happened **just as the psychic had predicted**.

We use *as if* and *as though* with the same meaning after verbs such as *feel*, *look* or *sound*.

21 Can I help you? You look **as if you're lost**. He sounds **as though he might be getting a cold**.

- **Other verbs used with as if/as though: *act*, *behave*, *seem*, *smell*, *talk*, *strut around*, *taste***

In informal situations, we often use *like* instead of *as* or *as if*.

22 No one will ever love you **like I do**. It feels **like winter has suddenly arrived**.

We use *as ... as* (= 'in the same way that') to say that two actions or situations are similar (or different) in a particular way. Between the first and second *as*, we can put adjectives or adverbs (23) and quantifiers such as *many* or *much*, with and without nouns (24).

23 It isn't **as hot as** it was last year. We didn't play **as well as** we did against France.

24 Were there **as many** problems **as** you anticipated? It didn't cost **as much as** he said.

Unit 11 Reported speech

Reported speech

We use reported speech (or indirect speech) to report the meaning of what was said, not the exact words. We begin reported statements with *that*, or no conjunction in informal uses.

1 'I'm going to win the prize.' → Michael **said** (**that**) he was going to win the prize.
'I can beat everyone.' → He **boasted** (**that**) he could beat everyone.

In reported speech, we change those words that refer to the speaker's situation (*I*, *my*, *this*) to words that reflect the different point of view of the person who is reporting (*she*, *her*, *that*).

2 '**I** don't like **my** hair in **this** style.' → She said (that) **she** didn't like **her** hair in **that** style.

We usually change words that refer to the place and time of speaking.

3 'It rained **here yesterday**.' → He said it had rained **there the day before/the previous day**.

- **Others: *now* → *then*, *tomorrow* → *the next/following day*, *two days ago* → *two days earlier***

We also change verb tenses. After a reporting verb in the past simple, we usually change present simple to past simple (4), present continuous to past continuous (5), and present perfect to past perfect (6).

4 'It **is** late and I **have** a headache.' → He complained that it **was** late and he **had** a headache.

5 'We**'re training** hard while he**'s** just **lazing** around.' → She pointed out that they **were training** hard while he **was** just **lazing** around.

6 'I**'ve** heard that they **have** been arguing.' → He said he**'d** heard that they **had** been arguing.

After a reporting verb in the past, we can use present tense for a situation viewed as current or unchanging (7). We can also report a past simple as a past simple or use a past perfect to emphasize that the event was earlier in the past (8).

7 'I **love** you.' → He said he **loves** me.
'Pluto **isn't** a planet.' → They said Pluto **isn't** a planet.

8 'I **didn't see** Mark.' → He said he **didn't see** Mark. / He said he **hadn't seen** Mark.

We usually change the modals *can* → *could*, *may* → *might* and *will* → *would* in reported speech. We don't change *could*, *might*, *ought to* and *should*.

9 'You **can** go.' → He said we **could** go.
'I**'ll** wait.' → She said she **would** wait.

Reported questions

We begin reported *wh*-questions with *wh*-words (10) and yes/no questions with *if* or *whether* (11). In reported questions, there is no question mark and we put the subject before the verb.

10 'Who is he?' → She asked me **who he was**.
'What does he do?' → She asked **what he did**.

11 'Is he a doctor or a nurse?' → She wanted to know **if/whether he was** a doctor or a nurse.

We can use *whether or not* (not *if or not*) as a phrase at the beginning of a reported question.

12 'Did he win or not?' → I asked **whether or not** he won. / **whether/if** he won **or not**.

We can report some *wh*-questions with *should* (about the right thing to do) by using an infinitive.

13 'When should I come and what should I do?' → I asked her **when to come** and **what to do**.

- **We don't use *why* in this way:**
I asked her **why I should do** that. (… ~~why to do that~~)

Reporting verbs

We can use verbs such as *explain* with a *that*-clause (14) or with *to* + an object before a *that*-clause (15) for reported speech. After a verb like *agree*, we can use *with* + object (16).

14 'I've been ill.' → She **explained that** she had been ill.

15 'I had the flu.' → She **explained to me that** she had had the flu. (~~She explained me that …~~)

- **Others: *admit*, *announce*, *boast*, *confess*, *mention*, *point out*, *propose*, *say*, *suggest*, *swear*, *whisper***

16 'You're right. There's a mistake.' → He **agreed (with me) that** there was a mistake.

- **Others: *argue*, *check*, *confirm*, *disagree***

After a reporting verb such as *promise*, we can use a *that*-clause or an infinitive.

17 'I'll fix it.' → He **promised that he would fix** it. / He **promised to fix** it.

- **Others: *agree*, *claim*, *guarantee*, *hope*, *swear*, *threaten*, *vow***

After some reporting verbs such as *offer*, we use an infinitive for reported speech (18). After other verbs such as *encourage*, we must include an object before the infinitive (19).

18 'I'll help you later.' → He **offered to help** us later. (~~He offered us to help us later.~~)

- **Others like this: *apply*, *decline*, *demand*, *refuse*, *volunteer***

19 'You shouldn't quit.' → She **encouraged me** not **to quit**. (~~She encouraged not to quit.~~)

- **Others: *ask*, *call on*, *expect*, *invite*, *order*, *remind*, *teach*, *tell*, *urge*, *warn***

After verbs reporting advice, such as *recommend* or *suggest*, we can use a gerund (20), or a *that*-clause with *should* or a present subjunctive (21).

20 'Let's go early and avoid rush hour.' → I **suggested going** early and **avoiding** rush hour.

21 The police **recommended that** all unnecessary travel (**should**) **be** avoided in the meantime.

After some verbs with prepositions, such as *boast about*, we use a noun phrase or a gerund.

22 He **boasted about his win**. He **boasted about winning**. He **boasted about having won**.

- **Others: *admit to*, *cry out against*, *go on*, *go on (and on) about*, *insist on*, *object to*, *own up to***

With some reporting verbs, we summarize what was said rather than use a *that*-clause.

23 Bob said to Mary: 'I'm sorry for the delay.' → Bob **apologised** to Mary for the delay.
Mary said to Bob: 'I'm grateful for your support.' → Mary **thanked** Bob for his support.

Unit 12 Conditionals

Unreal conditionals

There are two basic types of unreal conditionals. We can use a hypothetical conditional (***if*** + past simple, *would*) to connect two imaginary or unlikely future events (1), and a counterfactual conditional (*if* + past perfect, *would have*) to connect two imaginary events in the past (2). The contracted form *'d* can be *had* in the *if*-clause and *would* in the main clause (3).

1 If we **had** enough time, we **would go** off on a Caribbean cruise. (= imaginary future)

2 If we **had had** more time, we **would have gone** on a Caribbean cruise. (= imaginary past)
If I **hadn't gone** to the conference, I **wouldn't have met** all those really smart people.

3 If **you'd** seen him, **you'd** have laughed. (= If you *had* seen him, you *would* have laughed.)

The most common modal in the main clause is ***would*** (***have***), but we also use other modals such as ***could*** (***have***), ***might*** (***have***) and ***should*** (***have***).

4 If I went by train, I **could go** via Oxford.
If we had taken the bus, it **might have been** cheaper.

- **We don't usually put *would*, *could*, *might* or *should* (+ *have*) in the *if*-clause.**

In a hypothetical conditional, we can use the past subjunctive *were* or *were* + infinitive instead of *was* (5) to talk about an imaginary situation. We can also use *happen to*, *should* or the expression *by any chance* when we think the imaginary situation might occur by accident, often before we make a request, usually in an informal style (6).

5 If I **were** you, I wouldn't worry.
If I **were to go** off on holiday, who would do my job?

6 If you **happen to** run into Angie, please ask her to call me.
If, **by any chance**, you see Pete, let me know.

Mixed unreal conditionals

In hypothetical conditionals, instead of connecting an imaginary event to a possible present or future event using *would* (7), we can connect it to a possible past event with *would have* (8).

7 If we **didn't have** our own financial problems, we **would give** more to charity.

8 If we **didn't have** our own financial problems, we **would have given** more to charity.

In counterfactual conditionals, instead of connecting an imaginary past event to another past event using *would have* (9), we can connect it to a present event or situation using *would* (10).

9 If your parents **hadn't met**, you **wouldn't have been** born.

10 If your parents **hadn't met**, you **wouldn't be** sitting here now.

Special conditionals: *only if*, *even if*, *what if*, etc.

We use *only if* to emphasize a special condition (11) and *if only* with an unreal conditional to express regret (12).

11 These can be used **only if** there is an emergency.
He'll come **only if** he's ordered to.

12 **If only** she had been wearing a seat belt, she could have survived the crash.

We use *even if* ('despite the possibility that') to say that a condition may exist, but it won't affect the future or possible situation described in the main clause.

13 We'll have a great time **even if** it rains.
Even if I can afford it, I don't want to buy a car.

We can use *what if* to introduce a question about a possible situation, often followed by another question.

14 **What if** we can't come up enough money for the rent next month? Will they kick us out?

We can use the expression *it is/was not as if* when we want to be clear that, despite appearances, something is not true.

15 I've met Simon for coffee a couple of times, but **it's not as if** we're a couple or anything.

We can use the expression *if and when* to talk about a future event that may or may not happen.

16 There could be a problem later, but we'll cross that bridge **if and when** we come to it.

When we want to refer back to something that has already been mentioned, we can reduce the *if*-clause to the positive form *If so* (17) or the negative form *If not* (18).

17 Some books may have missing pages. **If so**, they can be exchanged.

18 Rules really must be enforced. **If not**, they can easily be ignored. (= If they're not enforced.)

Conditionals without *if*: *unless*, *whether*, *supposing*, etc.

We can use inversion of the auxiliary verbs *had*, *should*, *were* and their subjects instead of an ***if***-clause to express a condition, usually in a formal style.

19 **Had we** thought it through a bit better, it wouldn't have been so chaotic. (= If we had ...)

20 **Should you** need an extra key, let me know and I'll get you one. (= If you should ...)

21 **Were it all** to go wrong, it would be my head on the chopping block. (= If it were to ...)

We use *unless* to say 'except under the following circumstances', or 'except if'. It is used to draw attention to the condition as an exception and sometimes means the same as *if ... not*.

22 He won't come **unless** you ask him. **Unless** we can get some help, we won't finish on time.

We can use *whether*, meaning 'it doesn't matter if', when there are two or more possibilities (23). We use *whether* (not *if*) with infinitives as possibilities (24).

23 **Whether** we win or lose, we always enjoy playing.
I love soup, **whether** it's hot or cold.

24 She still hasn't decided **whether** to start university next year or take a gap year and travel.

Instead of *if* as a conjunction, we can use *assuming* (*that*) to talk about a possible condition (25) and *provided/providing* (*that*) to talk about a necessary condition (26).

25 **Assuming (that)** the weather gets really bad, how are you going to get back home?

26 **Provided (that)** you have a permit, you shouldn't have any problems with parking.

- **Others used like this: *as/so long as*, *given* (*that*), *on condition that***

We can also use the prepositions *but for* (27) or *without* (28) + noun phrase (not a clause), meaning 'if there isn't/wasn't ...', to say that something is/was necessary.

27 **But for** the intervention of the central bank, the currency would have suffered badly.

28 **Without** new investment, the company will soon have to close its doors.

Information files

Unit 2, Introduction page 21, exercise 1

1 Farming and ranching account for the majority of the world's water use.
2 It takes 3 litres of water to produce 1 litre of bottled water.
3 Producing potatoes is more environmentally-friendly because it takes only 89 litres of water to produce 500 calories of potatoes, 251 for rice, 1,515 for poultry and 4,900 for beef.
4 25% of the world's mammals are facing extinction. Here are some of them and their numbers:
the Iberian lynx (Central and Southern Spain): 100–150
the Saiga antelope (Russia, Kazakhstan): 42,000
the Sumatran tiger: about 400
the silky sifafka (a lemur in Madagascar): 100–1,000
the Java rhino: fewer than 60
the South China tiger: 60 in captivity
the Cross River gorilla (Nigeria and Cameroon): 250–300
the Amur Leopard (Russia): 135 in the wild
5 8%
6 25%
7 The Great Pacific Garbage Patch is a collection of marine litter in the central North Pacific Ocean. Estimates of size range from 700,000 square kilometres to more than 15,000,000 square kilometres or 0.41% to 8.1% of the size of the Pacific Ocean.
8 150,000

Unit 3, Writing page 39, exercise 3

Alex Sharp is a bright / smart / sharp Cambridge graduate who works for a US research company based in Cairo. During one of his regular weekend visits to the bazaar, he comes across a(n) ancient / faded / weathered parchment in hieroglyphics which the stallholder says came from an ancient tomb. At some time in the past someone has tried to decipher the symbols and has written a translation in Arabic underneath. Alex is fascinated by / captivated by the parchment and buys it, determined to unravel its mysteries. As he does so, he begins to experience eerie / odd / bizarre / uncanny / peculiar parallels between the events related in the parchment and his own life and work on genetic engineering. The novel takes us on a(n) gripping / engrossing / riveting / spellbinding /mesmerizing journey between the ancient and new cities of Cairo. Alex is faced with tough / formidable / monumental / daunting / nail-biting challenges and momentous / life-and-death / tough decisions. We follow him on his journey which lurches from exhilarating breakthroughs to the chilling / spine-tingling realization of the real message of the parchment.

Unit 3, Speaking, Part 3 page 40, exercise 4

Instructions for Student A

1 You are going to be the interlocutor. Follow the instructions below. This is the prompt card for Student B:

> How much easier is it to learn a language nowadays than it was in the past?
> - technology
> - travel
> - learning techniques

2 Read aloud the words in *italics*.
So (Student B), *I'm going to give you a card with a question written on it and I'd like you to tell us what you think. There are also some ideas on the card for you to use if you like. All right? Here is your card. Please let* (Student C) *see your card. Remember* (Student B) *you have about two minutes to talk before we join in. Would you like to begin now?*
3 Stop Student B after two minutes by saying *Thank you.*
4 Then ask Student C this question:
Why do you think some people find it more difficult than others to learn a language?
5 After about 20 seconds invite Student B to join in with the following prompt:
What do you think?
6 Let Student B and Student C talk together for about 30 seconds.
7 End the discussion by saying *Thank you.*

Unit 4, Speaking Part 3, page 45, exercise 2

Instructions for Student A

1 You are going to speak for about two minutes. Here is your prompt card:

> What can sometimes make international relations difficult?
> - language barrier
> - cultural differences
> - previous history

2 After about two minutes, ask Student B this question:
How easy do you think it is for people from different cultures to really understand each other?
3 Then, after about 30 seconds, briefly say whether you agree or disagree with Student B.

Unit 3, Speaking, Part 3 page 40, exercise 4

Instructions for Student B

1 You are going to be the interlocutor. Follow the instructions below. This is the prompt card for Student C:

> What cultural misunderstandings can arise when someone lives and works in a foreign country?
> – body language
> – greetings
> – customs and habits

2 Read aloud the words in *italics*.
So (Student C), *I'm going to give you a card with a question written on it and I'd like you to tell us what you think. There are also some ideas on the card for you to use if you like. All right? Here is your card. Please let* (Student A) *see your card. Remember* (Student C) *you have about two minutes to talk before we join in. Would you like to begin now?*

3 Stop Student C after two minutes by saying *Thank you*.

4 Then ask Student A this question:
How can we prevent cultural misunderstandings?

5 After about 20 seconds invite Student A to join in with the following prompt:
What do you think?

6 Let Student A and Student C talk together for about 30 seconds.

7 End the discussion by saying *Thank you*.

Unit 4, Speaking, Part 3 page 45, exercise 2

Instructions for Student B

1 You are going to speak for about two minutes. Here is your prompt card:

> How can governments help to improve international relations?
> – promoting learning of other languages
> – working together for the common good
> – preventing further conflict

2 After about two minutes, ask Student A this question:
How can individuals help to improve international relations? What do you think the future of organizations like the UN will be?

3 Then, after about 30 seconds, briefly say whether you agree or disagree with Student A.

Unit 5, Introduction page 51, exercise 1

Official statistical ranking	Days of life expectancy lost
being male rather than female	2,700
remaining unmarried	1,800
being a coal miner	1,500
riding in cars (15,000 kilometres per year)	200
choking on food	12
being struck by lightning	6
being bitten by an animal or insect	0.3
exposure to radiation	0.05

Unit 5, Speaking, Part 3 page 58 exercise 6

Instructions for Student A

1 You are going to speak for about two minutes. Here is your prompt card:

> What risks do people face in the modern world?
> – travelling
> – environmental problems
> – crime

2 After about two minutes, ask Student B this question:
To what extent do we have control over our own safety?

3 Then, after about 30 seconds, briefly say whether you agree or disagree with Student B.

Unit 8, Reading & Use of English Part 4, page 82, exercise 2

The jury retired, and coming to a decision was not difficult. The jury returned with a verdict of 'Not guilty' on all charges. Owen was relieved to leave the court a free man.

Unit 10, Introduction page 101, exercise 2

40% = Eating out
21% = Mobile phones
16% = Music
11% = Film
7% = Sport
5% = Video games / gaming

Unit 3, Speaking, Part 3 page 40, exercise 4

Instructions for Student C

1 You are going to be the interlocutor. Follow the instructions below. This is the prompt card for Student A:

> How has modern technology affected the way we communicate?
> - social life
> - education
> - work

2 Read aloud the words in *italics*.

So (Student A), *I'm going to give you a card with a question written on it and I'd like you to tell us what you think. There are also some ideas on the card for you to use if you like. All right? Here is your card. Please let* (Student B) *see your card. Remember* (Student A) *you have about two minutes to talk before we join in. Would you like to begin now?*

3 Stop Student A after two minutes by saying *Thank you*.

4 Then ask Student B this question:
Do you think that because of new technology we might lose the ability to communicate face-to-face?

5 After about 20 seconds invite Student A to join in with the following prompt:
What do you think?

6 Let Student A and Student B talk together for about 30 seconds.

7 End the discussion by saying *Thank you*.

Unit 5, Speaking Part 3, page 58, exercise 6

Instructions for Student B

1 You are going to speak for about two minutes. Here is your prompt card:

> In what ways are we exposed to fewer dangers than previous generations?
> - new technology
> - medical breakthroughs
> - rules and regulations

2 After about two minutes, ask Student A this question:
What dangers might our planet face in the future?

3 Then, after about 30 seconds, briefly say whether you agree or disagree with Student A.

Unit 1 Review

Vocabulary

1 Fill in the missing letters to write words and expressions meaning the *opposite* of the words below. (The missing words all appear in Unit 1.)

Example: *vivid: f u z z y*

a cherished/comforting: tr___m___c
b lingering/lasting: f___t__g
c disturbing/unwelcome: tr______d
d to conjure up: to bl__o__
e original/innovative: h__kn___d
f conventional/predictable: ec____r_c
g realistic/true-to-life: u_c_n______g
h wonderful/marvellous: at__c___s
i glamorous/extraordinary: m__d__e

Exam practice

Reading & Use of English, Part 1

2 Read the text below. For questions 1–8, decide which answer (A, B, C, or D) best fits each gap.

The sights and smells of Moroccan markets

As you approach the city of Fes, you are (0) ___C___ by the incredible noise of the traffic. Roads are unmarked, there are no traffic lights, and people are sounding their car horns all the time, (1) ______ a terrible din. The traffic noise abates once you enter the market, as the streets are too narrow for cars to get (2) ______.

The medina (market) of Fes has a unique smell that is hard to describe, and even harder to forget. It smells (3) ______ raw meat that has been in the sun too long, combined with the stench of (4) ______ oil and olives. The sound of flies buzzing is everywhere.

It is easy to escape from this smell if you enter a pharmacy. The shopkeeper speaks both Arabic and English fluently. He listens (5) ______ to his customers and then tells them what medicines they need. Giant bottles of herbs and spices give (6) ______ a fragrant scent of fresh mint and lavender.

There is a restaurant nearby, where lunch is being served. Big platters of fresh vegetables come out first, but many tourists (7) ______ clear of raw vegetables in case they get ill from the water they were washed in. Then, the main course is served — curried chicken. It looks and smells appetizing and tastes delicious. The diners eat it with relish, (8) ______ down with cola, even though many of them have seen chickens being killed in the market just a few minutes earlier.

	A	B	C	D
0	*A arrested*	*B dazed*	*(C) overwhelmed*	*D taken over*
1	A creating	B making	C leaving	D sounding
2	A by	B along	C across	D through
3	A as	B from	C of	D with
4	A old	B rancid	C acrid	D stale
5	A thoroughly	B fully	C fluently	D intently
6	A off	B away	C out	D up
7	A drive	B stand	C steer	D stay
8	A cooled	B poured	C washed	D glugged

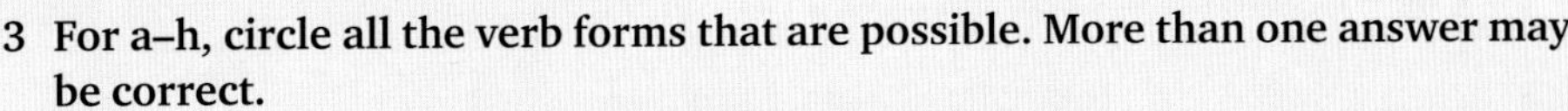

Grammar

Past tenses and *would*

3 For a–h, circle all the verb forms that are possible. More than one answer may be correct.

a I ________ with my parents when I met Carol for the first time.
1 lived 2 was living 3 had lived

b He ________ me just as I was about to have dinner. It was so annoying!
1 always phoned 2 would always phone 3 always used to phone

c I ________ that she would at least listen to what I had to say, but she didn't.
1 would hope 2 was hoping 3 had hoped

d I'm feeling really exhausted. Would you mind if we ________ go out tonight?
1 don't 2 didn't 3 wouldn't

e I ________ a big car when I lived in the country, but now I've got a smaller one.
1 used to drive 2 would drive 3 drove

f We asked them if we could pay for dinner but they ________ of it.
1 didn't hear 2 wouldn't hear 3 hadn't heard

g When I saw my first Harley Davidson, I knew that one day I ________ one.
1 would buy 2 'd buy 3 'll buy

h You ________ to bring your wallet. Typical! You're always forgetting it!
1 would forget 2 'd forget 3 've forgotten

Writing

Set text preparation

4 Choose the correct word in *italics* in each sentence to complete the advice on answering set text questions.

a Make notes on aspects of the *personality / setting*, such as the time and place.
b Compare the *attitudes / characters* in the book to those of the modern day.
c Make notes on the characters' *personality / relevance* and appearance.
d Make notes on how *settings / relationships* develop through the book.
e Watch a film *version / summary* after reading the book and note any differences.
f Write a *summary / quote* of each chapter.
g Don't spend too much time studying the minor *characters / attitudes*.
h *Suspense / Setting* is key to maintaining reader interest in any genre.
i Learn *quotes / relationships* about people, places and events to support your answer.
j It is important that everything you write has *relevance / suspense*.

5 Write a paragraph explaining your views on one of the following:

a Why is the setting as important as the characters and plot?
b Why is the opening as important as the climax?
c Why is suspense important in maintaining reader interest?

Speaking

Link words

6 Here are some candidates' replies to the question: *How important is it for you to travel?* Circle the best option from the words in *italics*.

a *Well, / So, / I have to say*, I've always enjoyed travelling.
b I want to go to an English-speaking country, *so / so that / because* I've got my heart set on a trip to America.
c I don't like long plane journeys. *Because, / So, / I must admit*, I'm a bit scared of flying.
d I wouldn't want to travel by sea. *Actually, / Well, / So*, I get very seasick.
e I really enjoy visiting big cities. *On the other hand, / I have to say, / I must admit* I love the countryside, too.
f I'd like to be near the mountains *because / so that / so as* I can go skiing.

Unit 2 Review

Vocabulary

1 Complete the definitions and sentences with words from Unit 2.

a Something that affects the whole world can be said to have a g .... i ....

b Cities that have g .... s .... are easier to live in than crowded ones.

c Resources which can be replaced are r ....

d When a piece of research affects how people think and behave, it can be described as i ....

e A group of animals or plants which can breed together is defined as a s ....

f We have detected increased levels of r .... near the nuclear reactor.

g Something with disastrous consequences can be described as c ....

h When animals are becoming extinct, we can say that they are d .... o ....

i S .... resources last for a long time; using them helps to protect the environment.

j Most scientists believe that human behaviour has an i .... o .... the environment.

Exam practice

Reading & Use of English, Part 2

2 For questions 1–8, read the text below and think of the word which best fits each space. Use only one word in each space. There is an example at the beginning (0).

The world about us

Pressure groups (0) *such* as Greenpeace and Friends of the Earth have done a considerable amount to change the attitude of the general public towards environmental problems. However, their once strident voices of protest now sound (1) .... from being extreme, and politicians from all parts of the world have begun to realize that global warming is a very real problem which they are having to (2) .... much more seriously now than they ever did in the past. Nevertheless, this is (3) .... the time to be complacent because (4) .... radical practical measures are put in place quickly, in years to (5) .... , the situation will only get worse. (6) .... the way things were in the past, from now on we will not be able to get (7) .... on our current reserves of energy sources and we will have to look (8) .... for substitutes.

Grammar

Future forms

3 Only two of the sentences in a–j are correct. Find the mistakes in the other sentences and correct them. More than one answer may be correct.

a Once supplies of oil will run out, we will need to find alternative sources of energy.

b The Environment minister is about to make an important statement tomorrow afternoon.

c By the time the government introduces a law to ban illegal fishing, fish stocks will have decreased significantly.

d Here's my prediction. Ten years from now we'll still have relied on oil for most of our energy needs.

e The conference on global warming is going to start on the 4th of June.

f Nuclear power is certainly to be a controversial issue in the future.

g If the panda is to survive as a species, we need to act to protect it now.

h I'm thinking of buying an electric car next year if it won't be too expensive.

i It's likely to be another volcanic eruption during the next ten years.

j Public transport will need to improve a great deal if more people will agree to give up their cars.

Writing

Paraphrasing

4 Paraphrase sentences a–d, starting with the words given.

a Research and development related to more environmentally-friendly products can have significant long-term benefits.

There are ....

....

b Currently, there is no reliable system to warn future generations about the existence of nuclear waste dumps.

We don't ....

....

c Scientists consider African elephants to be keystone species as they help to maintain suitable habitats for many other species in savannah and forest ecosystems.

The role ....

....

d It's high time that the government introduced legislation prohibiting the use of wild animals in circuses.

The government needs ....

....

5 Look at the following two opposing opinions on the environment. Paraphrase the one you most agree with and incorporate it into a paragraph on the topic.

a Hunting is completely necessary to ensure adequate protection of agriculture and the environment from animal pests or overpopulation.

b The basic interests of the hunted animals are seriously violated in order to satisfy less basic human interests.

Speaking

Generalizations

6 For a–e, rephrase the sentence below in six different ways by filling in the missing words. The first letter of each word is given.

People are aware of the benefits of recycling nowadays.

Example: G*enerally* s*peaking*, *people are aware of the benefits of recycling nowadays.*

a O.................... t.................... w...................., people are aware of the benefits of recycling nowadays.

b People are l.................... aware of the benefits of recycling nowadays.

c B.................... a.................... l.................... people are aware of the benefits of recycling nowadays.

d B.................... s...................., people are aware of the benefits of recycling nowadays.

e It s.................... a.................... i.................... people are aware of the benefits of recycling nowadays.

Unit 3 Review

Vocabulary

1 Complete sentences a–j with a suitable word from the list below, making any necessary changes to the word.

auspicious coherent care plausible grateful proportionate connect alcoholic literate relent

a The singer was worn down by the ______ pressure of work and the constant attention of his fans.

b The previous owners of the flat had had the phone ______ so we had to contact the telephone company to get it working again.

c She didn't even thank me for my present – I couldn't believe she was so ______.

d The barrister complained that the long prison sentence was ______ to the seriousness of the crime her client had committed.

e I don't really believe in fate, but even I felt that the fire at the theatre on the first night was a rather ______ start.

f He never learned to read or write and remained ______ for the rest of his life.

g As I'm driving, I'd rather have a ______ drink like orange juice or iced tea.

h I couldn't understand a word he was saying on the phone – because of the fever, he had become totally ______.

i The composition you wrote was interesting but it was spoiled by a number of ______ mistakes.

j Her excuse about having to work all weekend sounded a bit ______; I suspect she didn't really want to come to the party.

Exam practice

Reading & Use of English, Part 3

2 For questions 1–8, read the text below. Use the word given in capitals at the end of some of the lines to form a word that fits in the space in the same line. There is an example at the beginning (0).

A very Welsh poet?

Dylan Thomas (1914–1953) was born in South Wales. (0) *Unlike* many of his contemporaries, he knew	LIKE
no Welsh. He began to write poetry at school, and worked as a journalist before moving to London in1934; his	
first volume of verse, (1) ______ *18 Poems*, appeared that year. He then embarked on a career in the	TITLE
media, spending much time in the (2) ______ popular afternoon drinking clubs of the era.	INCREASE
In 1937, Thomas married Caitlin Macnamara; they settled temporarily at Laugharne in Wales, returning there	
permanently in 1949. There were some allegations that Thomas had deliberately sought obscurity, but these	
may well have (3) ______ Thomas's true motives for settling in Wales. Despite this, he gradually won an	REPRESENT
(4) ______ following for his writing. His manuscripts, evidence of his (5) ______ perfectionism,	DENY, RELENT
reveal him as a (6) ______, even obsessional, craftsman.	PASSION
He enjoyed (7) ______ popularity as an entertainer on radio. In 1950, he undertook the first of his	PRECEDENT
lecture tours to the United States. Legend grew about his (8) ______ habit of drinking at all hours of	VARY
the day and night. Shortly before his death, he took part in a reading in New York of what was to be his most famous single work, *Under Milk Wood*.	

Grammar

Focus and emphasis

3 Rewrite sentences a–g beginning with the words given to emphasize the words in *italics*. There may be more than one correct answer for each sentence.

a Not only the male but also *the female characters* in the novels are memorable.
It ______________________________.

b The public really appreciated *the writer's colourful style*.
What ______________________________.

c Many famous novels first appeared *in serial form in magazines*.
It ______________________________.

d *Both Dickens and Dylan Thomas* are famous for giving lectures in the USA.
It ______________________________.

e I don't understand *why it is so hard to make a living as a writer*.
What ______________________________.

f I only studied *works by Shakespeare and Dickens* at school.
All ______________________________.

g You must have read *the second volume of the series*, not the first.
It ______________________________.

Writing

Creating interest

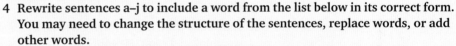

4 Rewrite sentences a–j to include a word from the list below in its correct form. You may need to change the structure of the sentences, replace words, or add other words.

claim chill ravel obsess expect reveal prime major passion title

a The book is called *A Mexican Adventure*.
b Jim never reads: all he ever thinks about is football.
c The author's latest novel is a love story full of deep feelings.
d The short story is a terrifying account of someone alone in a haunted house.
e We only discover the identity of the murderer in the last chapter of the novel.
f Brad said he had written a best-selling novel, but I'm not sure if he was being serious.
g Most of her novels were written several years ago.
h The ending of the story is a bit of a surprise.
i The plot of the story is a very difficult one to work out.
j The book is mainly about a revolutionary hero.

5 Look at the painting on page 37. Write a short paragraph describing it and saying what the artist is trying to achieve. Include your opinion of the painting.

Speaking

Introducing examples

6 Below is a transcript of a student responding to the question 'How important is speaking several foreign languages for getting a job?' Fill in the gaps with words and phrases from the list. You do not need three of them: which ones?

as as far as could say how in terms of it comes to
it goes to let me see suppose taking what

Well, (1)__________ . I believe that (2)__________ employability, languages are extremely important.

I (3)__________ that, (4)__________ companies are concerned, applicants who speak several languages have an advantage.

So, (5)__________ service sector jobs as an example, you (6)__________ that languages have a special role.

When (7)__________ a person's first job, there are a lot of different – (8)__________ can I put it? – factors to consider.

Unit 4 Review

s	t	i	c	k	i	t	o	u	t	r	n	o	e	t	l	t	e	m
h	s	s	e	e	e	o	d	s	s	h	s	o	o	t	i	e	t	y
t	u	c	s	e	v	a	w	g	n	i	k	a	m	s	p	v	i	t
u	s	e	h	y	e	f	e	h	o	u	s	e	o	n	f	i	r	e
r	t	t	f	r	i	o	u	n	s	i	e	s	u	n	i	t	c	t
t	a	s	d	a	r	s	e	h	y	e	s	n	h	c	i	r	o	h
e	i	e	s	e	e	h	c	d	n	a	k	l	a	h	c	e	p	e
m	n	w	c	s	s	e	n	s	s	e	l	t	c	a	t	s	y	r
o	f	f	y	o	u	r	c	h	e	s	t	e	a	r	e	s	h	v
h	m	e	u	y	n	i	n	u	u	m	c	o	c	e	i	a	o	s

Vocabulary

1 Find these words and expressions in the word square. The words go in any direction.

a When I first met my new neighbour, I really liked him straight away. In fact, we got on like a h__________. (3 words)

b My father hates confrontations. He really doesn't like m__________. (2 words)

c My sister and I are completely different from each other. People say we're like c__________. (3 words)

d What my boss said about me was true, but I didn't like it. She told me some h__________. (2 words)

e He's always upsetting other people. His t__________ is a real problem. (1 word)

f I'm not enjoying my new job, but I need the money so I've decided to s__________. (3 words)

g I d__________ being alone. I always need to have people around me. (1 word)

h You're much too timid. You need to be a lot more a__________ and tell people what you think and want. (1 word)

i She says she cares about the environment but she drives everywhere and never walks or cycles. She's such a h__________. (1 word)

j He is not good at talking to people, so he finds it hard to s__________ relationships. (1 word)

k The children are behaving so badly that I'm at the end of m__________. (2 words)

Exam practice

Reading & Use of English, Part 4

2 For questions 1–6, complete the second sentence so that it has a similar meaning to the first sentence, using the word given. Do not change the word given. You must use between three and eight words, including the word given.

1 Explaining what you mean to an audience can be difficult.
across
It's sometimes difficult ____________________ to an audience.

2 If something's worrying you, you should tell me about it now.
chest
If you have a problem, why don't you ____________________ now?

3 I think you should confront your boss right now with how you feel about this.
out
Why don't you ____________________ your boss right now?

4 Anna had decided Tom was not telling the truth about what happened.
teeth
Anna was sure Tom ____________________ about what happened.

5 Perhaps my sister was bad-tempered because she was tired.
fact
I put my sister's ____________________ she was tired.

6 I think you need to work hard to make a relationship a success.
more
I think ____________________, the better it will be.

Grammar

Perfect aspect

3 Which option in *italics* in each sentence is NOT correct?

a *Having travelled / Travelling / To travel* all over the world, I feel I'm a real global citizen.

b Lack of communication is known *to cause / to have caused / having caused* the breakdown of many a relationship.

c I'm always pleased *making / to make / to have made* new friends.

Perfect and continuous aspect

4 Put the verbs in brackets in the correct tense. More than one answer may be correct.

I (1) ______ (wait) for a bus for ages on Saturday when I suddenly (2) ______ (realize) that my friend Julia (3) ______ (stand) in the same queue. Julia and I (4) ______ (be) friends for a very long time. Ever since we (5) ______ (first/meet), we (6) ______ (always/confide) in one another. Julia has a fiancé called Bob. They (7) ______ (only/go) out for about six months when they (8) ______ (decide) to get engaged. They get on well together and for the last few months they (9) ______ (plan) their wedding, which is in two weeks. Unfortunately, Julia confessed to me that she (10) ______ (changed) her mind. She feels that she (11) ______ (lead) a very sheltered life so she (12) ______ (accept) a job in another part of the country. The problem is that she (13) ______ (not/tell) Bob yet and she (14) ______ (agonize) for weeks about how he'll take it.

Writing

Cause and effect

5 Use the words in the lists to complete the sentences below. You may need to change the form of the words.

be rooted in   respond to   on account of   hence   result in

a Genetics are the basic blueprint of life, ______ people argue this is strongly linked to behaviour.

b What triggers criminal behaviour is a challenging question to ______.

c The criminal behaviour of parents can ______ similar behaviour by children.

d Some argue that poor behaviour ______ society not genetics.

e It is ______ both genetics and environment that criminal tendencies occur.

mean that   account for   as   provoke   as a result of

f The laws of genetics ______ blue-eyed parents will often have a blue-eyed child.

g The nature versus nurture debate still ______ much argument and discussion.

h The extent to which the environment ______ the shaping of individual behaviour is difficult to determine.

i The argument is likely to continue, ______ it is impossible to prove conclusively that one element overrides the other.

j ______ scientific developments, we are starting to understand the influences of genetics on shaping who we are.

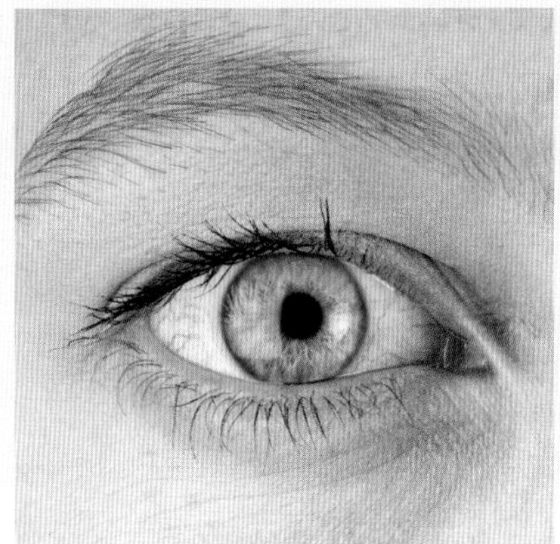

6 Write a paragraph discussing whether personalities are determined by nature or nurture. Refer to two people brought up in the same family. Use cause/effect expressions and vocabulary from the Unit 4 Writing section.

Speaking

Discourse markers

7 Fill in the missing words in these discourse markers.

a I'm not keen on meeting people at parties. Mind ______, I don't go to many.

b From my ______ of view, people are the same all over the world.

c As ______ as friendships are concerned, I prefer to have just a few close ones.

d He isn't very good at his job. ______ more, he's always late for work.

e ______ the way, did I tell you who I met on the train last night?

Unit 5 Review

Vocabulary

1 Fill in the missing letters to write words and expressions from Unit 5.

a He needs to s________ u___ f______ himself more, and not always agree to do what other people tell him.

b I'd like to do a bungee-jump, but at the moment it seems too d____________g.

c We felt so excited when we got to the top of the mountain – it was really e________________g.

d As we walked further into the jungle, I caught a g____________ of a snake moving slowly towards us.

e Even though I'm scared of heights, as we crossed the bridge I g____________ at the river below.

f I'm afraid I m________ h__________ weather of putting up the tent, as I'd never done it before.

g I think we might be running low on petrol, so we need to ________p a weather eye on the fuel gauge.

h Rumours of the accident s__________ like wildfire, so the company was forced to issue a statement.

i After the accident, the police carried out a p________________g search of the area where it had taken place.

Exam practice

Reading & Use of English, Part 1

2 Read the article below and for questions 1–8, decide which answer (A, B, C or D) best fits each gap. There is an example at the beginning (0).

Be safe, not sorry

Anyone (0) ____C____ in outdoor sporting activities, or (1) ____________ with a desire to outperform their peers, will be more aware that from a health and safety (2) ____________, they are (3) ____________ themselves to far more risks than the average person. After a recent slalom race, expert skier and free-rider Chris Mantaw declared that fear is an essential (4) ____________ of any sport, but injuries ought not to be regarded as unavoidable side-effects. When free-riding you can make use of the whole mountain, and can (5) ____________ conditions you do not find on the piste. However, with that freedom (6) ____________ added risk, so how do you cope with the visible and hidden dangers? Short of campaigning to have anyone with a (7) ____________ attitude banned from participating in sports, the best (8) ____________ is to buy a helmet, wear protective clothing and check your equipment regularly.

	A	B	C	D
0	*A connected*	*B embarked*	*(C) involved*	*D hooked*
1	A flaring	B driving	C flaming	D burning
2	A presumption	B probability	C perspective	D prospect
3	A uncovering	B exhibiting	C manifesting	D exposing
4	A point	B part	C period	D place
5	A experience	B live	C feel	D undergo
6	A falls	B comes	C brings	D renders
7	A careless	B negligent	C distracted	D reckless
8	A opportunity	B option	C selection	D preference

Grammar

Modal verbs

3 Choose the most appropriate modal verb to complete each sentence.

a I think this dead tree *must / should / ought to* have been struck by lightning.

b If the safety inspector isn't there when you arrive, you *might / would / could* always leave a message for him.

c If we'd known it was going to be too wet to walk today, we *shouldn't / wouldn't / couldn't* have brought our hiking boots.

d It *couldn't / shouldn't / mightn't* have been a wolf that you saw because there aren't any in this area.

e You *should have not / didn't need to have / could have not* bought travel insurance, as we are all covered by my company policy.

f They look as if they have sunburn; they *would / should / might* have used sun-lotion.

g If I'd known your email address, I *wouldn't / shouldn't / can't* have bothered phoning you.

h You *must / can't / could* have been terrified when you lost your way in the forest.

Writing

Expressing opinions

4 Complete the following sentences with words from Unit 5.

a ______ said that, it is also true that the use of cycling helmets has saved lives.

b I don't agree that legislation is the way forward. ______ we need is a public campaign.

c To ______ up, I think that people should not be encouraged to look for someone to blame when they have an accident.

d The council is keen to install more speed cameras, which are a complete ______ of time and money.

e It is ______ important that we tackle the issue of road safety.

5 Write sentences expressing opinions on the following topics.

a Health and safety legislation

b Drink-driving laws

c Banning tobacco

d Limiting road speeds

Speaking

Expressing opinions

6 Use the words in the list to fill in the gaps in the sentences below. Five of the words do not fit in.

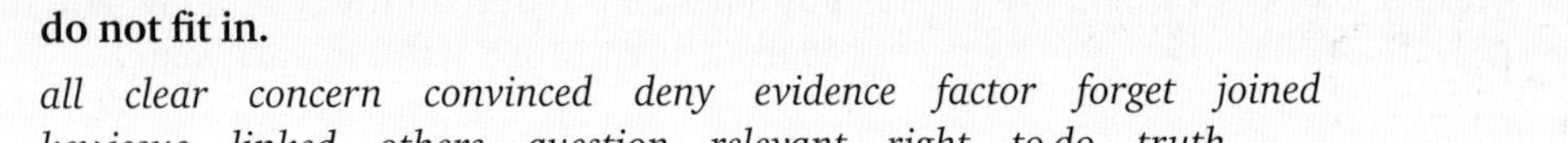
all clear concern convinced deny evidence factor forget joined key issue linked others question relevant right to do truth

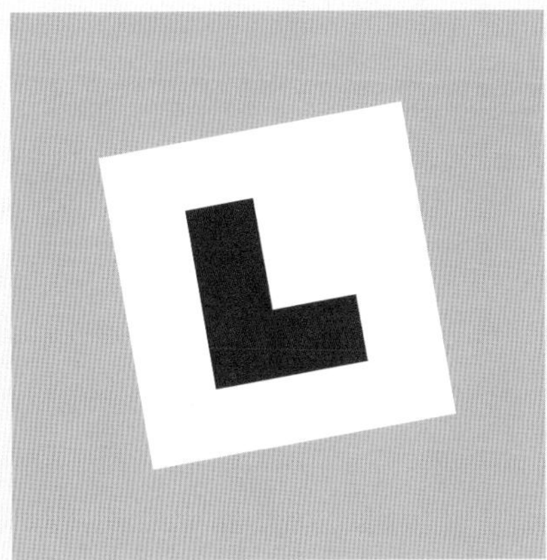

a I'm totally ______ that the driving test needs to be made more challenging.

b You can't ______ that the driving test needs to be made more challenging.

c It's absolutely ______ to me that the driving test needs to be made more challenging.

d For me, it's much more a ______ of individual responsibility.

e I think individual responsibility is a much more important ______.

f The ______ for me is that of personal responsibility.

g There is some ______ in that, I suppose.

h What you're saying might be ______.

i Maybe you're right in some ways, but not ______.

j I'm not sure how closely ______ it is to driving speeds.

k I'm not sure that driving speeds are especially ______.

l I'm not really sure that driving speeds have much ______ with it.

Unit 6 Review

Vocabulary

1 Complete the crossword using the clues below.

Across

4 In order to lose weight successfully, you need to reduce your calorie ________ and take more exercise.

5 Access to healthcare is unequal across the country, but the government wants to create a ________ playing field.

6 Adjective: someone (e.g. a gymnast) who is able to move and bend their body easily can be described as ________.

8 You shouldn't go back to work until you feel completely better. Flu can really take ________ you. (3 words)

10 The doctor explained the operation to me, but I was so anxious that I found it hard to ________ all the details. (2 words)

11 The government is keen to help people who are ________ to cigarettes to stop smoking.

Down

1 All nurses have to ________ rigorous training.

2 He tries to attend every match his team plays during the season. He's a real ________ of football.

3 The doctor told me that improving my diet would be ________ to my health.

6 I'm very ________ about trendy diets: to lose weight, you need to eat less and exercise more.

7 Tennis players are particularly ________ to arm and leg injuries.

9 I'm afraid I can't advise you on your child's health problems; that's not my ________. You need to consult a paediatrician.

Exam practice

Reading & Use of English, Part 2

2 For questions 1–8, read the text below and think of the word which best fits each space. Use only one word in each space.

Yoga

There can be hardly anyone who has not heard of yoga, and (1) ________ you are 16 or 60, you can reap the benefits of taking (2) ________ in a yoga class. Yoga is a system of training the body and the mind. Its goal is to (3) ________ it easier for people to remove all distractions preventing them living a life of the spirit in union with their Maker. Reaching this state is (4) ________ greater a challenge than might be imagined. The main emphasis of the physical training is (5) ________ bringing the body under complete control in such areas as the regulation of breathing and the flexibility of the muscles, (6) ________ of which are instrumental in controlling our overall movements. The mental training, as (7) ________ as the modifications to the behaviour of the physical body, make undisturbed concentration possible. So perhaps it's (8) ________ we all headed for the nearest yoga class and started training right now.

Grammar

Relative and reduced clauses

3 **Complete sentences a–h with one or two words. More than one answer may be correct.**

a That personal fitness trainer, ______ DVD made millions, is appearing on TV.
b Cycling and running, both ______ I enjoy, are effective forms of exercise.
c We all want better hospitals, but ______ money should they be paid for?
d The man ______ was recently appointed as our new team manager is well known to everybody.
e Tom goes jogging every day, ______ is obviously good for his fitness regime.
f The girl ______ came to see me last night is my cousin.
g The free concert ______ was held in the park last night was attended by hundreds of people.

4 **Rewrite the two sentences in exercise 3 where no additional words are needed.**

Writing

Exemplification

5 **Match the statements a–e to the examples 1–5.**

a Technology has introduced a number of conveniences that we now take for granted.
b Western diets are having a negative influence on those of other countries.
c Working life has become extremely sedentary.
d A number of changes have increased the time we spend on leisure activities.
e People now have a wider and more varied diet than in the past.

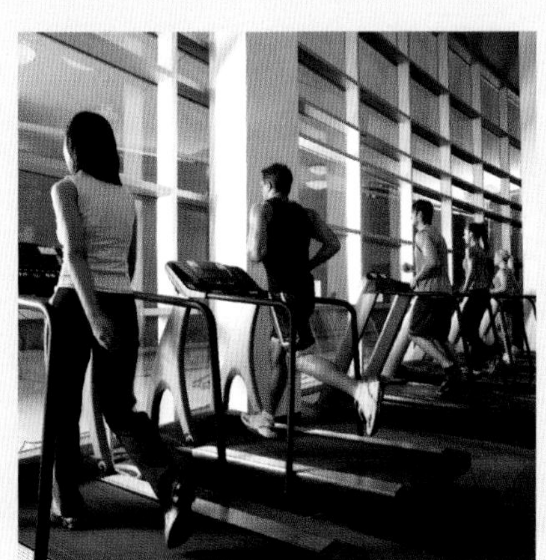

1 True, many people go to the gym, but this doesn't necessarily compensate for the loss of movement in our everyday routines.
2 Take my mother, for example. She'd never even eaten pasta until five years ago, and now she tries all cuisines.
3 Like most people, I just couldn't cope without a washing machine or dishwasher.
4 Just taking Japan as an example, the increasing number of fast-food joints there is being linked to the sharp rise in obesity among young people.
5 Gym membership is at an all-time high, for example.

6 **Write a paragraph of an article for a magazine on 'The division of labour within families and its effect on the amount of leisure time people have'. Use an informal style and include examples. Use vocabulary from the Unit 6 Writing section.**

Speaking

Suggesting alternatives

7 **Here are some ways of suggesting alternatives. Match a–e to 1–5.**

a I suppose we could …
b Maybe what's needed …
c Why don't we …
d I guess we need …
e I was wondering whether …

1 … is a government initiative to promote healthy living.
2 … new ways of encouraging people to eat healthier food.
3 … always increase the cost of unhealthy food, such as fast food and snacks.
4 … have a bicycle rental scheme in our cities?
5 … subsidizing gym membership might be a better solution.

Unit 7 Review

Vocabulary

l	l	c	a	t	a	s	t	r	o	p	h	e	a	q	e	t	a	l
d	i	s	e	n	t	a	n	g	l	e	p	l	l	t	r	a	i	n
e	y	g	y	q	e	s	t	e	t	m	t	t	a	n	e	s	t	k
s	h	n	h	a	t	g	l	w	r	e	k	c	i	l	f	e	a	n
e	n	i	i	t	w	l	e	t	r	e	o	e	n	l	i	o	r	l
i	v	s	l	g	y	h	p	a	e	l	m	u	t	n	a	u	q	t
o	s	o	u	n	s	e	t	t	l	i	n	g	p	h	t	l	l	v
l	m	p	l	n	e	i	a	a	o	l	s	l	l	s	g	y	e	a
n	a	m	n	v	o	n	e	r	p	e	t	l	c	e	o	u	h	t
a	q	i	v	n	e	r	l	t	s	e	u	q	h	y	t	a	i	r

1 Find these words and expressions in the word square. The words can go in any direction.

a The routes which connect one part of the brain to the other are known as neural p__________.

b A verb meaning *to change over a long period of time*: e__________

c A noun meaning *a change*: a__________

d A noun meaning *a disaster*: c__________

e If the government spends more on scientific research, it will need to r__________ resources from elsewhere.

f When considering the risk of the Earth being hit by an asteroid, we need to d__________ fact from fiction.

g A noun meaning *a search*; often used to describe something important, such as scientists' seeking knowledge: a q__________.

h An adjective meaning *impressive to look at*: i__________

i An adjective meaning *disturbing, worrying*: u__________

j The power supply suddenly dropped, causing the lights to f__________.

k A scientific expression, commonly used to mean *a big and sudden change*: q__________ l__________

l Our research programme will give us a huge advantage. It'll put us l__________ y__________ ahead of our competitors.

Exam practice

Reading & Use of English, Part 3

2 For questions 1–8, use the word in capitals at the end of some of the lines to form a word that fits in the space in the same line. There is an example at the beginning (0).

The difference engine

Charles Babbage was born in 1791, the son of a London banker. As a youth, he was his own instructor	
in algebra, of which he was (0) *passionately* fond. In his twenties, Babbage developed an interest in	PASSION
calculating machinery which became his (1) __________ passion for the (2) __________ of his life. In	CONSUME, REMAIN
1821, he invented the Difference Engine for compiling mathematical tables. On completing it, he conceived	
the idea of a better machine, the Analytical Engine, which is (3) __________, because it had some of the	SIGNIFY
(4) __________ of today's computers.	CHARACTER
(5) __________, little remains of Babbage's prototype computing machines. Throughout his life,	FORTUNE
Babbage worked in many different fields, and made contributions that would have assured his fame	
(6) __________ of his work on the Difference and Analytical Engines. However, despite his many	RESPECT
achievements, he was (7) __________ in constructing his calculating machines, and in particular the	SUCCESS
refusal of the government to support his work, left Babbage in his (8) __________ years a disappointed	DECLINE
and embittered man.	

Grammar

Stative verbs: simple and continuous

3 For each sentence a–j, choose the correct option: 1, 2, or 3.

a It ________ that the price of smartphones is going to fall dramatically.
1 seems 2 's seeming 3 Both are possible

b How ________ today?
1 do you feel 2 are you feeling 3 Both are possible

c The ________ of the new system has been put back until next year.
1 introduction 2 introducing 3 Both are possible

d What I ________ is that you get someone to install your new computer system instead of trying to do it yourself.
1 suggest 2 'm suggesting 3 Both are possible

e I ________ to buy a new television for some time now. Ours is just too old to cope with the new technology.
1 've meant 2 've been meaning 3 Both are possible

f I ________ astronomy at university, and this year the lectures are fascinating.
1 study 2 'm studying 3 Both are possible

g I can't remember whether James ________ computer games or not these days. Maybe he has other interests now.
1 likes to play 2 is liking playing 3 Both are possible

h His ________ to my letter does not mean that he accepts my concerns; it depends on what he actually does.
1 response 2 responding 3 Both are possible

Writing

Evaluative language

4 Complete sentences a–f with a suitable word. More than one answer may be possible.

a The author never br________ the question of cyber-crime and whether or not our systems are secure.

b His basic as________ is technology provides us with more free time.

c This summary only t________ on what is a much deeper issue.

d I w________ completely disagree with the a________ that the internet has been the greatest invention of our time.

e The argument r________ solely on the pr________ that we will still be using the internet in twenty years.

f He fails to c________ the impact this technology is having on our brains.

5 Using a range of evaluative language, write a paragraph responding to the comment below.

Technology is great. It saves time and increases productivity.

Speaking

Talking about consequences and effects

6 Choose the correct option in *italics*.

People's increased use of the car in recent decades …

a … has led *by / into / to* an increase in pollution in cities and towns.

b … has resulted *at / in / by* the growth of out-of-town shopping centres.

c … has had a rather negative effect *on / to / with* the development of railways.

d … has had a positive impact *for / on / with* the car manufacturing industry worldwide.

e … has been a positive step *in / to / towards* giving people more mobility and a greater sense of freedom.

f … has had negative consequences *for / in / with* the number of road accidents.

Unit 8 Review

Vocabulary

1 **Correct the mistakes in sentences a–l using words and expressions from Unit 8. More than one answer may be correct.**

a Once you are seventeen, you will be entailed to apply for a driving licence.

b You are issued with a passport by quality of being a citizen of the country.

c The jury took a very long time to find a verdict.

d He was convicted of attempting to enfraud a bank, by paying in a false cheque.

e Having crashed the car, he was convicted of unreckoning driving.

f He was found guilty of tax escape and had to pay a heavy fine.

g It's tempting to take revenge on someone who has harmed you, but you should never bring the law into your own arms.

h The judge told the jury not to be bent by their sympathy for the accused.

i We must be extremely careful to stick to the words of the law and not ignore any of the details.

j His lawyers are going to house an appeal against his sentence, which they think is too harsh.

k After a month-long trial, he was finally excused of all the charges and was free to go home.

l They have been remaindered in custody until they appear in court next month.

Exam practice

Reading & Use of English, Part 4

2 **For questions 1–6, complete the second sentence so that it has a similar meaning to the first sentence, using the word given. Do not change the word given. You must use between three and eight words, including the word given.**

1 The judge is not going to resign over the matter.
intention
The judge .... over the matter.

2 When confronted with his crime the accused was unrepentant.
remorse
The accused .... crime he had committed.

3 We aim to stamp out violent crime in this area.
put
Our aim .... violent crime in this area.

4 The judge sent Jones to prison for two years.
sentence
The judge .... prison.

5 People do not recover from a crime like this quickly.
over
This kind of crime is not .... quickly.

6 When I opened the door, I was surprised that no-one else was at home.
only
I opened the door .... nobody at home.

Grammar

Gerunds and infinitives

3 Complete sentences a–h using one of the verbs below in the gerund or infinitive form. In one of the sentences both forms are possible: which one?

lock see commit think phone make outline explain

a He told the judge that he regretted ______ the crime.
b Did you remember ______ the back door before you left?
c I tried ______ why I was parked illegally, but the traffic warden wouldn't listen.
d After talking about crime in general, the speaker went on ______ the advantages of the new crime prevention scheme.
e I dread ______ how much our new burglar alarm is going to cost.
f I've been meaning ______ you for ages, but just never got round to it.
g Please stop ______ that dreadful noise. I can't hear myself think!
h I rushed back to my car, only ______ the thief driving it away.

Writing

Hedging

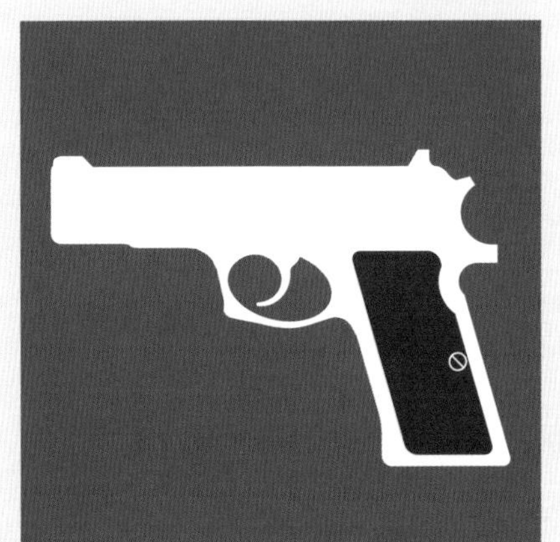

4 Rearrange the words to make sentences adding punctuation as necessary.

a ~~believed~~ that ~~it~~ on illegal urban areas ~~widely~~ a ~~is~~ crackdown firearms rates in our addressing the would go crime spiralling way in some ~~it~~
It is widely believed ______

b ~~it~~ raising the age should crime levels shown that principle reduce been school-leaving in ~~has~~
It has ______

c legal authority some handed down remote than those by criminal behaviour bearing on have more ~~it would~~ that punishments friends and family out by members seem meted
It would ______

d society by the operation limit the harm ~~it~~ kept to of ~~might~~ be possible illegal drug to caused markets of sight are out if they
It might ______

e where the establishment of a sense West frontier of the Wild ~~the internet~~ law and order reminiscent fully implemented has yet ~~is~~ in to be
The internet is, ______

5 Choose a subject from the list. Write a short paragraph. Describe some of the problems associated with it and then offer some solutions. Try to use a variety of hedges to soften your opinion.

Illegal firearms Anti-social behaviour Teenage gangs Corruption

Speaking

Speculating

6 A police officer is describing some closed-circuit camera footage of a bank robbery. Match the two halves to make complete sentences.

a It might be that …	1 … might be armed.
b I would say that those …	2 … waited until there were no customers.
c It certainly looks like they…	3 … out their faces.
d They might have …	4 … two men are the robbers.
e It all seems …	5 … they've seen the camera.
f I can't quite make …	6 … the police cars arriving.
g They look as …	7 … to be happening incredibly fast.
h Perhaps they heard …	8 … if they've just seen something.

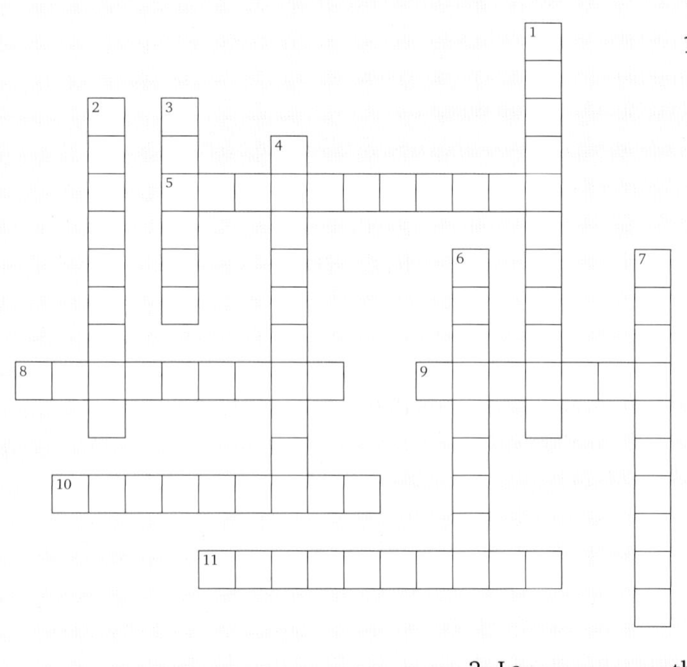

Vocabulary

1 Complete the crossword using the clues below.

Across

5 I was a builder and now I'm an actor. My old job bears little r________ to my current one.

8 Stealing company property will lead to instant d________.

9 It's important for you to realise that I don't e________ what you did. In fact, I think you behaved very badly.

10 He's quite loud and loves being with other people; he's a real e________.

11 When people sitting near me in my office are talking while I'm working, I get very d________.

Down

1 She d________ f________ me in many respects. For example, she's very sociable while I'm a bit of a loner. (2 words)

2 I do hope she gets the job. She's certain to be u________ a________ some strong competing candidates. (2 words)

3 I s________ through all the online job adverts every day, hoping to find a new job.

4 Another way of saying *reliable*: d________

6 Competing with colleagues often b________ o________ the worst in people. (2 words)

7 He doesn't care about earning a big salary; he isn't especially money-o________.

Exam practice

Reading & Use of English, Part 3

2 For questions 1–8, read the text below. Use the word given in capitals at the end of some of the lines to form a word that fits in the space in the same line. There is an example at the beginning (0).

Sigmund Freud

Sigmund Freud, father of psychoanalysis, is generally recognised as one of the most (0) *controversial* thinkers of the twentieth century. Working initially in a close (1) ________ with Joseph Breuer, Freud elaborated the influential theory of the mind as a complex energy system. He articulated and refined the concepts of the unconscious and of repression, and proposed a tri-partite account of the mind's structure, all as part of a radically new conceptual and (2) ________ frame of reference for the understanding of human (3) ________ development and the understanding of mental conditions such as hysteria.

Notwithstanding the multiple (4) ________ of psychoanalysis as it exists today, it can in almost all fundamental respects be traced directly back to Freud's original work. Moreover, Freud's (5) ________ treatment of human actions, dreams, and indeed cultural artefacts as invariably possessing implicit (6) ________ significance has proven to be (7) ________ fecund and has had important implications for a wide variety of other fields such as anthropology and artistic (8) ________.

CONTROVERSY
RELATE
THERAPY
PSYCHOLOGY
MANIFEST
INNOVATE
SYMBOL, ORDINARY
CREATE

Grammar

Using passives, *have* and *get*

3 Complete sentences a–j using the verbs in brackets in the correct form. Where there is a choice between *have* or *get*, choose the correct option.

Example: *The factory is about to (*have or get*?) (take) over by a competitor. = get taken*

a It (rumour) that the managing director (force) by the board to resign, but I found out later that this wasn't true.

b When I took the car in to (service), I (*have* or *get*?) the garage check the air-conditioning unit.

c I'm afraid that your application letter seems to (*have* or *get*?) (hold) up in the post.

d Once we've completed the first round of interviews, successful candidates (ask) back to attend a second interview next week.

e I spoke to my manager and (*have* or *get*?) myself (invite) to the annual sales dinner.

f We (*have* or *get*?) our office (break) into yesterday, but fortunately nothing was stolen.

g We always (*have* or *get*?) job applicants (fill) out a questionnaire after their interview.

h My cousin (*have* or *get*?) himself (fire) last week for failing to meet his work deadlines.

Writing

Giving reasons

4 Complete sentences a–e using an appropriate word or phrase. Use a different word or phrase for each one.

a She is highly deserving of a pay rise ________ she has gone the extra mile on this project.

b The company has been forced to outsource jobs ________ an increased demand from customers.

c The Indigo chairman has decided to step down ________ the recent media scandal.

d Participants of the meeting began nodding off in their droves ________ the monotony of the speaker's voice.

e He is an exceptional team player and ________ he will go far in the company.

Tact

5 Rephrase a–e to make them sound more tactful.

a He's just so downright rude.

b He just loves the sound of his own voice.

c She'll stop at nothing to get her own way.

d He's completely bone idle.

e He's stupid.

Speaking

Speaking strategies

6 Fill in the gaps in the notes about speaking strategies with words from the list. Three of the words are not used.

according to accurately confess consider idea in opinion pauses precise range repetition synonyms waits

Speaking strategies

- Avoid (a) ________: use a wide (b) ________ of vocabulary, especially (c) ________, (e.g. *proposal, concept*, (d) ________)
- Avoid long (e) ________ or silences: use 'filler' expressions such as 'Well,' 'So,' 'Let me see' to give yourself time to think.
- Be clear and (f) ________: try to use vocabulary and grammatical forms (g) ________
- Make it clear when you are giving your own personal (h) ________; use discourse markers such as: (i) ________ *my view* ..., *I suppose that*..., *I must* (j) ________ *that*..., etc.

Unit 10 Review

Vocabulary

1 Fill in the gaps with words from Unit 10 to complete sentences a–j.

a The children at school love to m................ their favourite singers. They dress like them and even talk like them.

b He has an unfortunate t................ to upset people; he needs to be more careful about what he says.

c Sentencing the footballer to three months in prison, the judge told him he was a bad r................ m................ for young people.

d When I discovered that my new colleague liked the same music as me, I b................ with her immediately.

e She isn't really a close friend of mine; she's really more of an a................ .

f I like going to the theatre, but I don't often go these days as the cost of tickets has become completely p................ .

g The creation of satellite TV was a real w................ in the history of television.

h The film industry in my country is absolutely c................ by a lack of investment and by competition from Hollywood movies.

i The most p................ prize for writers is probably the Nobel Prize for Literature.

j Making a TV series requires a huge initial o................ from investors and the production company.

Exam practice

Reading & Use of English, Part 1

2 For questions 1–8, read the text below and decide which answer (A, B, C or D) best fits each gap. There is an example at the beginning (0).

The Victorian music hall

In Victorian Britain, an (0) ....*D*.... popular place of entertainment was the music hall. Shows were full of songs of all kinds, in which the audience was (1) .... to join in the chorus. Between 1900 and 1910, however, music halls (2) .... a dramatic change in character and (3) .... their emphasis on eating, drinking and singing to variety shows, where families went to see, among other acts, great (4) .... like Roman chariot races, or diving contests. Although temporarily (5) .... by the 1914–18 war, the music halls were to (6) .... their popularity for many years after this. However, the advent of radio (7) .... to be increasingly detrimental to live entertainment and a further (8) .... was dealt with the arrival of the cinema.

	A	B	C	D
0	A overridingly	B overreachingly	C overpoweringly	(D) overwhelmingly
1	A indebted	B obliged	C constrained	D indulged
2	A subjected	B submitted	C underlined	D underwent
3	A rearranged	B fluctuated	C shifted	D relocated
4	A spectacles	B parades	C exhibitions	D displays
5	A obstructed	B halted	C terminated	D checked
6	A retain	B absorb	C grasp	D reserve
7	A claimed	B turned	C resulted	D proved
8	A setback	B disaster	C blow	D crash

Grammar

Adverb clauses

3 Complete sentences a–k using the words in the list. More than one answer may be correct.

even if despite while since now that as as if like in spite though as though even though

a Don't you think that film was very much ______ the last film she starred in?

b ______ the terrible traffic, we still arrived for the play with time to spare.

c ______ I can see your reasons for not liking modern art, there are lots of people who really appreciate it.

d It looks ______ there's going to be a tube strike next week.

e Much ______ I love the cinema, I don't go very often.

f ______ I've seen *King Lear* many times, I still love to see new productions of it.

g I enjoyed the film ______ of having to wait for half an hour to get tickets.

h ______ digital downloads are so popular, CD sales are going to continue to decline.

i Thanks for the invitation but ______ I'm not really interested in opera, I think you'd better find someone who would appreciate it more.

j ______ we have to queue for hours, I really want to get tickets for this concert.

k Difficult ______ it is for some people to understand, I really detest sport.

Writing

Complex sentences

4 Correct the mistakes in each sentence. One sentence is correct.

a Many young people no longer want to follow a traditional career, despite it may ultimately be more fulfilling.

b Celebrities do a lot of work for charity, which they should be praised.

c Aspirations such as happiness are still achievable, though unfortunately they are seriously undervalued in our society.

d Wealth and fame are high on many people's agenda, that explains why hard work is not a priority.

e Further more, the celebrity culture shows no signs of diminishing.

f Some people think they will be happy simply through to appear on TV.

g Hollywood movie stars and high-profile footballers who are all remunerated very handsomely are often the most vocal about not being paid enough.

5 Now write a short paragraph outlining the good and bad points of being famous. Include a variety of conjunctions to link ideas within sentences, and use vocabulary from the Unit 10 Writing section.

Speaking

Useful expressions

6 Circle which of the words and phrases 1–4 are correct. More than one correct option is possible for each item.

a There's no ______ that TV has changed the way we live.
1 alternative 2 debate 3 doubt 4 question

b That's ______ true.
1 absolutely 2 certainly 3 definitely 4 rather

c I'm ______ agree with that.
1 not sure I'd 2 sure I don't 3 not going to 4 afraid I don't

d I ______ we've become more reliant on TV.
1 consider 2 'd say 3 suppose 4 suspect

e You ______ that TV has improved communication between people.
1 'd say 2 could say 3 might even argue 4 might think

Unit 11 Review

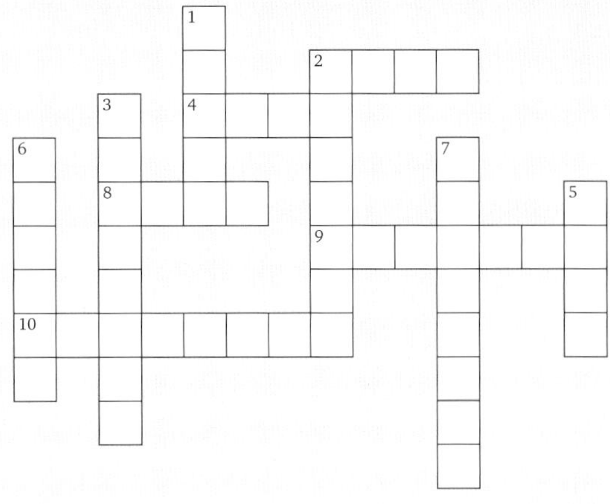

Vocabulary

1 Complete the crossword using the clues below.

Across

2 Buying expensive items can give you a short-term b__________, but it can cause you problems later on.

4 The company is now in debt to the t__________ of over a million dollars.

8 Given the current economic crisis, our priority must be to k__________ the company afloat and not let it sink.

9 At the supermarket I try only to buy the items on my shopping list. Buying things on i__________ costs far too much.

10 Our competitors are f__________ the market with cheap goods.

Down

1 Our house is now o__________ market, as we want to move. (2 words)

2 It's hard for her to see a reason to work harder, when how hard she works seems to have no b__________ on how much she earns.

3 Their new business has really t__________. They never expected to be so successful so quickly. (2 words)

5 He has a h__________ for business and an eye for a bargain.

6 This new TV was so expensive, and it stopped working almost as soon as we got it home. What a complete r__________! (2 words)

7 We only buy necessities and try not to s__________ our money on luxuries.

Exam practice

Reading & Use of English, Part 2

2 For questions 1–8, read the text below and think of the word which best fits each space. Use only one word in each space. There is an example at the beginning (0).

Bad business

I sold funeral insurance to North Carolina black people to put myself through college. I myself am not black. I still feel bad about what went (0) ***on***. But my parents worked at the cotton mill.

I grew up in one of these employee row-houses. Our shrubs were always tagged with fluff blown off stacked bales. You didn't understand that you'd steadily breathed fibres – not (1) __________, like Dad, you started coughing at age forty and died at fifty-one. First, I tried peddling the *Book of Knowledge*. I attended every training session. The sharp salesman showed us (2) __________ to let the 'T' volume (3) __________ open at the Taj Mahal. Our company had spent a lot extra on that full-page picture. In a living-room the size of a shipping crate, I stood before my seated parents. I practised. That should have helped, but if (4) __________, it made me worse. Before I hiked off with my wares, Mom (5) __________ pack a bag-lunch.

Other sales kids owned cars. I had to walk lugging my sample kit; twenty-six letters' (6) __________ of knowledge gets heavy pretty fast. My arms and back grew stronger but my spirits sort of caved in. I hated the thought I was about to trick them (7) __________ buying something they didn't want or need. The only thing worse than facing strangers door-to-door is finding people you know there. Grinning, they'd ask me in. When I finished, my hosts sighed, said this book-set sure sounded great. Then they admitted what I knew (8) __________ along – they just couldn't afford it.

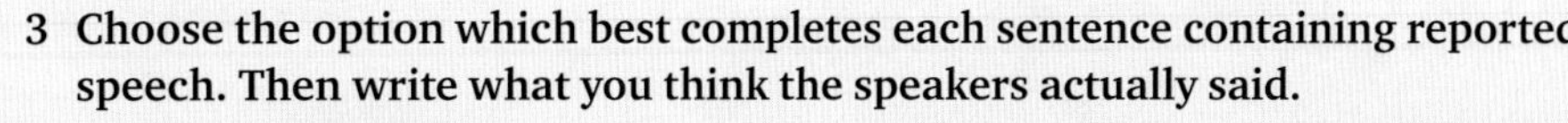

Grammar

Reported speech

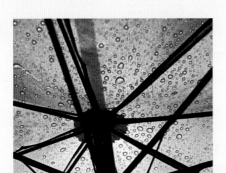

3 Choose the option which best completes each sentence containing reported speech. Then write what you think the speakers actually said.

a The bank manager .... me if I was interested in opening a business account.
1 asked 2 enquired 3 wondered 4 checked

b The head teacher suggested .... a sponsored walk to try and raise money for my children's school.
1 us to hold 2 to be held 3 holding 4 to hold

c The manager of the shop guaranteed .... the difference if we found that make and model of TV on sale cheaper elsewhere.
1 refunding us 2 to refund us 3 us to refund 4 that she refund us

d He swore .... everything he owed me by the end of that month.
1 to pay back 2 me to pay back 3 that he pay back 4 that he'd pay back

e Claire insisted .... a new umbrella to replace the one she had lost.
1 buying me 2 on buying me 3 to buy me 4 to buy for me

f She urged .... invest my money in such a risky business.
1 not to 2 me not to 3 me to not 4 that I don't

Writing

Nominalization

4 Rewrite a–e using a nominalized form of the underlined words.

a The two companies have <u>merged</u> and this is an important milestone.

....

b Insider trading at the bank has been <u>discovered</u> and this is affecting their share values.

....

c The government has <u>decided</u> to attract new investment, which has been welcomed by the private sector.

....

d The industry sector <u>grew</u> faster during March, which indicates that the economy is on the up.

....

e Industry leaders have <u>withdrawn</u> their support for revised tax laws, causing unrest in markets.

....

Speaking

Qualifying a reply

5 Fill in the gaps in a candidate's reply to the question 'Do you think advertising aimed at children should be banned?' using the expressions below. Three of them are not used.

already just on balance on reflection one hand
put it say say it suppose the one hand

I have to (a) ...., my initial reaction is yes, it should definitely all be banned. But (b) ...., I realize it's quite a complicated issue. I (c) .... if we completely banned adverts aimed at children, sales would go down, which would hurt the economy. On (d) ...., children are consumers, just like adults. But on the other, they (e) .... aren't as sophisticated. Compared with adults, children are – how can I (f) ....? – rather vulnerable. So (g) ...., my view is we should allow advertising for children, but we should control it strictly.

Unit 12 Review

Vocabulary

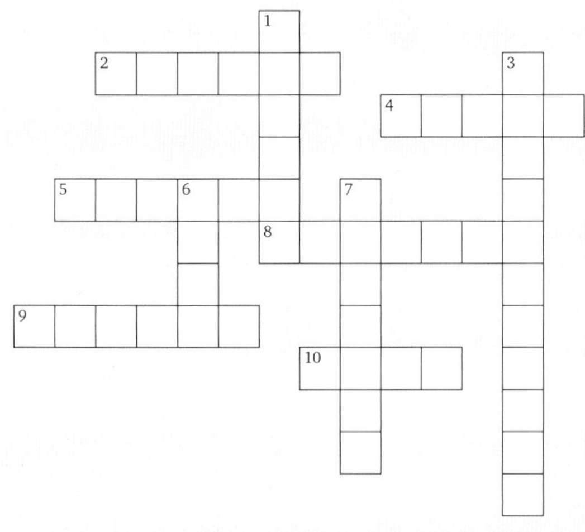

1 Complete the crossword using the clues below.

Across

2 I suffered an unfortunate m__________ on my last trip: I lost my passport two days before I was due to fly home.

4 My family left China when I was quite young, but I still have v__________ memories of my life there.

5 I find living in the countryside boring; I much prefer the hustle and b__________ of a big city.

8 We looked up, and suddenly the kangaroo was blocking our path. It seemed to jump up out of n__________.

9 We hired a jeep so that we could get off the b__________ track.

10 She's followed a very unusual career p__________. She started out as a ballet dancer; now she's a tour guide.

Down

1 There was no sign of any plants or trees as far as the eye could see; the landscape was completely b__________.

3 My Asia trip was great: I wouldn't have m__________ it for anything. (3 words)

6 He isn't the adventurous t__________; he prefers to spend his holidays on the beach.

7 I looked up and saw my ex-wife: she was staying at the same hotel as us. It was a really a__________ moment.

Exam practice

Reading & Use of English, Part 2

2 For questions 1–6, complete the second sentence so that it has a similar meaning to the first sentence. Do not change the word given. You must use between three and eight words, including the word given.

1 We should have bought cheaper tickets.
opted
I wish __________ such expensive tickets.

2 It was incredible that there's absolutely no tarmac on the roads.
lack
I was amazed __________ of tarmac on the roads.

3 I was determined to take advantage of the experience.
out
I would __________ such an experience for all the world.

4 We knew we would probably get stuck in the mud.
high
We knew that there __________ stuck in the mud.

5 The country my friends and I were visiting made a deep impression on us.
skin
The country we were visiting __________ me and my friends.

6 We knew that the journey would be long and arduous, but we weren't expecting it to be so dangerous.
said
We knew that the journey would be long and arduous, but __________ about it being so dangerous.

Grammar

Conditionals

3 Complete sentences a–j with a suitable word or phrase.

a I've never visited Bolivia but ...., I'm sure I would have enjoyed being there.

b If we went there by bus instead of by plane, we .... a lot of money.

c .... the noisy hotel, that would have been a perfect holiday.

d .... I told you a secret, could you keep it to yourself?

e .... you get yourself a tourist visa, you won't be able to come with us next month.

f .... I have to walk there myself, I'm determined to visit the Valley of the Temples tomorrow.

g If I .... ask you very nicely, would you upgrade my seat to business class?

h It doesn't make any difference to me .... you come or not. I'm quite happy to visit the museum on my own.

i .... in advance how expensive it was here, I might have booked a holiday somewhere else.

j We're going to Spain next month .... that my new passport arrives in time.

Writing

Descriptive language

4 Use the words from the list below to replace the word *got* in each of these sentences. Three of the words are not used.

wangled prevailed accessed clambered gleaned gained fetched transported

a We *got* out of the car.

b He *got* his way out of a difficult situation

c They *got in* the house via the back window.

d We *got* our water from a well each morning.

e His grasp of the language was so poor that he *got* very little from the conversation.

5 Replace the verbs in italics in sentences a–e with words from the list below. Three of the words are not used.

a desolate drifted squeezed an oasis a respite stretch swept brushed

a A cool breeze *entered* through the open window.

b Everyone stood as the bulls *ran together* through the streets.

c The building stood in *an empty and unattractive* landscape.

d The café was *a calm and pleasant place* in the heart of the packed city centre.

e The last *part* of the race was the hardest.

6 Choose another common verb in the English language such as *put*, *give*, *take*, etc. Think of as many synonyms for these verbs as you can. Write a paragraph describing your first impressions of a place you have just arrived in, using the synonyms of the verb you have chosen. Use vocabulary from the Unit 12 Writing section.

Speaking

Evaluating and suggesting alternatives

7 Match a–g to 1–7 to make complete sentences.

a Yes, I see …	1 … case, cost isn't the only factor.
b You do have …	2 … fact, I think you're right about that.
c There is some …	3 … same, I think there's more to it than that.
d As a matter of …	4 … where you're coming from.
e For one …	5 … thing, you haven't mentioned the effect on the environment.
f In any …	6 … truth in that, of course, but I'm not sure I agree completely.
g All the …	7 … a point there, I must admit.